DIRECTING WITH THE MICHAEL CHEKHOV TECHNIQUE

DIRECTING WITH THE MICHAEL CHEKHOV TECHNIQUE

A Workbook with Video for Directors, Teachers and Actors

MARK MONDAY

Series Editors: David Carey and Rebecca Clark Carey

Bloomsbury Methuen Drama
An imprint of Bloomsbury Publishing Plc

B L O O M S B U R Y
LONDON • OXFORD • NEW YORK • NEW DELHI • SYDNEY

Bloomsbury Methuen Drama
An imprint of Bloomsbury Publishing Plc

Imprint previously known as Methuen Drama

50 Bedford Square	1385 Broadway
London	New York
WC1B 3DP	NY 10018
UK	USA

www.bloomsbury.com

BLOOMSBURY, METHUEN DRAMA and the Diana logo are trademarks of Bloomsbury Publishing Plc

First published 2017

© Mark Monday, 2017
Foreword © Seth Gordon, 2017
How the World Began © Catherine Trieschmann, 2011, Bloomsbury Methuen Drama, an imprint of Bloomsbury Publishing Plc.
Family Portrait © H. G. Clarkson. Quoted by permission of the author
Magical Clay Imaginary Body Sculpture reproduced by permission of Melissa Owens
Three Sisters by Anton Chekhov, translation © Michael Frayn, 1983, Bloomsbury Methuen Drama, an imprint of Bloomsbury Publishing Plc.

Mark Monday has asserted his right under the Copyright, Designs and Patents Act, 1988, to be identified as author of this work.

All rights reserved. No part of this publication may be reproduced or transmitted in any form or by any means, electronic or mechanical, including photocopying, recording, or any information storage or retrieval system, without prior permission in writing from the publishers.

No responsibility for loss caused to any individual or organization acting on or refraining from action as a result of the material in this publication can be accepted by Bloomsbury or the author.

British Library Cataloguing-in-Publication Data
A catalogue record for this book is available from the British Library of Congress.

ISBN: HB: 978-1-4742-7963-5
PB: 978-1-4742-8403-5
ePDF: 978-1-4742-7965-9
eBook: 978-1-4742-7964-2

Library of Congress Cataloging-in-Publication Data
A catalog record for this book is available from the Library of Congress.

Series: Theatre Arts Workbooks

Cover design: Louise Dugdale
Cover image © Great Lakes Michael Chekhov Consortium

Typeset by Deanta Global Publishing Services, Chennai, India

To find out more about our authors and books visit www.bloomsbury.com. Here you will find extracts, author interviews, details of forthcoming events and the option to sign up for our newsletters.

For

Don Nance (Coach)

CONTENTS

Acknowledgments ix
Foreword *Seth Gordon* x
Prologue to using this book xiii
Preface to using this book xxii

1 Preparation—Analysis and Composition 1

2 Casting and Classwork Using Archetypes 19

3 Creating the Ensemble 37

4 Establishing the Language of Class and Rehearsal 53

5 Using Psychological Gesture as Action 67

6 Putting it all Together Thus Far 87

7 Character Relationships 99

8 Work on Soliloquies 123

9 Characterization 135

10 Scenes and Blocks with Multiple Characters 143

11 Tempo/Rhythm and Atmosphere 157

12 Spy-back 181

Appendix I: Links to Workbook Videos 191
Appendix II: Concept Statements and Casting from Other Plays 192
Appendix III: Sample Scores from Other Plays 204
Appendix IV: Additional Exercises and Helpful Documents 224
Appendix V: A Brief History of Michael Chekhov 233
Appendix VI: How this Book Came to Be 235
Appendix VII: Additional Notes on *A Midsummer Night's Dream* 238
Index 246

ACKNOWLEDGMENTS

The first acknowledgment must, and should, go to my wife, Kathryn. She has supported and bolstered my artistic career for many years and continues to do so.

The second acknowledgment and thanks go to all the folks who have been a part of the vision of the Great Lakes Michael Chekhov Consortium (GLMCC). They are my colleagues and friends: Catherine Albers, Lionel Walsh, and Lavinia Hart. My colleagues have much passion for the Chekhov Technique and we work together every day in our effort to accomplish our goals at GLMCC. I wish to also mention our organization's fine staff of teachers—many of whom are former students of my colleagues or my own: Susan Cato-Chapman, Nicole Perrone, Melissa Owens, Jennifer Tuttle, Jamie Koeth, Billicia Hines, James Haffner, Eva Gil, and Chris Bohan.

Many many thanks go to Joanna Merlin, Mala Powers, Jack Colvin, and Lenard Petit, who were my first formal teachers in the Technique. They initially inspired me with their teaching, which has brought me to this point in my journey.

Kudos go to my editor, David Carey, and publisher, Bloomsbury, and especially John O'Donovan, who believed in this book from the beginning and have been so encouraging. Thanks, too, to Patrick Hawks who has been a diligent reader of this manuscript and helped greatly in its clarity.

Finally, thanks to my students from GLMCC who have collaborated with me in coming to the conclusions I have thus far. There are more acknowledgments in Appendix V and are most special because those named helped frame the artist I have become (for better or worse).

FOREWORD

As a director, I often feel the two hardest things to accomplish when taking on a production are closely related. One is an accurate reading of the text, and the other is articulating that reading—that vision for the production—in a way that is simple and clarifying to everyone who requires it. That's what I love about this book: it is a very simple and comprehensible explanation of a technique for acting, and for the art of theater making, that is itself a very honest, pure way to express the truth.

There are plenty of valid approaches to acting that are Stanislavski based, Chekhov certainly being among them. When I mention Stanislavski, however, I'm thinking of two things he emphasized in his teaching: that everything is rooted in psychological truth, and that everything is the product of an artist's imagination. Some techniques emphasize one over the other. As described here by Mark Monday, Chekhov marries them in a way that gives the artist a path to both. Early in the book is my favorite sentence in it, "When we fantasize, we transport ourselves to a world that feels very real."

Have any of us ever heard a better description of what happens on stage when what's happening is magical? In the book, Mr. Monday emphasizes all the things I find most important as a theater artist. He admonishes us to root all our work in what the playwright provides, describing the Technique as being "immediately applicable to the text." He describes the Technique as one that encourages collaboration and equality in the rehearsal room. And he celebrates the use of a rehearsal room as a "safe space," where artists can work, and sometimes fail, as they slowly and painstakingly discover the best way for a production to unfold. He urges everyone, be they an actor or director approaching a play, to read it aloud when working on it at home. Plays, like poetry, are

FOREWORD

not constructed to be read silently, they are meant to be performed, so of course that's the best way to study a script, but who among us actually does that? He provides for a level of specificity in acting choices that I can say, having directed countless actors and auditioned countless more, is rare. I suggest looking especially carefully at the section in which having a beginning, middle, and end to every moment in the play, to every action an actor plays, is addressed. This level of specificity is, for me, often the easiest way to distinguish a professional, fully trained, and formed actor from one who is less so.

Here's another telltale sign that an actor is of less than polished, professional quality: you see their technique on stage. You see the struggle, rather than simply seeing the magic. Imagine watching Fred Astaire's greatest dance routines. Now imagine what must have been involved in developing these dances—the choreography, the rehearsal, the endless repetition, and oh, the physical pain. Now erase all that once again and just see the effortless smile on his face as he shows you the very best of life in his dance. That's the magic an actor must deliver. In this book, Mr. Monday reminds us repeatedly that the techniques in the book are just that—techniques to be perfected as exercises either in rehearsal or in preparation for rehearsal. If the audience knows your psychological gesture, something is terribly wrong with your performance.

I admire all this about Mr. Monday's book, and more. I admire his observation that theater is not an intellectual exercise. Great theater, one hopes, moves us, and makes us think about the world in some new way. That's for the audience. For the artist, the work is always happening now, in the moment, and therefore cannot be intellectualized. That's where the term "spy-back," used often here, comes in. Spy-back allows you to act *now*, by providing a way for you to talk about it—and therefore to think about it—later. I admire how he urges directors to listen to actors from the heart first. It integrates the director into the ensemble and makes him or her a more trustworthy leader. He urges directors to guide actors to discoveries using this technique, rather than providing them with direct answers to their questions.

Finally, I admire how he urges us to continually expand our technique, regardless of how experienced we may fancy ourselves. It's so true that an actor who can sing and dance well is a very hirable one, but an actor with this and outstanding acting technique is truly rare. This field is so competitive, and one who wishes to excel in it ignores this observation at one's peril. We must always be learning. Who knows what opportunities might present themselves because we've developed the skill necessary to take advantage when they do? As Mr. Monday observes, "I certainly never thought I would write a book." Well, I never thought I'd write a foreword.

During the course of the book, Mr. Monday uses Shakespeare's delightful *A Midsummer Night's Dream* as a sample text of sorts, as he demonstrates various techniques in both acting and script analysis. He also uses, to a lesser degree, Anton Chekhov's *Three Sisters* and other works. You would be wise to read these plays (aloud!) and be very familiar with them while reading this book. He mentions a variety of other plays and playwrights. I would suggest considering any mention of any play, author, or other theatrical figure in the book about which you're not familiar an assignment to read more about it. The book will serve you best that way.

The best description I've ever received for why we rehearse plays is this: to remove the barriers to excellence. Perhaps, like me, excellence is your goal when approaching a production, or any endeavor, for that matter. Use this book, and the Technique it describes, as a tool to smash that barrier. But never forget that every project is its own journey toward excellence; the struggle begins anew each time, and that's where technique comes in. Enjoy the journeys.

Seth Gordon
Associate Artistic Director, The Repertory Theatre of St. Louis

PROLOGUE TO USING THIS BOOK

Who can use this book

This book is meant to be a guide for teachers, directors, and actors who are interested in building a more collaborative process through play analysis and rehearsal using the Michael Chekhov Technique. Playwrights, dramaturges, and designers will also find value in the work to aid in a better, more productive process of script analysis when working in collaboration with a director. The process described within is somewhat different from the norm of play production. Plays are traditionally rehearsed from beginning to end, not as described in this book. I think, as does Michael Chekhov, there is a better path for the journey of discovering a play. It begins with a fresh way of looking at script analysis. However, in Chekhov's *To the Actor,* there is only one brief chapter that theater artists can apply to analysis. In my career as an actor, director, and teacher, I have discovered ways to utilize and expand the theories in this chapter—not only in analyzing the play but in rehearsing it as well. *If you are searching for a more organic process to your acting, teaching, and directing, this book is for you.* (For a brief history of Michael Chekhov, please see Appendix V.)

What I have learned through the study and practice of the Michael Chekhov Technique is, more than any other major methodology based in the Stanislavski approach, how immediately applicable the work is to text. From the actor's and director's standpoint, the work, especially on action, is immediate because it begins in the imagination and is executed in a physical form—a "psychological gesture" or PG.

When I refer to the imagination, I do not mean that the artist must do a lot of thinking, or visualizing, before doing. Imagination, in the Chekhov work, engages the world of fantasy. For today's youth the fantasy is created for them through technology. Theater artists need a mechanism to help open the door to rediscover the life of fantasy. If you, as a theater artist, are willing to leap into the world of the play through fantasy and imagination, this book will be of use to you.

When we fantasize, we transport ourselves to a world that feels very real. This is the beauty of the Chekhov Technique. In this book, theater folk will find tools to create truthfully in this world of fantasy. It is a world in which the whole being of thinking, feeling, and doing is engaged at the same time—a visceral psychophysical process. As theater is a heightened and not realistic world, truly living in a place of fantasy is the only way to take an audience on the roller-coaster ride that a good play can and should do. By being willing to fantasize, the artist can work in what Chekhov calls the "Higher Ego," a state in which the artist abandons everyday life and commits to work in a creative place. It is in this state where we truly make art. It is a place beyond our everyday ego and is only attainable through imagination and fantasy life.

Here I may commit a sacrilege to many of my fine teachers as they have repeatedly said, "The answers are always in the text." I don't believe the answers are always in the text. We "must go beyond the playwright," said Michael Chekhov. What does this mean?

It is the director who must aid the actor to the Higher Ego. The director uses the tools of atmosphere and improvisation, among others, to help the actor achieve this highly creative state. We often talk, in the acting studio, about creating a "safe" place in which to work. To me, this simply means creating an environment where this highly creative state can exist without fear of failure. If the director/teacher does this, actors are willing to let go of their daily selves, which must be done to achieve Higher Ego. This extremely playful state is exactly what Chekhov means by going beyond the playwright. In this state the actor discovers more about the character than is written. In this state the director learns more about the play than exists on the written page.

Very few characters are completely fleshed out in any text. I don't think playwrights set out to define characters in that way or to solve all the problems of the story they are telling. Shakespeare surely doesn't do it. There is lots of room for interpretation as long as we stay grounded in the given circumstances of the script.

WORD OF CAUTION TO THE DIRECTOR OR TEACHER

Going beyond the playwright and going beyond the play are vastly different things. It is easy, when working in the Higher Ego, to go too far and beyond the play itself. This is when we have to bring actors, and ourselves, back to the given circumstances.

For anyone who has taken a course in script analysis—using traditional methods to discover the themes, motifs, and symbols of the play—the analysis portion of this work offers a different approach that you may find refreshing and inspiring. This is why it appears near the beginning of this book. It can be inspiring because the work leads to a workable visual chart of how a play is structured. Creating this chart is a hands-on experience and therefore forces the whole being to be involved— so important for the artist. The chief outcome of this work is that it allows all involved to begin "on the same page." All theater artists begin the production journey with an analysis of the script, and it is crucial the production team understands the director's vision. The vision, of course, comes from a deep and personal analysis of the play.

Often, I am asked if the Chekhov Technique works for everyone. The answer is unequivocally yes—and no. In Chekhov's *On the Technique of Acting*, Mala Powers provides, in the preface, a chart of eighteen separate areas of the work. In fact there are many more in the subcategories of each. I know of no other acting technique with the depth that Chekhov explores and explains. Yes, there are many aspects of the work that will appeal to all. They vary from person to person. There are aspects of the Technique that may not work for an individual. The point is there is enough technique in the work of Michael Chekhov that everyone can apply. The Technique can be applied to any genre of theater as well.

By the way, this is not meant to be a text for the first book a directing student encounters. It does not address blocking, creating lovely stage pictures, or "tying down your corners." There are good books on the market for those fundamentals. Instead, use this book as a supplement to Directing I, in advanced directing, script analysis, monologue classes, character and scene study, and as a glimpse into the director's work for any design course.

Not everything in this book comes directly from the writings of Michael Chekhov. Rather, a good bit of it is derived and evolved from his Technique. Since Chekhov died in 1955, many of the pupils he taught, and those who have taught me, have expanded the Technique in exciting ways. It is of utmost importance to realize that this evolution is exactly what Stanislavski hoped would happen when he taught Chekhov, Vakhtangov, and others. Much of the work in this book expresses that evolution while remaining rooted in the Technique.

It has been suggested by peer reviewers of this book that I include critical comments concerning the sources I have used to complete it. The writing of Michael Chekhov is the chief source of this book, yet I should be clear that his writing has been interpreted through his students. I have been fortunate to have worked with several of them.

The Technique, as all good art does, evolves. All of the exercises I describe contain the essence of Chekhovian principles. They are not necessarily the way in which Chekhov taught them, nor are they all created by Michael Chekhov. When I was taught the Technique, my teachers were interpreting and creating in their own voices, not regurgitating former lessons. The Technique is not meant to be standardized. What is most important for the reader is to realize that everything in the book is rooted in Chekhov and Stanislavski. It would be a good exercise to constantly reference Chekhov's *To the Actor* to recognize the foundation of the work and understand that the evolution of the Technique is imperative.

A critical analysis of source material would be an interesting academic exercise. That exercise is not the point of my work. My work describes an artistic journey. The source material I have used comes from years of study and practice in the Technique. However, because this is chiefly a book about directing in the theater, the source material has mostly been derived from a vast amount of time experimenting on how to use an acting technique to aid in directing a play. There is little source material on directing with the Chekhov Technique.

Where appropriate, I do acknowledge sources and suggest further reading. The director/educator must ultimately get the actors off the page and on their feet. Written words on pages are theories and theories are proven with results. Results are action and action is the artistic journey of the actor and director.

It has also been suggested that I provide an outcome of the process I used in directing the production of *A Midsummer Night's Dream* chronicled in this book. I honestly do not know how to go about that. The reader will not know the outcome unless he or she witnessed the production. My opinion of the outcome is completely subjective. I can say the rehearsal process was filled with joy and the audiences seemed engaged in the performances. I can also say the actors involved in the production loved rehearsals and the way in which they were conducted. The only complaint was that rehearsals were too long in terms of the number of weeks we worked. Well, I like to rehearse. I teach, in rehearsal, as much as I direct and that is my own journey.

If the teacher/director works in the way I propose in the book, he or she will experience, as did I, a consistency and growth from the actors throughout the run of the production. That is the beauty of the Michael Chekhov Technique and of having a technique to rely on.

I recall Joanne Woodward saying, "I am an intuitive actor, which is fine as long as I have something to intuit." To me, in this statement, Ms. Woodward relies on instinct, and she has great instinct indeed. Yet, what happens when an actor doesn't intuit? A strong technique, for most of us, is essential.

What this book is about

This book obviously concerns how to apply the Michael Chekhov Technique to directing, acting, and teaching. It means to be a guide to a completely collaborative and creative rehearsal and teaching process. The director works with many artists other than actors. So, in essence, the book is about the process of production from creating the vision through performances before a live audience. It is about getting the entire production team looking at a play through the same artistic lens. Beyond that point it is chiefly about how the director works with actors to achieve the concept agreed upon with designers and how a teacher of acting/directing may offer a fresh approach to his or her classes.

In the book *Michael Chekhov's To the Director and Playwright*, compiled and written by Charles Leonard, there is a short chapter named "Toward Better Rehearsals." Chekhov states in the first sentence of the chapter, "As practiced throughout the world today, the stage rehearsal is perhaps the greatest area in which the theatre has remained at a standstill." Chekhov presents arguments in the chapter as to why the rehearsal process should not be conducted in a linear fashion—from beginning to end. I wholeheartedly agree with Chekhov's thesis, which serves as my foundation for directing. This concept is of major focus in several chapters.

In Chekhov's *To the Actor*, the chapter on "Composition" has also served as an inspiration, especially these lines, "This chapter will also endeavor to draw closer together the different psychologies of the actor and director. For a good actor must acquire the director's broad, all-embracing view of the performance as a whole if he is to compose his own part in full harmony with it." The creation of the composition of the play, using Chekhov's principles, leads the director to a collaborative process through his or her Higher Ego.

In this book I explore, with you, the mechanics of composition, according to Chekhov, and how to employ the concepts throughout the play. It is an unconventional approach and therefore a bit daunting at first. Yet, discoveries in art are often unconventional. Look at the unconventional *Hamilton* which took Broadway by storm! We must continue to "push the envelope" of art, and Chekhov does this. Perhaps this book is really about "pushing the envelope" of conceptualizing and rehearsing in harmony with all artists involved in the process.

How and when to use this book

In *The Shakespeare Workbook and Video*, a book in this series, authors David Carey and Rebecca Clark Carey share articulately about actors speaking the text aloud. Directors should adopt this policy. During the early analysis process, as a director, I always not only read the play aloud, but also *act* all the roles. This helps me attain my Higher Ego and I make amazing discoveries. I talk much more about this in early chapters. Yet, it is worth mentioning here because much of this book should be read aloud. There is a great amount of text from plays that demand of the reader to discover not only the character's "actions," but also the "quality of actions" as well. Actions are seen. Qualities must be heard and they can only be heard aloud.

As you begin to apply the techniques and exercises in this book, you might also read Chapter 8 of Chekhov's *To the Actor*, "Composition of the Performance." It is, however, not necessary to become an expert on Michael Chekhov to use the concepts written herein. When working with the Chekhov Technique you'll find, as have I, the beautiful simplicity in his genius. Artists have a tendency to complicate their craft by overthinking. Chekhov teaches us to feel first and think after. This is imperative in the "how" to put this work to its best use.

Chekhov's life goal was to create an "Ideal Theatre of the Future." Chekhov believed the ideal begins with actors. While I believe that everyone involved in a theatrical endeavor is imperative, there is no one more imperative than the actor. The playwright creates the story. The director interprets the story from a unique perspective. The designers and other artisans bring to life the director's concept. The actor is the *teller* of the story. What a responsibility the actor takes on! He or she is responsible for bringing together the "whole" of the entire production team.

Directing with the Michael Chekhov Technique is about *how* a director/teacher collaborates with actors in the studio or a production team to present a story. The director's responsibility is to present the story in a coherent manner that an audience can easily follow. Ultimately, the director, designers, property artisans, stage managers, run crew, and board operators give the stage to the storytellers. The teacher's responsibility is to guide his or her student actors toward how to become a good storyteller.

Working with *Directing with the Michael Chekhov Technique*

The following preface and Chapter 1 of the book are admittedly more theoretical than practical. Understanding the theory is vital before moving on to the chapters that follow. The subsequent chapters consist of how to put the theory into practice. They employ a "framework," which gives the participants an overview of the work to be covered and a series of explorations and exercises to get the work into the body.

The book chronicles a single production from conception through performance. There are also suggested "scores" from *Three Sisters* and other plays in Appendix III. They are included here because the Technique is applicable to any play of any style including musical theater and opera. Each chapter builds upon the previous one and introduces new concepts and exercises—always adding on to what has been covered.

The majority of the exercises must be done on your feet. They are mostly full-bodied exercises so your class or your cast should be prepared by dressing to move. When you read an exercise that has an accompanying video, I suggest you view the video immediately before and after your reading. You'll find the link to the video, if there is one, in Appendix I. The exercises are too numerous to have a video for each. When you view the videos, you'll notice many of them will include work on two things: a specific form and a quality that emerges from that form.

Take care that the gestures remain archetypal in form. There should not be a great amount of variety in creating the form itself. They should not vary physically too much from person to person. You'll find the quality of the form will appear naturally depending on the given circumstances and the tempo/rhythm derived from the text. There are "rules" on creating form especially in the chapter on psychological gestures. Adhere to the rules and watch the videos and you'll experience the Technique in the way Chekhov intended.

Chekhov's exercises are rarely brief. He created them to be a full immersion in self-discovery of the topic at hand. Fortunately, while not necessarily brief, the exercises are simple. The concepts are simple. Where appropriate, I suggest the length of time that should be spent on the exercises. Don't, however, take the suggested time as set in stone. As they are designed for making discoveries, remember each artist discovers in her own time. You must be willing to experiment, improvise, and take the time necessary for actors to discover the lesson. In the studio, I have often abandoned my entire lesson plan because discoveries were being made.

The beauty in the work is that the actor and director can use text while practicing the Technique. This is important because in many methodologies you do an exercise and then apply its lessons to text. There is a gap you have to traverse between the exercise and the chosen text. Here, you will make discoveries about the text while you are deepening the Technique in your body. You'll find numerous examples of this throughout the book. Chekhov said, "Repetition is the

PROLOGUE TO USING THIS BOOK

growing power." Repeating the exercises several times always leads to new discoveries. It is vital to have a journal nearby and to write down your discoveries after each exercise. We call this the spy-back. Resist the temptation to write about something you want to try the next time through. This will "put you in your head." Instead, only write about the discovery in the exercise just performed.

When to use this book is *now*. The Ideal Theater of the future can only be accomplished when commercialism in our theater takes a backseat to Chekhov's statement, "Our theatre has become a dry business. . . . The theatre is not solving any problems. It is not interested in the future, in what shall happen." Perhaps this is because our current theater belongs to the director. Simon Callow talks about this in the foreword of *To the Actor*. I think his words get to the heart of the matter and to the heart of this book—collaboration.

I learned from an early age about team effort and I know from forty-five years of theater experience that the best results come from creating a community where everyone has a feeling of importance. Yes, in the end, we give way to the storytellers—the actors. In a good collaboration the actors understand that they only get to an artistic experience because the production team has truly collaborated. Otherwise, it is just "another op-nin, another show" for everyone. The show may run for many performances. Does a long run mean we have reached Chekhov's goal? No—it means the show is commercially viable. It means that artists are working. Does it mean that those artists are fulfilled to their Higher Ego, the highest creative state?

I don't intend to downplay the importance of the business aspect of theater. I do intend to strongly suggest that our theater has become more business than art. Surely, artists must understand the business of how to be a professional. Beyond the business, we become artists when everything and everyone teams together. Theater is not about the one, it is about the whole. That is *how* to use this book.

As a teacher, I am comfortable stating that every student, to whom I teach the work, IF he or she commits fully to it, finds the Technique applicable and necessary to create truthfully in the fantastical world that is theater.

Finally, in the preface and Chapter 1, please study the theory and practice explorations carefully. This will prepare you for the in-class and rehearsal exercises that follow. The work in the preface and Chapter 1 must precede working with actors. Enjoy your journey!

PREFACE TO USING THIS BOOK

Developing the concept

As I mentioned in the prologue, this preface and Chapter 1 are meant to be more theoretical than practical. That said, I have added some *practice explorations* to prepare for the work to come in subsequent chapters. Consider the preface and Chapter 1 as "what" to do, using practice explorations, and the following chapters as "how" to do the work.

When a director receives an assignment he or she must first consider the culture, period, given circumstances, and themes of the play. This work must be done prior to developing a concept. What is a concept? The concept is the director's vision of the play. It is an interpretation and the interpretation must be clear and consistent for the play to succeed. As I have already said, there is only one good way to discover a play and that is to read it aloud. Reading aloud sparks the imagination. One begins to hear, see, and feel the characters at the sound of one's own voice. I recall being in a class taught by Rosemary Harris in which she spoke of rainy days. Ms. Harris is an avid gardener. She said she loved rainy days because she could retreat from her garden into her den, open her Shakespeare, and play all of the characters reading them aloud. We should all take that story and realize that plays are meant to be heard. The exercise of reading aloud invites the reader to be engaged in all three centers—the thinking center (the neck and above), the feeling center (shoulders to waist), and the willing center (from the waist down—from where we move). Not only should plays be read aloud they should also be read on our feet. We discover so much more when we are fully engaged. Sitting at a table and reading/analyzing the

PREFACE TO USING THIS BOOK

play only engages the thinking center and does not engage the body. It is very difficult to receive a feeling, what we strive for, from the thinking center alone. All theater artists should put reading aloud on their feet into practice.

Reading aloud and on your feet is also of extreme value in script analysis courses. Script analysis should be taught in an acting studio and not in a classroom with desks cluttered everywhere. The same themes will be found, the same character development, and the same through line but in an organic, artistic way. The chief point here is that discussion should be conducted after acting—after discovery. "What did you discover in embodying the text aloud?" is the best leading question the teacher or the director could possibly ask.

Of course the teacher/director must have a clear understanding of the main themes of the play if he or she is to aid students toward discovery. Students in script analysis should be guided to discover for themselves. Actors should be guided to discover for themselves via the director's vision of the play. The actor's job is to tell the story the playwright has written, within the director's concept. This requires discipline and collaboration between actor and director. If the director is clear about the concept and the work that needs to be accomplished from rehearsal to rehearsal then there can be meaningful collaboration.

Great collaboration can only occur if the seeds are sown from the beginning. The beginning is the development of the director's concept. If the concept is not clear to everyone involved, there can be confusion between directing, design, and acting elements. It is the work of the director to inspire the entire team by developing a cohesive plan and yet leave latitude for all artists to create within the parameters of the written concept.

How does a director arrive at a clear concept of a production? After reading aloud the play several times, and incorporating the tools I offer herein, I ask myself a series of questions:

What are the chief themes of the play?
How did I arrive at the decision of the chief themes? (Justify.)
Where in the play, specifically, do these themes manifest?
What do I consider to be the main theme of the play and why?
> (When the audience leaves the theater what do I want them to be thinking about)? This will become the plays superobjective and will include the overall atmosphere.

How can the main theme be best represented visually?
Is this a play that can be reimagined—set in a time period other than it is intended? (This is possible with many plays and especially Shakespeare.) What drives me to think about this?
Why are we doing this play now? Are there events happening in the world that makes this play timely? How can I connect our play to those events?
What music might I use to enhance the themes?
What colors do I see—especially on each character? Why?
What is the overall atmosphere of the play and in each scene?

> ***Teaching Tip:*** Once I have completed a concept statement, I e-mail it to the stage manager who then sends it to the entire production team. I do this at least two weeks prior to the first production meeting. This gives the designers time to consider the concept and develop some initial thoughts/questions. In those weeks prior to the first production meeting I usually meet with the scenic, costume, and lighting designers individually to listen to their responses. Inevitably some things change in the concept from their responses and usually for the better. Directors must give designers room to practice their own art. Since I chiefly work in academic theater, mentoring designers is extremely important. I love this early part of the process.
>
> When we get to the first production meeting everyone is already excited and the meeting is lively. Instead of presenting the concept at the meeting I can look at the designers' early visual images from their research and listen to their ideas. When I have responded to these ideas, I then check in with each designer frequently until the final production designs are due. Ideas breed more ideas (and positive changes) and being a hands-on director in the design process always produces better results. The concept evolves with lots of conversation and creative collaboration.

Here is my concept for *Midsummer*. (How I arrived at the themes occurs at the end of the concept.)

A MIDSUMMER NIGHT'S DREAM BY WILLIAM SHAKESPEARE DIRECTED BY MARK MONDAY

Concept statement

"The course of true love never did run smooth." Lysander

We are telling a story about love and all that love entails—fear, jealousy, sex, compromise, exhilaration, and sacrifice. Our story ends in very happy circumstances and leads me to think Shakespeare means for us to consider that *Love Conquers All*. (The theme "Love Conquers All" is our "superobjective," or what we want to communicate as the overriding theme of our story.)

The time of the action is 21–24 June (summer solstice). In Elizabethan England, Midsummer Day—the feast of St. John the Baptist is 24 June. Midsummer night is the preceding evening. It was a time of feasting and merriment. On midsummer night, fairies, hobgoblins, and witches held festivals. The action takes place at the palace of the Duke of Athens and a forest somewhere beyond the palace in Ancient Greece, or in actuality, a thinly disguised Elizabethan England made from fantasy and mythology.

The design depends on the chiaroscuro of night and day: daylight for opening scenes in Athens; moonlight followed by fog and then dawn in the woods; day for Bottom's return to the other mechanicals, night (torchlight) for the married couples in the palace, with "moonshine" (and starlight) in *Pyramus and Thisbe*. Finally, the fairies enter to give "glimmering light by the dead and drowsy fire."

Cupid, the love god, is important to represent as he is mentioned several times in the play. Perhaps our floor treatment could be a portrait of "Cupid painted blind." As we will stage the play in a thrust configuration, I feel there should be a "forest canopy" above and behind the audience to give the feeling of enclosure and intimacy. I'd like the audience to feel as if they are part of the forest. Perhaps also represented on the floor or otherwise may be images of Theseus overcoming Hippolyta in the war with the Amazons. Other scenic elements might include a bridge in the upstage portion of the space serving as part of the palace and a footpath or footbridge in the forest. Titania's bower could come from below the bridge and be stored behind when necessary. Vine-covered columns could serve as architectural elements of the palace and trees in the forest. The columns could mask ladders and fire poles, which the fairies use for entrances and exits. Three downstage benches located near the vomitorium and stairs on either side complete the mise–en–scène.

Costumes reflect the period of Ancient Greece yet in a fantasy or dream. For an *image* let's think of Ancient Greece meets Fredericks of Hollywood. What does sexy lingerie look like in a dream/fantasy of the period? As the "lovers" pursue each other in the forest, their garments become dirty, ragged, until they are left with almost nothing at all. Theseus and Hippolyta will also play Oberon and Titania. We will need to transform the characters on the stage in full view of the audience. The four speaking fairies should be costumed according to their names, which reflect elements in nature. The character of Moth should have wings that can be manipulated by another fairy who serves as a "shadow." The rude mechanical's clothing is rough-hewn and patchworked and should also have an element of fantasy. It is important, when designing the ass's head for Bottom, to remember that the actor must be able to speak with clarity and ease.

Lighting should clearly define the four days and nights of summer solstice described above. Beyond the specific definition of days and nights, especially in the forest, texture and color should enhance the theme of dream/fantasy. Muted lighting, filtering through the canopy of the forest comes to mind. The play begins with an "old moon," meaning (for dramatic purposes) a full moon, and ends on the cycle of a "new moon," or slightly crescent moon. Finally, there is one scene in the play that requires fog. It must come in quickly and from at least four locations.

As to sound—since this is leaning toward a more traditional production of *Midsummer*—I am listening to Mendelssohn and especially harp music from the Celtic tradition for the fairy world. (The fairies are Celtic inspired in the play.) At this point I am not "married" to Mendelssohn, and welcome input. We will need incidental sounds (possibly harp) to accentuate the magic spells as they occur. There may be some underscoring during certain speeches.

Note: Luckily, we did not use Mendelssohn. Instead, the actor playing Quince—Jamie Koeth—wrote original and beautiful music for the production. This is an example of how the director profits from flexibility. The original music was a highlight of the ensemble experience. Actors profited greatly, as did the audience, with the collaboration of the composer who also acted as music director. The music also inspired many choices from this director.

Props

One very important prop is a puppet of the "little Indian boy." He is so important to the plot between Oberon and Titania, I believe he needs to have a presence. The puppet should have some physical articulation to be manipulated by one of the fairies. As to size, the puppet should be able to be hidden in the wings of Moth. Other props include lanterns mounted on long sticks for scenes in the forest to be carried by fairies. These lanterns could be surrounded by moths, bees, etc. mounted on wires. Titania and Oberon should have bows and arrows in the scene in the forest. Philostrate should have scrolls at the end of the play. The rude mechanicals should be outfitted with their respective accoutrements as described in the play within the play.

Note for scenery, props, and lighting

One Greek celebration was to take down the Mayday wreaths at end of summer solstice and burn them in large communal bonfires. This would feature dancing, music, and jumping over flames. It may be interesting at the end of the play, during the fairy dance, to have the fairies remove the wreaths, "set them on fire," and perform their dance during Oberon's final speech.

Major themes of the play

1 Love's Difficulty: Love is out of balance for much of the play.
2 Love Is Blind.
3 All's Fair in Love and War.
4 Magic: Supernatural power of love—the love potion. Misuse of magic.
5 Dreams: Explanation of strange events; time loses its normal sense of flow, illusion. Dreams are often fantasy/fantastical.

- 6 Feminism/Male Dominance. (Father's don't always know best.)
- 7 Love Conquers All.

Scene breakdown

Act I, scene I—The Royal Palace of Theseus in Athens, Greece
Act I, scene II—The home of Peter Quince in Athens
Act II, scene I—The Magical Kingdom of Oberon (the forest)
Act II, scene II—The same (Titania's bower)
Act III, scene I—Before Titania's bower
Act III, scene II—Another part of the forest
Act IV, scene I—The same
Act IV, scene II—The home of Peter Quince
Act V, scene I—The Royal Palace of Athens

> **NOTE TO DIRECTORS**

You'll see in the concept statement there are specific wants from the director and also hints to the designers. Give designers, through these hints, leeway to surprise you. These surprises, when designers respond to the concept, always excite me and give me more ideas. The concept should always send a clear message and allow other artists to practice their art. It really is a matter of respect not only for all theater artists but for theater itself.

How I arrived at the themes of the play

Theme: Love's difficulty (love is out of balance for much of the play)

1 Egeus is outraged that his daughter Hermia would defy him by wanting to wed someone other than his choice for her husband. Why would a daughter defy her father in this period of history given the circumstances?

PREFACE TO USING THIS BOOK   xxix

2 Demetrius loves Hermia, and once loved Helena. Helena and Hermia are best friends. Now, there is strife between Hermia and Helena, which sets their relationship out of balance.

3 There can be an interesting dynamic between Theseus and Hippolyta. Theseus has recently conquered the Amazons in battle. He must be a mighty force indeed for Hippolyta, Queen of the Amazons, to have fallen in love with him so quickly. This tells me that "Love Conquers All."

4 Looking at the rude mechanicals, it is interesting to consider their history together. From my reading, I wonder about their backstory. What brought these artisans together? One can conclude from the text that they have some sort of prior relationship and at the root of it all is their love of theater. They are dilettantes; they aspire to more, yet without much talent. So, their love of theater is out of balance with what they can possibly achieve.

5 The relationship of Puck to everyone in the play is out of balance. He or she is full of such mischief, and mistakes, for example, his or her administering a potion to the wrong person, throws Oberon's plan out of kilter.

6 Oberon's anointing of his potion to Titania—making her fall in love with an "ass." This introduces a theme of lust, and possibly even bestiality that is definitely out of balance.

Theme: Love is blind

> Things base and vile, holding no quantity,
> Love can transpose to form and dignity
> Love looks not with the eyes but with the mind,
> And therefore is wing'd Cupid painted blind.

This excerpt from Helena's speech in Act I, scene I, is the crux of the entire play, for love is often illogical.

1 It is not logical for a father, Egeus, to bring his own daughter before the highest court in the land where she may be sentenced to death.

2 It is not logical for a Queen to fall in love with a donkey.

3 It is not logical for four young people to flee from trouble into a forest for the sake of love.

All's fair in love and war

1 Helena concocts a scheme to win back Demetrius from her oldest and most dear friend.
2 Oberon concocts a scheme to punish Titania for not giving him a small boy to attend him.
3 Theseus conquers Titania and woos her to be his wife.
4 Puck goes to great lengths for his love of Oberon—his master.

Magic

1 My gentle Puck, come hither. Thou rememberest
Since once I sat upon a promontory,
And heard a mermaid on a dolphin's back . . .
That very time I saw (but thou couldst not),
Flying between the cold moon and the earth,
Cupid all armed.

In Oberon's speech, Act II, scene I, we begin to get the sense of how powerful the theme of magic is in the play. Magic is something we all believed in as children and many of us still do, or at least want to believe. Regardless, we are drawn to the power of magic even if it is on the stage and we suspend our earthly beliefs because of it.

2 Puck's ability to "put a girdle round about the Earth in forty minutes."
3 Puck's ability to make magic potions.
4 The magic of turning Bottom into an ass and having Titania fall in love with him.
5 The magic that helps bring to fruition the main theme of "Love Conquers All" when the three couples are married.

Dreams

1. This play could begin with Bottom awakening and delivering his famous "Bottom's Dream" speech from Act IV, scene I. From there it could unfold from the beginning. It would set up the notion that the play reveals the dream that Bottom had and what transpires is the enactment of that dream.
2. *Midsummer* is a play that might come from dreams and of which dreams are made.
3. Dreams are often our fantasies.

Feminism/male dominance

1. Egeus brings to the highest court his argument of the law of Athens, which is that the father has the right to choose the husband of his daughter.
2. Hermia, daughter of Egeus, has the gumption to argue the law.
3. Hippolyta doesn't utter a word in the matter of the argument put before Theseus from Egeus and Hermia concerning the marriage. Hippolyta is a conquered Queen and is probably wary of interfering with matters of court. She does, however, make her status known in her speech late in the play, "I was with Hercules and Cadmus once." This indicates the relationship between the two have grown together in sharing conversation and are on a more equal footing.

Love conquers all

1. There is the triple wedding near the end of the play. Love has conquered even the most strained of circumstances.
2. Oberon and Titania have been joyfully reunited.
3. Egeus, at least in this production, gives his blessing to Hermia following the wedding.
4. With the success of the play at court, Bottom and Quince overcome their differences and express their love for each other.

Practice exploration

Choose a play you're working on now or have recently done and develop a concept with justifications for the themes you wish to explore.

Follow-up

When reading your play aloud it's best to keep a journal handy. Jot down any thoughts or images you discover. This will aid you in developing the concept. Once you have an initial statement you will be ready to continue your preparatory work. I prefer to write my concept statement and then do the work in the next chapter. Following that, I can refine the statement and then share it with the production team. It may seem excessive but this work usually takes me six to nine months. Some of that time is spent cutting if I'm working on a classic play. Regardless, we cannot be too prepared as directors or teachers.

The material in Chapter 1 is filled with important concepts and definitions. I urge you to proceed slowly as the work is the foundation for all that follows. It may be beneficial for you to analyze a play of your choosing while delving into the material.

1
PREPARATION — ANALYSIS AND COMPOSITION

Framework

The work in this chapter is concerned with the elements of composition. The composition of a play, in Chekhovian terms, results from careful analysis. Chekhov says in *To the Actor*, "The same fundamentals which govern the universe and the life of earth and man, and the principles which bring harmony and rhythm to music, poetry and architecture, also comprise the *Laws of Composition* which, to a greater or lesser degree, can be applied to every dramatic performance." As I mentioned earlier it would be a good idea to read Chapter 8 of *To the Actor* before tackling this work. Not all of the principles of the Laws of Composition are explored here. I've found, in my directing, that certain individual laws take care of themselves if you adhere to the major ones we will explore.

Before we begin, I've provided definitions of the terms we'll be using for easy reference.

Definitions

Composition: combining elements to form a whole. Creating the composition of a play consists of finding tempo, polarity, transformation, and identifying themes, atmospheres, artistic frames, and the major and auxiliary climaxes. The other definitions that are included are not germane to Chekhov.

Atmosphere: the overall mood of the play and individual scenes, for example, fear and hate. Atmosphere permeates the play and each scene and also exists in individual characters dependent on the given circumstances. We term the overall atmosphere of the scene, or the play, "the objective atmosphere." The atmosphere of the individual is the subjective atmosphere. It is the collision of atmospheres that create conflict.

Polarity: contrast. Polarity, in a well-written play, can be best observed by comparing the beginning and the ending. In *Midsummer*, for example, we begin with dire circumstances and end in a joyous triple wedding. What happens in between is the *transformation* of evil to good. In the beginning of *King Lear*, we witness a despotic king who, in the end, experiences his final moments in redemption. While it may be too little, too late, it is regardless a journey that exemplifies the struggle of good and evil. Polarity also includes choices an actor can make to reach his or her objective. By varying choices to reach an objective the actor helps in creating the rhythmical wave.

Rhythmical Wave: a literal wave, a roller coaster, created by all components of composition. (See example later in this chapter.)

Tempo: a rate of movement/speech between the slowest and the fastest. In Chekhovian terms this is "staccato-legato."

Transformation: the longest part of the play. The play progresses from the initial climax near the beginning and transforms to a polar climax near the end.

Artistic Frame: similar, yet more profound, to Stanislavski's "beats." The artistic frame has a beginning, middle, and ending (B-M-E). The B-M-E can also be thought of as preparation, execution, and sustaining. The preparation begins in the fantasy—imagining, at Chekhov's direction, to see the objective achieved before we actually make an attempt of action. The execution is the action. Sustaining is maintaining the action(s) with your scene partner until the frame is completed.

Arc of action (AoA): the titling, naming, or "baptizing" of an artistic frame, such as, "The confrontation," "The set-up," etc. Baptizing an artistic frame with an AoA is extremely important for the director and actor. What is an "arc" in our terms? It is an unbroken line, like a rhythmical wave, that gives the actor a clear indication of how the artistic frame should be constructed with action. After baptizing the artistic frame, the director need only guide the actor by keeping his or

PREPARATION—ANALYSIS AND COMPOSITION 3

her actions within the title of the AoA. Baptizing the artistic frame with an AoA is a time saver because the director offers minimum instruction and allows the actor to create in those given parameters.

Blocks: division of the text for rehearsal purposes.
Action: what I do to get what I want; a verb, for example, I lift.
Qualities of action: how I do what I do to get what I want; an adverb, for example, joyfully. Action and qualities are always combined, for example, I lift, joyfully.

Note: Actions and qualities are explored in depth later. They are mentioned here only as a precursor of the work to come with actors. Don't be overly concerned about them in the analysis portion of your work.

We can now move on to identifying the climaxes for *Midsummer* and creating a rhythmical wave for the play. If you have written your initial concept for the play you are working on, you already know where the climaxes occur.

In a well-written play there are usually three major climaxes (CX). In *Midsummer*:

CX1—1st major climax—Act I, scene I—the plea from Egeus to Theseus.
CX2—2nd major climax—Act III, scene I—Bottom is transformed into an "ass."
CX3—3rd major climax—Act V, scene I—the play within the play.

This is somewhat of a subjective exercise and lies within the director's vision. For the sake of learning the basic theory of composition let's agree on this division. Then, there are the auxiliary climaxes (ACX):

ACX1—1st auxiliary climax—Act II, scene I—Titania's line "Not for thy fairy kingdom. Fairies, away!" Titania recognizes that the situation is hopeless and exits.
ACX2—2nd auxiliary climax—Act II, scene II—Lysander awakes and professes his love to Helena.
ACX3—3rd auxiliary climax—Act III, scene II—the fight between the lovers.
ACX4—4th auxiliary climax—Act IV, scene I—Titania wakes and sees Bottom as he truly is.

ACX5—5th auxiliary climax—Act IV, scene II—Bottom's return to the other mechanicals.

Admittedly, *Midsummer* is different from a Shakespearean tragedy in that the tragedies and the histories have more auxiliary climaxes and mainly because there are fewer scenes in each act in *Midsummer*. This makes the play a good example to study in that it is not overwhelming. Here we must again agree, for our purposes of study, on the major climax—"the play within the play."

Abbreviations:

CX1 = Climax 1, etc.

ACX1 = Auxiliary Climax 1, etc.

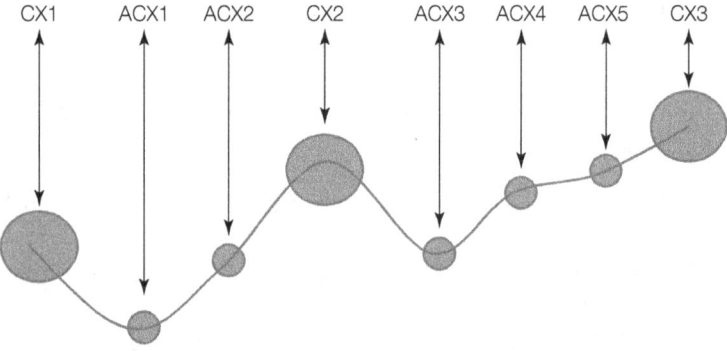

A crucial element of composition the director must consider and communicate to the designers and cast is that of *polarity*. A well-written play ends at the polar opposite of how it begins and, according to Michael Chekhov, represents the fight between good and evil—another aspect of Higher Ego. In *Midsummer*, the first major climax occurs when Egeus brings his daughter Hermia before the Duke of Athens. In essence, Egeus brings "charges" against Hermia, which she attempts to defend. This is serious business and should be played so. It is a trial of sorts with an overall atmosphere of fear. Egeus wants Hermia to marry as he chooses or else be put to death or banished. There is nothing more serious than life or death and these are the stakes being played. There is the sense of evil present.

Practice exploration

Using the same play you worked on for developing your concept statement, create a rhythmical wave and identify the climaxes.
  Then the journey begins toward the end of the play. The audience rides the wave to the ending which is filled with the atmosphere of joy and the representation of the journey from evil to good. The play ends exactly opposite from where it begins—with weddings, the play within the play, a celebration with the fairies—and is an example of perfect polarity. Of course there is the middle to consider—that place where plots unfold and intertwine. This is the transformation. It is best, I believe, to truly understand the polarity of beginning and ending before delving too deeply into the middle. It is the middle that is most difficult to construct, considering that it should constantly be connected to both ends. It is also the longest period of the play. Themes reinforce themselves in the middle period or give a glimpse of the ending. I think of it as building a bridge where we have a solid foundation on both ends and slowly work ourselves from both these ends to an eventual meeting in the middle. The director should work with the actors on the climaxes of the beginning and ending in the first week of rehearsal. It is not important that we find a performance in rehearsing this way. That's impossible in the first week. Rather, let's find the commitment to reach the Higher Ego. We improvise, we rid ourselves of our daily lives, we plunge headlong into the highest points of the play and explore where we "let go" the most—emotionally and physically. It is good to indulge at this stage for there is a freedom in indulgence. Push the boundaries! If we don't find where the boundaries are, we'll never know how far we can go.
  What one finds in this exercise of charting a rhythmical wave is that the themes, more often than not, reveal themselves within these major and auxiliary climaxes. We can now revisit our work on our written concept and develop it even further.
  Finding the major and auxiliary climaxes of the play is the foundation of composition, which strengthens the concept. The next step is to divide the play into rehearsal blocks. These blocks are sometimes French scenes (entrances and exits) or simply sections of text that constitute a logical rehearsal section comprised of 20 to 90-minute increments. In *Midsummer*, I divided the play into 88 blocks.

First of all the stage manager makes a list of each character in each block and posts it on the production callboard. At the beginning of the week the stage manager posts the rehearsal schedule for the entire week—the breakdown of each day with the blocks we'll be rehearsing. The actors can reference the schedule to the list of blocks. For instance, I may call a rehearsal on Tuesday for blocks 1, 2, and 3. I might schedule block 1 for 20 minutes, block 2 for 30 minutes, and block 3 for 1 hour. Only the actors who are in those blocks are called for that period of time. This saves a tremendous amount of time if all actors are punctual and prepared and if the director is also well prepared for the work.

This type of scheduling is initially difficult for the director. Once you get used to it, you'll find it makes preparation easier. The director is forced to make a rehearsal plan that is based upon the specifics of what needs to be accomplished. Actors appreciate this type of structure. I believe that calling actors to wait in the studio for a lengthy period of time without getting on stage is counterproductive to the feeling of the whole. This type of scheduling also gives actors time to prepare.

The blocks are comprised of artistic frames. The chief element of the artistic frame, for analysis and scoring purposes, is a clear beginning, middle, and ending baptized with an AoA. Some blocks are a single artistic frame, others longer with several or many frames. This is the subjective work of the director. You'll find various examples forthcoming.

Practice exploration

Please read the following scene aloud and on your feet now. You can come back to it later and "score" the scene with added tools for a very different kind of reading. Have your journal handy and jot down anything that gives you a visceral reaction. Make a note where you feel a change in the text. The change can be an indication of the beginning of a new artistic frame. You'll feel the changes if you read slowly and are open to discovery. In your reading especially note where you feel the climax may be.

Act I scene I. Athens. The palace of THESEUS.
Block 1
Enter **Theseus**, **Hippolyta** *followed by* **Philostrate**

Theseus
Now, fair Hippolyta, our nuptial hour
Draws on apace; four happy days bring in
Another moon: but, O, methinks, how slow
This old moon wanes! She lingers my desires,
Like to a step-dame or a dowager
Long withering out a young man's revenue.

Hippolyta
Four days will quickly steep themselves in night;
Four nights will quickly dream away the time;
And then the moon, like to a silver bow
New-bent in heaven, shall behold the night
Of our solemnities.

Theseus
Go, Philostrate,
Stir up the Athenian youth to merriments;
Awake the pert and nimble spirit of mirth.

Exit **Philostrate**

Block 2.
Hippolyta, I woo'd thee with my sword,
And won thy love, doing thee injuries;
But I will wed thee in another key,
With pomp, with triumph and with revelling.

Block 3.
Enter **Egeus, Hermia, Lysander,** *and* **Demetrius**

Egeus
Happy be Theseus, our renowned Duke!

Theseus
Thanks, good Egeus. What's the news with thee?

Egeus
Full of vexation come I, with complaint
Against my child, my daughter Hermia.
Stand forth, Demetrius. My noble lord,
This man hath my consent to marry her.
Stand forth, Lysander. And, my gracious Duke,

This man hath bewitch'd the bosom of my child.
Thou, thou, Lysander, thou hast given her rhymes,
And interchanged love-tokens with my child.
Thou hast by moonlight at her window sung
With faining voice verses of feigning love,
And stolen the impression of her fantasy.
With cunning hast thou filch'd my daughter's heart,
Turn'd her obedience (which is due to me)
To stubborn harshness. And, my gracious Duke,
Be it so she will not here before your Grace
Consent to marry with Demetrius,
I beg the ancient privilege of Athens:
As she is mine, I may dispose of her;
Which shall be either to this gentleman,
Or to her death, according to our law
Immediately provided in that case.

Theseus
What say you, Hermia? Be advised fair maid.
To you your father should be as a god:
Demetrius is a worthy gentleman.

Hermia
So is Lysander.

Theseus
In himself he is;
But in this kind, wanting your father's voice,
The other must be held the worthier.

Hermia
I would my father look'd but with my eyes.

Theseus
Rather your eyes must with his judgment look.

Hermia
I do entreat your grace to pardon me.
I know not by what power I am made bold,
But I beseech your grace that I may know
The worst that may befall me in this case,
If I refuse to wed Demetrius.

Theseus
Either to die the death or to abjure
Forever the society of men.

Hermia
So will I grow, so live, so die, my lord,
Ere I will my virgin patent up
Unto his lordship, whose unwished yoke
My soul consents not to give sovereignty.

The blocks above are examples of very short, short, and long blocks. I divide the play into blocks before rehearsals begin. Part of the analysis is dividing the blocks into artistic frames. This work is all the subjective work of the director and his or her vision.

Once I have broken the play into blocks and decided the climaxes, I determine each block's artistic frames and baptize (label) each AoA and atmosphere. An AoA is the overall theme or umbrella, including action and atmosphere, of each artistic frame in each block. What do I want the audience to know? In other words, I come up with a brief description of the AoA and the atmosphere/mood of each artistic frame. This exercise of labeling the overall AoA gives the actors and designers a guide to help construct the rhythmical wave. The actors should structure objectives, actions, and qualities according to the label of the AoA following work on psychological gesture (see Chapters 4, 5). I offer the concept here because it is part of the initial process of the director.

Determining the AoA is an interesting process. First, you must experience the artistic frame by acting it. Then, your brain takes over. Ask yourself, what was that experience? What did I feel? What did each character feel? What is the argument? What is the overall arc of the frame? From here you can create a label, or baptism, for the frame. I have found it wise to keep the baptism of the frames brief as actors only need a guide to their actions and qualities—not paragraphs of director dialogue. Asking and answering these questions as you act the play on your feet is the key to continued development of the concept and choosing artistic frames.

Atmosphere, or mood, is ever present in the play and in characters. In *Lessons for the Professional Actor*, Chekhov says, "Each creation starts with atmosphere . . . it always starts with atmosphere." We are always in some sort of mood. Actors, directors, and designers must realize this. We recognize atmosphere can be labeled most anything—atmosphere of the circus, hate, love, or sexuality. I believe we can reduce atmospheres to their "lowest common denominators." Audiences respond emotionally to *archetypes* (form and psychology) that are universally recognizable. You should be aware that reducing the atmospheres to their lowest common denominator is not Chekhov's teaching. Rather, the idea comes to us through psychology and, I believe had Chekhov known this, he would have embraced the idea.

The archetypes of atmosphere (in their essences and according to psychology) are: glad, mad, sad, bad, and fear. These five moods represent the archetype, or the *essence*, of the thing itself. The practice of reducing to the essence of atmospheres is useful in beginning rehearsals. Actors and directors may, as is their prerogative, be more specific about atmosphere according to their needs or given circumstances as rehearsals progress. A director/teacher, in the beginning, should serve to guide the actor via archetypes. Chekhov suggests that we read the play, at first, forgetting about all that we know about it and consider only the atmospheres. It makes good sense to me to identify the atmospheres, at first, as essences.

Atmosphere is an integral part of Higher Ego in that it affects our feelings. The danger, for the actor, is attempting to *act* or *play* an atmosphere. It is not something one can play or indicate, as we know (indicating is not truthful acting). Rather, atmosphere is created in the imagination and *influences* our actions and qualities of action. The director should always be aware of this "trap." We'll consider more about this in a later chapter. Also, see below a sample exercise for atmosphere.

Practice exploration

In Quince's prologue in the play within the play (from his demeanor), we observe he is quite nervous. The essence of nervousness is fear. As the speech progresses, his subjective atmosphere changes in tune with the given circumstances. A gateway to creating atmosphere begins before reading.

Walk about the room before you speak and treat objects with the chosen atmosphere. Lift a chair within the atmosphere of fear. You are

PREPARATION—ANALYSIS AND COMPOSITION

not necessarily afraid of the chair—simply work in the atmosphere. Just imagine a room filled with fear and your behavior will change. Imagine lifting the chair as your action. Once you have created the atmosphere, begin to speak. Repeat the exercise when you reach a new atmosphere in the speech. Read this speech aloud and imagine each atmosphere. Speak the title of the atmosphere, with its inherent quality, before you speak the lines:

Prologue
(*Fear*) Gentles, perchance you wonder at this show;
But wonder on, till truth make all things plain.
This man is Pyramus, if you would know;
This beauteous lady Thisbe is certain.
This man, with lime and rough-cast, doth present
Wall, that vile Wall which did these lovers sunder;
And through Wall's chink, poor souls, they are content
To whisper. At the which let no man wonder.
(*Glad*) This man, with lanthorn, dog, and bush of thorn,
Presenteth Moonshine; for, if you will know,
By moonshine did these lovers think no scorn
To meet at Ninus' tomb, there, there to woo.
This grisly beast, which Lion hight by name,
(*Sad*) The trusty Thisbe, coming first by night,
Did scare away, or rather did affright;
And, as she fled, her mantle she did fall,
Which Lion vile with bloody mouth did stain.
Anon comes Pyramus, sweet youth and tall,
And finds his trusty Thisbe's mantle slain:
Whereat, with blade, with bloody blameful blade,
He bravely broach'd his boiling bloody breast;
And Thisbe, tarrying in mulberry shade,
His dagger drew, and died. (*Glad*) For all the rest,
Let Lion, Moonshine, Wall, and lovers twain
At large discourse, while here they do remain.

Quince stumbles over his words and "his speech is like a tangled chain." As the speech progresses, he gains more confidence and the atmosphere changes to joy or "glad." The speech turns "sad" in the middle which affects the tempo/rhythm of the scene. All things in comedy are not "faster and funnier." How many plays and musicals have you seen that are all one tempo—fast? There is no journey in one tempo—only a flat line.

> **ATMOSPHERE**
>
> In the definitions in the framework of this chapter, I indicated there are two kinds of atmosphere: personal atmosphere (subjective) and an atmosphere that exists in the space itself (objective). As an example, before the play within the play begins, the couples just married enter the space of the court and fill it with "glad." They are, after all, pretty much just biding time before bedtime. There is an air of joyful anticipation—glad! Then Quince enters as the Prologue filled with the subjective atmosphere of fear. The atmospheres collide, which creates conflict. The courtiers find this collision humorous as does the audience. It is this collision that the director must be aware of and guide accordingly.

The score

What follows is a scene from the play that I have divided into blocks and artistic frames. I have also labeled the AoA and atmosphere. *Note: In this particular example the blocks and artistic frames happen to be the same. Again, this is not always the case.* This is the director's score.

The work on artistic frames, atmosphere, and AoAs is what the director would bring into the rehearsal. It gives the actors a rubric to work with. It doesn't interfere with their work on actions and qualities. The director should not identify actions and qualities as that is the work of the actors (within the director's vision). Where does this work come from for the director? It comes from reading aloud and recording the "clues" as he or she works through the play.

PREPARATION—ANALYSIS AND COMPOSITION

Practice exploration

Read this scene aloud and on your feet. You should also read aloud the AoA and the atmosphere. Again, when you speak the AoA and atmosphere try to find the quality they suggest in your voice (your vocal quality).

Block 12.

Enter, from one side, **Oberon**, *with his train; from the other,* **Titania**, *with hers*

Arc of action = The confrontation. Atmosphere = Mad.

Note: Artistic frames are enclosed in brackets.

Oberon
[Ill met by moonlight, proud Titania.

Titania
What, jealous Oberon? Fairies, skip hence:
I have forsworn his bed and company.

Oberon
Tarry, rash wanton: am not I thy lord?

Titania
Then I must be thy lady: but I know
When thou hast stolen away from fairy land,
And in the shape of Corin sat all day,
Playing on pipes of corn and versing love
To amorous Phillida. Why art thou here,
Come from the farthest step of India . . .?

Oberon
How canst thou thus for shame, Titania,
Glance at my credit with Hippolyta,
Knowing I know thy love to Theseus?]

Clues to AoA = "proud Titania," Titania confronts Oberon who is obviously jealous.

Clues to Atmosphere = "ill met," "jealous Oberon" Titania orders the fairies to leave, "rash wonton," which means a skittish and willful creature.

Block 13.
Arc of action = The truth. Atmosphere = Mad.

Titania
[These are the forgeries of jealousy:
And never, since the middle summer's spring,
Met we on hill, in dale, forest or mead,
By paved fountain or by rushy brook,
Or in the beached margent of the sea,
To dance our ringlets to the whistling wind . . .
We are their parents and the original.]

Clues to AoA = Titania is accusing Oberon of being the source or instigator of all of their confrontations for a long time. She is telling the truth from her perspective and we have reason to believe her.

Block 14.
Arc of action = The challenge. Atmosphere = Mad.

Oberon
[Do you amend it then; it lies in you. . .

Titania
Set your heart at rest:
The fairy land buys not the child of me. . .
. . . And for her sake I will not part with him.

Oberon
How long within this wood intend you stay?]

Clues to AoA = Oberon challenges Titania to give up the boy and says all will be well. Titania refuses and challenges him by saying no. She knows there will be repercussions and yet stands steadfast.

Block 15.
Arc of action = The attempt. Atmosphere = Bad.

Titania
[Perchance till after Theseus' wedding-day.
If you will patiently dance in our round
And see our moonlight revels, go with us;
If not, shun me, and I will spare your haunts.

Oberon
Give me that boy, and I will go with thee.]

Clues to AoA = "patiently," Titania is making an attempt at reconciliation. She also issues an ultimatum with her final line.

Block 16.
Arc of action = The final word. Atmosphere = Mad.

Titania
[Not for thy fairy kingdom. Fairies, away!
We shall chide downright, if I longer stay]. *Exit* **Titania** *with her train.*

Clues to AoA = "Not for thy fairy kingdom," or, not for all the world would I do this. "Chide downright" is also a clue. Titania and Oberon are powerful fairies. Oberon has already changed the weather to the detriment of the humans. Imagine if the two really got into a physical confrontation!

As I said, the above work is what the director brings to rehearsal. It is a vision derived from the study of the play and its superobjective—Love Conquers All. The scene is the first meeting of Titania and Oberon in the play. It begins and ends with the atmosphere of mad. It is in perfect contrast to the opening scene of the play with Theseus and Hippolyta where we saw a glad atmosphere. Therefore, polarity is present and important.

Notice that the objective atmosphere does not change in the scene. The conflict (atmosphere) is ominous. Neither Titania nor Oberon gives way to the objective atmosphere, and so a parting is inevitable. Is there a clear winner? Titania does use better judgment and decides to depart. This may be interpreted as reinforcing the theme of Feminism in the play and is important for the director to note because, in my opinion, the women in the play have the most logical point of view.

The director brings to the rehearsal an overall guide for the actors to follow. There is so much more to discover when actors bring their talents to the vision. We will look at the rhythmical wave of this scene later in the book after the actors have found their actions, qualities, and subjective atmospheres. The rhythmical wave is not only the overall wave that we create for the climaxes. There must be waves within the overall wave.

While thinking about composition, consider my "umbrella" analogy:

The canopy of the umbrella represents the overall objective atmosphere of the play.
The handle, top to bottom, is the *spine*, or superobjective. It connects everything and without its support the form is difficult to recognize.
The rods are AoAs that support, inflate, and deflate the canopy.
The ring (the device that connects all the rods and raises the canopy) can be the objective. In this case it is to protect the user from the elements.

Once the concept is initially scripted and I have studied the composition of the play, it is time to think about casting. The casting process is often stressful. It doesn't need to be if the director always keeps the concept in mind. Chapter 2 discusses the casting process and hopefully a way to make the process easier.

Other practice explorations for preparation

Read aloud and on your feet blocks 1–3 in this chapter playing all the roles. Have your journal accessible. Record any images that come to mind as you read. (Example: In my prework on this play I was excited to finally get to the forest in scene III so that I could play all the fairies. I knew it would be easy to work in my Higher Ego. Puck speaks to the fairy, "How now, spirit, whither wander you?" For whatever reason, I spoke loudly as Puck and I, as the Fairy, was startled. This led me to a wonderful image that was a highlight of the production. I discovered an image, as the Fairy, that I was gathering flowers while dancing on the moon. In the production we accomplished this having the Fairy appear prior to Puck's entrance. She was discovered dancing on a projection of the moon on the stage floor. Puck's entrance frightened her as she was caught up in her actions. This also led us to a change in atmosphere. Upon her entrance, I allowed the image of the beautiful Fairy to linger. There was often an audible gasp by the audience when the Fairy was discovered as the picture was so lovely. The atmosphere we established was "glad." When Puck interrupted the scene the atmosphere changed to "startled" or "fear." When I first read this opening I simply stopped and wrote down, "Fairy dancing on the moon.") We don't need to be elaborate in our notes in the beginning. Because we are working our Higher Ego, we have a feeling. Feelings are always stored in the body. When we revisit our notes the feeling will return and details can be fleshed out.

Practice exploration

After you've read Act I, scene I twice, divide the scene into artistic frames. Work through one artistic frame at a time and discover and record the AoA and atmosphere. (Note: I provide an alternate way to label the AoA in Appendix III if you wish to "cheat" forward.) Force yourself to begin at the climax of the scene. It will be the easiest artistic frame to label. Don't work from beginning to end. Read the scene again and pay attention to all you've recorded. You'll discover by adhering to your work that actions and qualities will occur naturally.

Note: The atmospheres listed in the scene included do not dictate actions. Remember that atmospheres are the canopy under which our actions are influenced. There are a multitude of actions that can be found in any specific atmosphere by the actors. Instead of dictating, guide. Just remember that atmospheres are not actable. Once you understand the process of the work in this chapter you are ready to begin your work with actors. Yet, first you must cast the play and Chekhov provides us unique tools to do so.

2
CASTING AND CLASSWORK USING ARCHETYPES

Framework

The focus of this chapter is chiefly dedicated to how a director can use archetypes as a tool in casting a play. Yet, the exercises described herein are easily adapted to acting and directing classes and to a rehearsal as you will note.

Now that we've explored developing a concept, we turn our attention to how the director comes to a conclusion in casting. Obviously, the director cannot move into the casting process without a thorough study of the play. I don't cast until I've established the concept and the overall rhythmical wave of the play. I need to decide the superobjective so that I can begin to understand how each character fits into the overall theme. All actors/characters should fit under the "umbrella" of the vision.

In looking at individual characters the director has clear clues from the playwright on how to cast the play. These clues are: what the characters say, what others say about them, and, most important, what the characters *do*. In Lenard Petit's book *The Michael Chekhov Handbook*, Petit refers to what the characters *do* as "deeds done." Recording the deeds done and other clues will help lead you to character archetypes. Archetype, again, means essence. At the very core of each character, and each human being, there are certain essences that determine archetypes. The Chinese refer to essence as "the spirit of the spirit." The director should search through the clues of the play and determine the archetypes of each character prior to going into the casting process.

The question becomes, "Does the actor possess these essences and/or can s/he incorporate them into the character?"

When working with the Chekhov Technique we are always searching for the essence of what it is we are doing in a given exercise, rehearsal, or performance. Find the essence of what you are physically doing and you will find the psychology. The essence appears as a physical form (which goes back to Plato's philosophy). The psychology appears in *how* we manifest the form. We'll explore this idea much more later on in the book.

We often talk about "typecasting" in our business. It is much more than the looks of the actor. What we are really talking about is looking for the essences of the character in the actors we audition and eventually cast. *Actors should know their own archetypes.* Knowing one's own archetypes and the archetypes of the character is a powerful thing. Actors may possess some aspects of character archetypes and directors call them back generally because of that. It just makes sense for the actor to choose audition material, or structure a callback, to suit the character's archetypes for which he or she is auditioning. Actors must learn to look for what is similar to themselves in their characters and what is different. It is the differences they should learn to embrace.

Note: I have found it rare in plays that characters possess more than 3–5 archetypes. Archetypes help determine several things: the physicality of the character, habits, status, actions, and qualities of action. Refer to a dictionary for the definition of each archetype. (I always keep a dictionary and thesaurus on the production table during rehearsals.)

Teaching Tip: A great source for a list of archetypes is *Archetype Cards* by Caroline Myss. The cards come in a box of 80 and list the "light" and "shadow," or polarity in each archetype. I have found these cards extremely useful in identifying the archetypes for each character in a play. There is a guidebook included in the box. You may be surprised at how closely Myss aligns with Chekhov in the introduction of the guidebook. Of course the internet is a logical source for lists of archetypes as well. Chekhov provides us no such list.

I am not endorsing the work of Myss. I am giving you a tool for a comprehensive listing of archetypes to use in our work in identifying

CASTING AND CLASSWORK USING ARCHETYPES

> character essences. Myss's work in energy medicine and human consciousness, while related, is nothing in our focus. The light and shadow aspect of archetypes is most interesting. We tend to look at the term "lover," for example, with all positive attributes: passion, devotion, affection. We should also consider the shadow or dark side of "lover": jealousy and dominance. Incorporating all of these archetypal elements into the work, at appropriate moments in the play, helps lead to a truly well-conceived characterization.

Exercises

The exercises in this section are all concerned with discovering the archetypes of self and character. They should be done in the order presented as they build in complexity.

Pre-class/rehearsal exploration

- Provide the class or cast a list of archetypes prior to your first meeting.
- Also, they should have read *Midsummer*, if you're using this play for class, another play you have assigned, or obviously the play you're working on if you're in rehearsal.
- You can use this chapter for a directing class, adapt the content for rehearsal purposes, or adapt it for an acting class. Regardless, we all should understand the value of archetypes.
- Have each participant make a list of his or her archetypes.
- Make a list of your own and share them at the beginning of class. Mine are: father, teacher, eternal child, storyteller, visionary.
- Make certain everyone chooses a child archetype.
- The child archetypes are: wounded child, eternal child, abandoned/orphan child, magical/innocent child, nature child, and dependent child.

In-class/rehearsal exercise

- Of the archetypes each person has chosen have them shrink the list to four including the child archetype. I might choose eternal child, storyteller, visionary, and father for the sake of the exercise.
- While standing in a circle have each participant, one at a time, create a large and full-bodied gesture for each archetype.
- At the end of the gesture say the name of the archetype.
- Pause at the end and radiate the inner energy into the space for a brief period. To radiate means to send the energy created from the gesture into the space. The energy is comprised of the physical gesture and the quality that emerges from it. Radiation springs from the imagination. It is a simple thing to imagine the energy permeating throughout the space.
- The sound of the voice reveals the specificity of the quality of action. The emotion is "coaxed," as Stanislavski suggests, from a commitment to the action (gesture) and the quality.
- Each participant creates one gesture and then the next person in the circle creates her gesture, etc.
- Continue this until everyone has created four gestures.
- Once all gestures are created instruct each participant, one at a time, to do all four gestures in sequence and again say the name after each archetype.

WORKING ALONE

(Actors) You can easily, and should, do these exercises on archetypes for all your characters. In fact, it should become a part of your homework. Unfortunately, you'll rarely find this kind of work being done in rehearsals. Make it part of your regimen.

CASTING AND CLASSWORK USING ARCHETYPES

> *Teaching Tip:* You'll note the participants will want to return to a "neutral" stance between gestures. You should discourage this. The gestures will create a more dynamic story if one gesture springs from another. You may side-coach by reminding the participants to radiate between gestures and be certain to imagine the gesture before actually doing it. Spy-back following the exercise. Ask the participants what they discovered about themselves and what they learned about others while observing. Depending on the number of participants you can anticipate this exercise to take 45 minutes or more.
>
> You can lengthen this exercise by replacing the naming of the archetype with a line of text. The sequence then becomes: imagining the gesture inwardly, executing the gesture physically, speaking the text, and radiating. You'll hear the quality of the text in the voice. Continue until all participants have four lines of text. Finally, after you have completed the circle of gestures at least twice, drop the physical gesture but maintain it inwardly and speak the text. Take time to imagine each gesture before speaking.
>
> **Archetypes** (https://vimeo.com/188675546)

In-class/rehearsal exercise

- If you are using the *Archetype Cards* as a resource, you can distribute a number of them (2–3 suggested for each participant) to the class and have the participants create a light and shadow gesture (as explained on the cards) using this same exercise.
- Using the light and shadow aspects of the archetype will create two gestures.

In-class/rehearsal exercise

- Have each participant choose a character from *Midsummer* or the play you're working with.

- Determine and justify the character's archetypes, as I have done below, and repeat the above exercise.
- Use the name of the archetype first and then choose single lines.
- Participants should cast themselves according to the chosen character's archetypes.

If you are casting a play, as I was for *Midsummer*, it should be noted that the work below was done prior to auditions. If you are working with a cast, the exercise simply becomes about finding the archetypes of each character and exploring them in rehearsal. If you're in a directing class this could be a written assignment that should be followed by the physical exercise in class. Again, just adapt the work for your purposes.

Determining archetypes of the major characters in A Midsummer Night's Dream

Theseus—archetypes and clues:

> King—He is the ruler of the realm. He is powerful, authoritative, and benevolent.
> Warrior—He conquered the Amazons. He represents the invincible and the theme "Male Dominance."
> Lover—He is in love with Hippolyta and is betrothed to her. He is passionate.
> Judge—He stands as the final judge of the law concerning Hermia's fate. He rules justly. From these archetypes I look for a man of authority, over six feet tall, with a masculine build and handsome. Ideally, he would be in his mid-late thirties. As a ruler (he is a duke but his archetype is king) the actor/character must be able to adapt quickly to any given situation. In the beginning of the play he interacts with Hippolyta as a lover. His wooing is interrupted first by Philostrate and then by Egeus and his train. Theseus "changes hats" quickly from lover to king, back to lover, and again to king. I would use this information when giving an actor an adjustment in a callback to determine how quickly the actor can accommodate the necessary shifts.

CASTING AND CLASSWORK USING ARCHETYPES

Hippolyta—archetypes and clues:

Queen—She is queen of the Amazons. She can be powerful and authoritative. She represents power in women.

Warrior—She has commanded an army of women and has just been conquered by Theseus.

Lover—She is in love with Theseus and is betrothed to him. She represents equality in love.

Mother—She says nothing in the scene in which Egeus is presenting his case to Theseus against Hermia. In Athens, this is a man's business. She is used to, as queen of the Amazons, leading and speaking her mind. Therefore, we can surmise, she is choosing to be silent. Her silence might be interpreted as having motherly instincts in that she may choose to speak with Theseus about the issue in a more private atmosphere. This idea, as a direction, gives the actress playing Hippolyta an opportunity for active listening during the scene. She may occasionally whisper to Theseus or gently touch him when she has a point but is reluctant to speak. (Perhaps she chooses her battles or at least when and where to fight them.) By not speaking, she has acquiesced, at least in this scene, to her role as a future wife and mother—reinforcing one aspect of the theme "Feminism."

The roles of Theseus and Hippolyta are relatively small in the play and this explains why these roles are often double cast with Oberon and Titania. The archetypes of both sets of characters justify double casting and support the themes of the play.

Before the wedding of Theseus and Hippolyta the couple goes out hunting. Hippolyta has a speech during the hunt that shows how their relationship has progressed:

Hippolyta
I was with Hercules and Cadmus once,
When in a wood of Crete they bay'd the bear
With hounds of Sparta: never did I hear
Such gallant chiding; for, besides the groves,
The skies, the fountains, every region near
Seem'd all one mutual cry; I never heard
So musical a discord, such sweet thunder.

Hippolyta is proving her equality by describing this most masculine of sports with the most masculine of men. At this point in the play she feels she can speak more openly with Theseus. She mentions Hercules and challenges Theseus to a kind of duel of masculinity. It is a brief, yet very important, moment to illuminate the theme "Feminism."

From these archetypes and given circumstances from the text I look for a woman of authority, with long hair—preferably red—in contrast to the actor playing Theseus, and because Helena is blonde and Hermia has dark features. She should be between five feet six inches and five feet ten inches depending on the height of Theseus. She should look to be a formidable opponent yet alluring. The actor should be capable of getting what she wants in a variety of ways. In a callback, I would give the actor adjustments by asking her to speak a block of text three times while using the same action but to change qualities each time. Perhaps: to acquiesce angrily, to acquiesce lovingly, and to acquiesce reluctantly.

Egeus—archetypes and clues:

> Father—Hermia is his daughter. His actions are parental in nature. He represents male authority.
> Politician (Lawyer)—He presents a solid "case" in the beginning of the play.

From these archetypes I look for a man in his late forties to mid-fifties. He should have an authoritarian presence, confident, demanding, and articulate. He should also be able to move easily and quickly between qualities of actions as this is his chief device to convince Theseus of his argument. In a callback I would give each actor adjustments in qualities to make certain he is capable of fast changes. The actor must understand the use of polarity in making choices. Also, in a callback, I would make certain the actor understands that I don't see Egeus as a comedic role. The play, for example, begins in the realm of evil and ends in the realm of joy.

Helena—archetypes and clues:

> Lover—She is in love with Demetrius. Jealousy drives her. Jealousy is a "dark side" of this archetype.

Slave—She surrenders her power, willing to give her virginity to Demetrius.

Teacher—She has several speeches wherein she discovers and imparts knowledge to the audience. She eventually finds the essence of true love.

From these archetypes I look for a young and determined woman. She must be capable of handling long speeches very important to the play. She should have a keen sense of comedy with the ability to quickly change her actions and qualities. In a callback, I would have her work on the "How happy some o'er other some can be" speech. What I would work for is the actor "discovering" the thoughts rather than, as we see it done mostly, knowing what she is going to say beforehand. According to the text she is "tall and fair." She should be blonde between five feet four inches and five feet eight inches tall.

Hermia—archetypes and clues:

Lover—She is in love with Lysander. Passion drives her.

Martyr—She is willing to subject herself to the law of Athens, meaning death, or to escape with Lysander from her family and lifestyle. She has courage.

Rebel—She challenges the law of the land in a public forum.

From these archetypes I look for a young woman with spirit who can bring to the text a sense of inner fire—being "short of temper." She should have dark features according to the given circumstances. She is referred to as an "Ethiope" in the play, which opens the possibility of diversity in casting not only Hermia but Egeus as well. In contrast to Helena, she should be smaller in stature between four feet ten inches and five feet two inches as she is called a "dwarf" by Lysander. In a callback I would have her read the following with Helena:

Hermia
I frown upon him; yet he loves me still.

Helena
O that your frowns would teach my smiles such skill!

Hermia
I give him curses; yet he gives me love.
Helena
O that my prayers could such affection move!
Hermia
The more I hate, the more he follows me.
Helena
The more I love, the more he hateth me.
Hermia
His folly, Helena, is no fault of mine.
Helena
None but your beauty; would that fault were mine!

Note: I would point out to the actors there is a lot going on in this confrontation. It is filled with jealously, justification, and love for each other. The actors must search for polarity from line to line.

Lysander—archetypes and clues:

Lover—He is in love with Hermia.
Gambler—He plots with Hermia to flee Athens and be married outside of the city where the laws against them do not apply. He is a risk taker.
Knight—He is doing a chivalrous deed for Hermia.
Poet—He has several highly poetic speeches in the play. He combines lyricism with insight.

From these archetypes I look for a young man compatible with Hermia. He should be handsome with darker features and not as tall as Demetrius. Lysander needs to handle verse well and have high energy. Above all he should be capable of sincerity. Perhaps, at a callback, I would look at the scene where Lysander awakes, after Puck has applied the magic potion, and immediately sees and falls in love with Helena. While this can be broadly played, the actor must be totally sincere. The audience needs to feel genuinely moved because of his emotional state.

Demetrius—archetypes and clues:

Lover—He is in love with Hermia at the beginning of the play.
Thief—He intends to steal Hermia from Lysander.
Addict—He is addicted to his cause and it makes him selfish. Before he fell in love with Hermia he was in love with Helena. At the end of the play he falls in love with Helena again. This also shows a kind of addiction.

From these archetypes I would look for a young man of fairer features to compare with Helena. He should be taller than Lysander. He should be handsome and athletic. Demetrius, like Lysander, should be capable of deep sincerity. I would approach his callback in the same way as Lysander.

Titania/Oberon:

I would double cast these roles with Hippolyta and Theseus. These characters share archetypes.

Puck—archetypes and clues:

Child/Magical—We all have a child archetype. Puck is immature, plays tricks on humans, and has magical powers.
Bully—He takes delight in frightening and intimidating others. There is often a coward underneath the bully.
Companion—He is loyal to Oberon.
Poet—He is insightful through poetic language.
Servant—He serves Oberon. He is not an indentured servant. He believes his servitude enhances.

From these archetypes I look for a highly energetic man or woman capable of making lightning-quick action and quality changes between the child, bully, companion, and poet. Puck's speeches can contain all four archetypes in one. He or she should be very athletic as the text demands it. He or she should have some gymnastic abilities. In callbacks I would address these archetypes in Puck's speech, "Through the forest have I gone. . . ." All of his or her archetypes can be found in this speech and I would point out to the actor where the changes occur prior to the reading.

> **NOTE TO DIRECTORS**

I think we spend too little time in callbacks with actors. If possible, you should callback fewer actors, taking into consideration archetypes, and spend more time with each.

Bottom—archetypes and clues:

> Clown/Fool—He is fearless in his actions without considering consequences.
> Child/Eternal—He is very young in spirit and strives to remain so.
> Dilettante—He loves the theater but is not a professional.
> Hedonist—He uses creative energy to embrace the good things in life.
> Lover—He has great passion and devotion.
> Bully—He bullies Quince and the other mechanicals by wanting to play all of the roles.

From these archetypes I look for a man with a great sense of humor and comic timing. He should have high energy and enthusiasm and read the text with deep passion and truth. He should also have improvisation skills. I would cast a large man, as his actions are so large and to contrast with Quince. In callbacks, I would stress the energy and enthusiasm I believe Bottom possesses. I would have the actor do the speech from the play within the play, "Sweet Moon, I thank thee for thy sunny beams. . . ." I'd stress broadness, tremendous energy, and a sense that Bottom *loves* what he is doing. All of this escalates as the speech progresses. I would work with the actor on "building" the speech.

Quince—archetypes and clues:

> Storyteller—He is the author of the play within the play.
> Advocate—He inspires the mechanicals to their best.
> Companion—He acts unselfishly.
> Mentor—He mentors all the mechanicals as he serves as director for the play.

From these archetypes I look for a man who is able to take charge in a gentle way. He should especially understand the role of mentor and direct the mechanicals in subtle actions and qualities. This is to contrast Bottom who always attacks his actions in a bombastic way. Quince should be thin and shorter than Bottom. Quince should also be clever. He can manipulate Bottom for results. In callbacks, I'd look for an actor who can change actions and qualities via the "thinking center," an actor who can assess a situation quickly and make an adjustment.

As directors, we should look for creativity and the ability from actors to take direction in the callback. In callbacks, I always give an actor an adjustment after his or her first attempt of the reading to determine if the actor is really capable of making inspired choices. What the director wants to do is guide the actor to his or her own choices within the essence of the archetype. As an example, look at this Lysander speech:

In-class/rehearsal exercise

Read the speech aloud and record your initial thoughts and images in your journals.

Lysander
A good persuasion; therefore, hear me, Hermia.
I have a widow aunt, a dowager
Of great revenue, and she hath no child.
From Athens is her house remote seven leagues;
And she respects me as her only son.
There, gentle Hermia, may I marry thee,
And to that place the sharp Athenian law
Cannot pursue us. If thou lov'st me then,
Steal forth thy father's house to-morrow night;
And in the wood, a league without the town
(Where I did meet thee once with Helena
To do observance to a morn of May),
There will I stay for thee.

This is a speech that I would consider good for a callback because it is a "trap" speech. In essence it is a proposal of marriage. The trap many actors choose is to have already considered the proposal as a plan instead of it occurring to the actor in the moment. Discovering the proposal in the moment is a more active choice.

If the actor falls into the trap, the director can guide toward the more active choice by suggesting the archetype of the lover and the gambler. The director might say to the actor reading for Lysander, "Lysander is so in love he is willing to take a tremendous risk (Gambler). The stakes are high. What choice might you make that would be risky and prove your devotion to Hermia in the moment of this speech?" In this way the director is giving the actor a path to follow and allowing the actor to discover organically a strong and bold choice. The director should always first ask questions of the actor rather than dictating a choice. The acting is always stronger when found through collaboration with the director. If the actor can make the adjustment then he or she and the director will most likely have a productive relationship. Good directing means guiding actors. Using archetypes is one tool in the beginning process that makes sense to both actors and directors. It is an excellent way to establish common ground. Through the essences of characters we find freedom to create. If the actor reads the speech without a specific action, give him the *action—to propose*. Giving the actor an adjustment of action is another good way to guide rather than dictate.

In-class exercise

Read Lysander's speech with the archetype of a gambler in mind. Like the archetype, take risks with your actions!

Teaching Tip: Objective—To get Hermia to say yes! Action—To propose. Try to guide the actor to the objective through working with the archetype. If the student doesn't find a specific action then the next best thing is to give it to him. You're teaching a process and the process is learned through repetition. With enough repetition students will learn the process and will no longer need too much guidance.

> **Teaching Tip:** Working with archetypes is obviously useful in initial auditions, callbacks, rehearsals, and as a class exercise. Actors can easily derive actions and qualities of action from archetypes without the director actually stating them for the actors. (Review: Actions—*what* the character does to get what he or she wants, a verb. Quality of action—*how* a character does what he or she does to get what he or she wants, an adverb. To seduce, tenderly—for example, combining the action and quality.)

Follow-up for directors

I believe it is important for the director to make all auditions as actor-friendly as possible. As directors, we make it easier on ourselves when we provide an environment for actors to do their best work. I prefer not to work from behind a table in auditions and I never take notes while an actor is working. In a monologue or brief scene there is no need for note taking. There are only a handful of things that can go wrong. Learn to give adjustments in auditions using clear and brief language. Sticking with actions and qualities for adjustments usually tells you all you need to know. You can suggest action but never qualities. Qualities are emotions and cannot be manufactured through the intellect or direction. They must be discovered through action. Make your brief notes on the actor's exit.

Note: I personally dislike when a director reads my resume during my audition. This tells me that the director is more interested in what I've previously done than what I am doing in the moment. It also is a clue to me that the director may not be a true collaborator. As an actor's career progresses, choosing who to work with is part of the artistic journey.

My preference is to sit to the side of the table so that when I greet or work with an actor there is no semblance of a divide between us. Collaboration begins with the initial meeting of actor and director. Actors should always leave the audition feeling good about the experience and that is all in the hands of the director.

Exploration

Choose either the *Three Sisters* or *Grapes of Wrath* and "cast" the main characters according to archetypes. You can compare with examples in Appendix II of this book.

Continued follow-up for directors

When the callbacks are complete the director has choices he or she must make. Here are some questions to ask:

> Which actors most closely embraced the archetypes?
> Which actors made the boldest choices?
> Which actors were able to make adjustments?
> Who are the actors I feel can work most collaboratively with and embrace the world of the play within the concept?

Casting is easily more than 50 percent of the success of the production. Answering the last question to the best of your ability supersedes everything else.

Follow-up

In every exercise described in this book you should lead the spy-back session following each exercise toward self-discovery for each participant. Students tend to recount what they did in the exercise rather than explore what they learned. Learning to spy-back is of paramount importance. Guide students toward what they felt and not toward a retelling of what they did. Connecting students back to their feeling centers will lead them to the discoveries of self and character. They should have their journals in hand, ready to write, for the spy-back session. Resist the temptation to allow your students to ask too many questions prior to each exercise or let them take notes during the work. Instead, allow plenty of time to spy-back.

In exercising on archetypes of self and character, listen for the quality of action at the end of each gesture. You can mentally record examples of particularly strong connections from quality and form and share this in the spy-back.

We cannot play archetype as an action or quality, yet we must recognize that we all are made of these universal truths. We should recognize where in the play these archetypes appear and embrace them. Back to my own archetypes: I am speaking here as a father: "Full of vexation come I with complaint against my daughter, Hermia." Knowing this archetype gives me great insight into my objective, actions, qualities, and status.

Further reading

Chekhov, Michael, *To the Actor*, Routledge, 2002. Chapter 1 "The Actor's Body and Psychology."

Chekhov, Michael, *Lessons for the Professional Actor*, Performing Arts Journal Publications, 1985. Third Class "The Actor as Director," p. 54.

Chekhov, Michael, *To the Director and Playwright*, Harper and Row, 1963. Chapter 12 "Toward Better Rehearsals," pp. 85–88.

Petit, Lenard, *The Michael Chekhov Handbook for the Actor*, Routledge, 2010. Chapter 4 Part 15 "Characterization: Archetype, The Psychological Gesture," pp. 66–71.

3
CREATING THE ENSEMBLE

Framework

Whether in rehearsal or in class the director or teacher must establish the ensemble early. In either case the group is often made up of strangers. Even if the group knows each other, every ensemble is different in that they are embarking on a new journey. We are concerned in this chapter with creating the ensemble—what Chekhov would term as establishing the "feeling of the whole." When we create the ensemble early a positive working bond is formed that will last through the entirety of the work—if the director or teacher continues to stress ensemble. Every person in the ensemble must be equal and that is a major part of our work here.

Theater is, or should be, our most collaborative art form. Directors are under extreme pressure from critics, producers, people who are reviewing them for tenure in academic institutions, or parents (perhaps especially parents). Actors are under pressure because—well—that is the nature of the business and where we put ourselves. Perhaps this is not necessary. Our job as directors, designers, and actors is to tell the clearest story possible. What I mean by this is clarity in concept, directing, design, and acting. It must all fit together and can be likened to a jigsaw puzzle. To complete the puzzle, we must collaborate. There must be a sense of trust. Trust begins with creating an ensemble. In professional theater, the cast, as an ensemble, may be assumed and not cultivated by the director. Sometimes, individual actors reject exercises the director introduces to create the ensemble and the result is counterproductive. Have we lost our art? Have we lost the art of collaboration in order to get the best reviews, create a long run, or to appease the parents? Have we lost the *art* of theater? Chekhov certainly believed that the art of theater was lost. Simon Callow, in his foreword to *To the Actor*, reinforces Chekhov's beliefs in a very convincing argument. Certainly, actors on every level can be critical of the process and damage collaboration. Creating an ensemble that is truly working for the feeling of the whole aids greatly in telling a clear story.

Actors love direction given in a particular manner. Actors, at least American actors, hate direction that approaches line readings or that is extremely specific. Directors should realize that acting is a craft and an art. To create a cohesive production the director must develop a concept and atmosphere in which designers and actors can practice their craft. It must be an atmosphere of trust. Creating a positive atmosphere in which all can work collaboratively is the director's job. And it all begins and ends with the way in which the director/teacher creates and maintains the ensemble.

Exercises

The exercises in this chapter are designed to help to initially establish an ensemble with the class or cast. Just as important, the exercises help to discover the play, or class work, in a physical way. Our work on the stage requires the entire body to be involved. The body tells the story—it is the form—and the voice reveals the emotion, which has been coaxed by physicalizing the action. The exercises presented here are the substance of the first two rehearsals. The following is easily adapted to scene study for acting or directing classes and is extremely useful in a script analysis course.

Prerehearsal or class exploration

If you are in rehearsal for a production, make sure your stage manager has sent the concept statement to the cast. There is no need for the cast to do anything other than read the statement at this point. We will be exploring the concept in the first rehearsal through two exercises.

If you are working in a directing class you may consider sending the students several examples of concept statements. (See Appendix II for other concept statements.) In an acting class you can adapt these exercises as noted.

Exercise—in-class/rehearsal

The first rehearsal

Design presentations, read-thru, and "The Palace" exercise

I believe it is important for the design presentations to occur at the beginning of the first read-thru (if the final designs are ready). This gives the designers a feeling of being an important part of the ensemble, tells the actors that the designers are part of the ensemble, and may give the actors some thoughts before the read. (I am constantly amazed at how actors respond to costume renderings.) The actors have read the concept statement, sent from the stage manager, and the director needs to speak little. The director shouldn't talk about the themes of the play before the read-thru. It is best to save that for the exercise described below. The designers should stay and be a part of the read-thru and exercise as they are an integral part of the ensemble.

> ***Teaching/Directing Tip:*** **Actors are at their best when encouraged to act. Yes, there is pressure to perform, which is not encouraged by most directors in the first read-thru. As an actor I've often sat at a table, reading and "discussing" the play for two full days of rehearsal. This practice can set up a noncollaborative scenario from the beginning. Actors in this scenario look to the director for answers, which is not good. When actors do get on their feet their choices tend to generate from the thinking center only. Engaging all three centers is the psychophysical process that goes back to Stanislavski and evolved through Chekhov. We have all seen plays where the actors' speeches seemed disengaged from their bodies. To proceed in a more productive way the director might**

consider saying to the actors, "Let's read this on our feet. Don't be afraid to move, make eye contact with your partner, go ahead and act and see what you discover. This is not a final performance or any kind of performance at all. Just have fun and allow yourselves to make choices. It doesn't mean that you should be 'married' to those choices. By beginning this way, I want you to feel that you are free to make choices at any time. Act! Act poorly, act brilliantly, act foolishly, but act!"

Designers should attend the first read as well. When designers see actors on their feet and engaging in the Higher Ego, an amazing thing happens: the designers view the work in their own Higher Egos! Images appear and, most important, their "feeling center" is engaged.

Many directors, following the first read-thru, will have a discussion, entertaining reactions. I do not. Instead, I take the actors, with designers observing or preferably participating, through an exercise called "The Palace." This exercise was taught to me by Mala Powers and I have modified it to suit a rehearsal process.

In-rehearsal/class exercise: The Palace

- The Palace exercise is designed to "turn-on" the actor's imagination/fantasy and to help them explore the play's themes on their feet rather than with their intellect only. (Other than the initial read-thru, I tend to do very little table work. The exception to this is work on individual speeches, usually in Shakespeare or solos in musical theater.)
- "The Palace" gives the participants the opportunity to work immediately in the Higher Ego.
- The actors are instructed that this is an individual exercise.
- While they will be aware of each other they are not to interact.

CREATING THE ENSEMBLE

Instructions from the Teacher/Director: *Find your own space in the studio. Imagine before you is a beautiful palace. Take time to create in your imagination your palace that would exist in the world of* A Midsummer Night's Dream. *Consider your palace from the point of view of your character in the play. (Designers should participate as themselves working from their perspective.) The majority of the exercise is done with your eyes open. Take time to create your palace with all of your senses. Is there a particular smell in the air? What do you hear around you?*

Consider the size of your palace. Is it surrounded by trees, a moat? Is it covered with vines? What is the color? Is it multicolored? Consider the lines of the palace. Is it a normal building with sharp lines and arches? Could your palace be round or even look like a jigsaw puzzle? It is your palace as Bottom, Titania, Oberon, Puck, Demetrius, Helena. . . ?

There are several rooms in the palace we will explore. When I ask you to 'cross the threshold' into the first room of the palace, I will give you the theme of the room and you should explore it by looking, feeling, smelling, and tasting if appropriate. Allow yourselves to play and discover as your character.

Teaching Tip: To aid the atmosphere of the exercise, I use a Zenergy Chime with three tones to signal the actors when to cross the threshold. I do this to keep my direction to a minimum.

Now, take a walk across the space to the front doorway of your palace. When I play the first chime, I will ask you to first close your eyes and then cross the threshold through the doorway into your first room. I will then tell you the name of the room. When I play the second chime, open your eyes and begin to play and explore.

> *Teaching Tip:* Play "chime"—the actors cross the threshold with eyes closed. Announce the first room—The Room of Magic—play "chime." The actors open their eyes and begin. I have found that the actors need about 7 minutes per room to fully explore. The teacher/ director must observe the actors carefully. This is the beginning of creating the ensemble and it happens quickly, this feeling of the whole. The director will observe an expansion of the ensemble, or an excitement radiating into the space created through fantasy/imagination. Then, after a time, there is contraction from the ensemble, a sort of air being released. The director does well to recognize when the actor's imagination begins to wane. Radiating one's imagination into space is not something an actor can sustain indefinitely. Watch the body language of the ensemble. This is the time to move on to the next room.

Pause and notice a doorway where you have not noticed one before. Walk to the doorway and stop. Close your eyes.

> *Teaching Tip:* Play "chime"—the actors cross the threshold with eyes closed. Announce the second room—The Room of Jealousy—play "chime." The actors open their eyes and begin.
>
> Repeat the steps above with the following rooms: Dreams, Sensuality, Fear, and finally Love Conquers All. The final room is special. Following the exploration, instruct the actors to continue working while forming a large circle. Have them pause and close their eyes. Ask them to imagine a "psychological gesture" (a full-bodied gesture that is the essence of the theme). Then, tell the actors when they hear the chime they are to embody the

CREATING THE ENSEMBLE

> gesture with eyes closed and hold the form until further instructed. Play the chime and when all of the actors have embodied the form ask them to open their eyes. Inevitably the gestures will be universal and there is a wonderful moment—the ensemble is created!

The spy-back

Following the exercise we sit in a circle and share our discoveries with each other. This always deepens the bond of the ensemble and prompts lively discussion. At first it is important to allow each actor to share individual experiences. At a proper point the director begins to guide the spy-back toward the themes and superobjective of the play. The director asks the actors to use these experiences to help realize the overall concept. While the director wants the actors to create freely, he or she also wants the actors to work within the superobjective and artistic frames of the play.

Once the ensemble is created it is another thing altogether to maintain and grow it throughout the rehearsal process. The last thing I do in the first rehearsal is to give the actors an assignment. I ask the company to give thought to their individual characters and why their character is the most important person in the play. I ask them to prepare an argument as to why this is so. We will have a debate at the beginning of the next rehearsal in an exercise called "Ladies and Gentlemen."

Working alone

The Palace exercise can easily be done on your own. Explore the rooms as your character after deciding which themes you wish to employ.

> *Teaching Tip:* You can use The Palace exercise in class as a general exploration as well. Here are the rooms I have my classes explore: Water, Music, Vegetation, Laughter, Knowledge, Stars and Planets, Sensuality, and finally the Empty Room—where the students create a gesture of joy ("glad"). In the spy-back, guide your students to how they may use this exercise when they are in production concerning the themes of the play and how their characters illuminate those themes. Give examples of plays you are doing in the season. In *The Crucible*, for example, you might suggest the rooms of Truth, Faith, Lust, Fear, and Redemption.

The second rehearsal: The "Ladies and Gentlemen" exercise

Maintaining the feeling of the whole begins at the second rehearsal and every subsequent rehearsal. In the early rehearsal period, when I have the entire cast together, I will begin with some sort of exercise to gain focus and energy toward our task. (See more exercises in Appendix IV.)

Following the warm-up I ask the cast to sit in front of three chairs I have provided for the exercise.

Instructions from the Teacher/Director: *Good evening. We're here to discover the story of A Midsummer Night's Dream through the eyes of each individual character in a debate format. I will act as the moderator of tonight's debate. In a moment I'll ask for a volunteer to begin. The volunteer will take a chair and start the debate by saying, "Ladies and gentlemen, good evening. I'm here to tell you why (Bottom) is the most important character in the play." You'll continue your argument until someone comes up and says, "Excuse me, ladies and gentlemen, I beg to differ. I'll tell you why (Oberon) is the most important character in the play." At this point (Bottom) will yield the floor to (Oberon) until (Bottom) says, "Excuse me, ladies and gentlemen please, I beg to differ." (Bottom) continues to present his argument or may choose to pick up on something (Oberon) said so as to challenge the point. The debate* *continues and someone else (Titania) may take a chair and say, "Excuse me, ladies and gentlemen, I beg to differ. I'll tell you why (Titania) is the most important character in the play." The floor must be yielded to the person who says, "Excuse me ladies and gentlemen." You may interrupt each other politely with that phrase. It is up to the moderator to either allow an argument to continue or to be interrupted. The moderator determines if someone has interrupted too quickly.*

> ***Teaching Tip:*** At this point all chairs are occupied. At an appropriate time in the debate another person will want to join. To do so the actor moves to a person already seated, places his or her hand on his or her shoulder and politely says "Excuse me ladies and gentlemen I beg to differ. I'll tell you why (Mustardseed) is the most important character in the play." The actor Mustardseed touches must yield his or her chair. As the debate progresses all actors present their arguments. Allow actors to take the stage more than once. As moderator the director can control the number of times a particular actor takes the stage. The moderator is also responsible for the debate not turning into a heated argument with actors not giving each other time to make their statements. This is why we set the exercise up with polite words. It helps keep the exercise light and easy. At the end of the exercise the moderator takes the stage and says, "Excuse me ladies and gentlemen. Thank you for your attention and debate. That concludes the wonderful story of *A Midsummer Night's Dream*." This exercise replaces intellectual table work and allows the actors to explore the play through an improvisation.
>
> During the spy-back the actors will want to know who the moderator thinks made the best argument. Don't give in to this request. The moderator should say, "I believe you all are the most important characters in the play. And that is the point of the exercise."
>
> You'll find the ensemble has bonded even more. They will feel that the rehearsal process has been a good one and will be excited to continue.

> Stanislavski said, "There are no small parts, only small actors." The "Ladies and Gentlemen" exercise empowers the entire cast or class and reinforces this famous concept.

The Second Rehearsal continues.

Rehearsal/class exercise: The four qualities of movement

This is an exercise I always introduce at this point in the rehearsal process. It is Michael Chekhov's *Qualities of Movement (QoM)*—*molding, flowing, flying, and radiating*.

- Once again, schedule plenty of time for the exercise.
- The first introduction should be at least 45 minutes.
- Radiating is the most difficult part of the exercise to understand for most actors. It is therefore important to introduce this concept first.
- Remind the actors about the definition of radiation.
- In our actor fantasy we can imagine constantly sending out "rays" from our feeling center to our scene partner and to the audience. Essentially, this is our personal atmosphere—how we are feeling at any given time.
- Again, atmosphere is not an actable thing for an actor. Rather, it is something to be imagined.

Whatever our atmosphere or mood may be, we are always, consciously or subconsciously, sending out our feelings. At times we try to hide our feelings. In Chekhov's terms, we call this "veiling." Regardless, those feelings are ever present and often easy for others to comprehend. Radiation should be considered and imagined to happen in a 360-degree radius. We don't just radiate forward, our entire being radiates, including

CREATING THE ENSEMBLE

our "backspace." To solidify the importance of radiation, I have the actors pause (in stillness) throughout the entire exercise and radiate their movements, feelings, and energy into the space.

In this exercise, and in all Chekhov exercises, we work from the Actor's Ideal Center. The Actor's Ideal Center ("feeling center") is located in the chest, in the area of the heart. In Chekhov's *On the Technique of Acting*, he suggests, "Imagine that invisible rays stream from your movements into space." The key here is to imagine! Realistically, there is nothing to see. The actor should imagine that all movement initiates from the "feeling center." In each movement, described below, if the actors are engaged with the imagination, qualities will emerge. It is these qualities that will evoke and entice feelings. Feeling is what we are radiating via our imagination. I have found that trying to visualize what we are radiating is not as useful as "feeling" these movement sensations. Once the actor begins to experience the quality, or feeling, images begin to appear on their own.

Before you begin to work on the four QoM, first introduce the Actor's Ideal Center by having the ensemble simply walking through the space, moving and radiating from the center. All movement should initiate from this center. The actors should imagine this movement prior to actually moving. They should feel the movement inwardly before the physical movement begins. Have them stop at points. Have them change direction, including walking backward without looking in that direction. Constantly remind them to imagine the movements initiating from the center—sending out "rays." You can actually see this working when actors are truly engaged in their Higher Ego.

Exercise:

- Have the cast, or class, walk the space and greet each other, with eye contact only, without any sentimentality.
- They are simply recognizing each other in the space.
- Begin from the Actor's Ideal Center before walking by radiating energy into the space.
- Remind the actors to radiate whatever they are feeling all around them: forward, backward, up, down, and side-to-side.

- The director/teacher may find the actors begin to "act" by manufacturing emotions. Discourage this and instruct instead to concentrate on radiating what is already present and *only* what is present.
- Following this exploration begin with the exercise below.

Instructions from the Teacher/Director: *We will begin with molding. While standing, using just your arms and hands, and while working from your Actor's Ideal Center, begin to make movements as if you were working in soft clay. Your movements should leave impressions in the air. They should have a clear beginning, middle, and ending. The movements can be staccato or legato (fast or slow). These are movements we can identify with the earth. Now begin to move through the space and mold with the entire body. You are literally molding your way through this world of clay. Concentrate on engaging your whole being. Pause occasionally and allow your energy to fill the entire space. Don't imagine you are creating a sculpture in the clay. We are working to comprehend the essence of molding. Our bodies experience the physicality of molding and we are working for an inward feeling as well. There should be no tension in this or any aspect of our work. It is this inward feeing that is most important. If the exercise is lacking in feeling inwardly, then we are simply doing the exercise for a physical reward. Our work must always be toward the psychophysical. That is the actor's work. The physical form must always contain psychology. The psychology comes from the quality that evokes the feeling. Constantly check in with yourself and record what these movements are doing to you inwardly. If you truly commit to molding you will experience a different psychology.*

Teaching Tip: Have the actors pause while molding, and while practicing all QoM, and radiate that feeling into the space—and then begin the movement again.

Once the actors have fully experienced molding have them stop that movement and just walk through the space. Always remind them of the Actor's Ideal Center. When the molding movements have left the bodies, pause and introduce flowing.

CREATING THE ENSEMBLE 49

The next quality of movement we will explore is flowing. Unlike molding, these movements move freely without an ending. Again, begin with the arms and hands. Identify these movements with water—like a gently flowing stream or gushing river depending on tempo. Gradually move through the space exploring physically and psychologically the experience of flowing. Remember that you are always radiating into the space and pause occasionally to simply send your energy into the space. There is nothing to restrict your movements. They should be free-flowing.

Teaching Tip: Make sure all movements remain in the world of flowing and are not married with molding or flying. Also, encourage the use of the full body. At a proper point stop the work as above. Encourage the actors to explore movements while working with their bodies on the floor and not just on their feet.

The final quality we will explore is flying. Obviously, we identify these movements with air. Everything that can live in the world of air flies differently. A bird flies differently from a butterfly. The common housefly flies differently from the soaring eagle. A word of caution: we are exploring the psychology of flying and not mimicking any creature. Creatures are not the only things that fly. Think of clouds, tornadoes, feathers, etc. Remember to pause occasionally and radiate.

Teaching Tip: Remember to go back to the Actor's Ideal Center between each segment. At the proper time have the actors pause and walk normally. Then have them sit in a circle for the spy-back session.

Qualities of Movement (https://vimeo.com/188813894)

The spy-back

As I said earlier, actors will speak of their personal experiences during the work. There will be insightful comments. Most actors will report a deep connection to two of the QoM and not so much to the others. This will vary from actor to actor and it is completely normal. A point to be made is that whichever movement was the least successful is the movement that should be attended to most. These are archetypal movements and must be mastered. They must be mastered because we have to apply them to text.

Teaching Tip/Exercise: Following the spy-back have the actors think of a few lines from a play or an entire short speech. Begin the exercise again with molding. Once the actors are engaged in the movements have them begin to say the lines. Direct them to vary the tempo and radiate. Have them pause as before. Using the same lines move on to flowing and flying. You will hear many varied qualities emerge and be impressed at the freedom the movements give the language. Have a spy-back session following the exercise and allow the actors to speak about their sensations. You can guide the actors to the chief points of the work. It is imperative for the teacher/director to listen for the individual qualities in the actor's voice. The movement and vocalization must be linked as one.

Instructions from the Teacher/Director: *Consider if your character is chiefly a molding, flowing, flying, or radiating one. Characters usually fall into one or two of these qualities. Consider your individual speeches. They can be explored through a quality of movement according to the arc of action in the artistic frames. Using QoM can aid in adding variety and polarity to your work. You can create a fully realized physical character using qualities of movement.*

CREATING THE ENSEMBLE 51

> *Teaching Tip:* This exercise is just one example of good collaboration between teacher and student or actor and director. The teacher/director provides guidance and allows the student/actor to discover for themselves. There is specificity in the guidance and freedom in the spy-back. The participants are totally invested and their discoveries will inform all of their choices in the work. Allowing discoveries from the class or cast is far more productive to the process than too much teaching or too much directing.
>
> It is important for the teacher/director to allow actors, in the early going, to play in rehearsal with the techniques introduced in this book. To introduce something is one thing. To allow actors the freedom to play is a great step toward the Ideal Theater. So, directors, go ahead and block the scene if you feel you must. Following that, allow your actors to radiate, mold, flow, and fly through the scene! Yes, it takes time and I promise the rewards are many.

Follow-up

Actors in training and actors in rehearsal want answers from their teachers/directors. "Was that better?" is the question most frequently asked by actors. Acting is not math where there usually is a correct answer. We, as acting teachers and directors, have chosen to work in a subjective field. We share our opinions. Resist sharing your opinion too frequently. Instead, guide your students to spy-back about how they felt, where (in their work) they had an organic feeling, and why they had that feeling at that particular time. Reinforce in students the necessity to know their own work through the spy-back. No amount of affirmation from a teacher or director can give an actor the ability to repeat that organic feeling night after night as is the actor's job in live theater.

Musicians and dancers work on their fundamentals every day for hours. It is this repetition that makes them or not. Actors don't really do this. Oh, we actors may work on our vocal exercises and run our lines. Daily voice work is only a part of the repetition. The Chekhov Technique gives us the tools to work on our own and work our art like musicians and dancers. The best the teacher can do is offer the technique to students and instill in them the worth and love of repetition.

Further reading

Chekhov, Michael, *To the Actor*, Routledge, 2002. "Foreword," Simon Callow, pp. xi–xxiv.

Chekhov, Michael, *On the Technique of Acting*, HarperCollins, 1991. Chapter 4 "The Actor's Body," pp. 43–57.

4
ESTABLISHING THE LANGUAGE OF CLASS AND REHEARSAL

Framework

As an actor, I have worked with many directors and teachers who did not possess the language, or terminology, to help me translate their directions or instructions into something playable, as in an action or a quality. Sometimes directors simply don't know "actor-speak," as they may not be trained actors. Directors/teachers often talk in terms of visual images or give the actor an analogy. Images and analogies are fine if the actor can turn them into something actable. It can be a guessing game that may cause the actor and director some anxiety. How does the director/teacher know if he or she has been clear? Answer: only if the actor nails it. But then how does the actor know how to replicate the direction?

As a director, I have worked with companies of actors with training so eclectic there is not a common terminology with which to begin. Actors are trained in many different approaches—all of which attack text somewhat differently and offer varying terms for the same thing. Some methodologists say tactic, which means action in other methods. Others say victory, intention, or goal for objective.

Other than Michael Chekhov, no methodologist talks about the quality of action. This can be confusing. Without a common terminology, directors, teachers, and actors can be at a disadvantage. Or, at worst, the teacher/director, because of lack of common vocabulary and time restraints in our modern theater, does not allow collaboration. The director sometimes dictates as if he or she is acting the role instead of the person cast. (This is as true in scene study class as it is in rehearsal.) The director also sometimes, due to this lack of common communication, allows the actor to create outside the parameters of the concept or even the play by allowing choices that do not fit the given circumstances or by not adhering to the arcs of action. Either scenario is not fruitful to creating a story that is cohesive—as a play should be. There can be a void between actor and director—between the space where the actor works and the table behind where the director sits—and it may be all due to terminology. The worst that happens is that actors become fearful of directors because the former feel they cannot communicate or are not given the opportunity to be heard. It is something that prevents good theater from being made, but it can be remedied.

Actors are sometimes defensive with directors—another sad scenario. Actors can come to their convictions and choices too early and hold onto them with such stubbornness that collaboration cannot occur. There is much to go wrong. There is a creative way for all to go right and it is through the use of the Michael Chekhov Technique. Not all actors, of course, will have been exposed to the work of Chekhov. It doesn't matter. The work is simple and immediately applicable. There is no time in the rehearsal process, or in a single semester acting class, to teach the entire technique. The director can, however, choose a few of the major tools of the technique that all actors will grasp immediately and thereby develop common territory—a territory of collaboration between actor and director. Slowly, we will realize Chekhov's Ideal Theater.

To maintain the ensemble, I have found in my directing and teaching that shared terminology is a powerful tool. I'm not talking about terms such as stage right, upstage, or downstage. I'm referring to more specific language between actor and teacher/director. When we all speak with the same terminology an atmosphere of equality is created. Equality is the real power. Equality, for our purposes, means respect for each other and our respective crafts.

Pre-class/rehearsal exploration

You might consider emailing your cast or class the list of "action words" from Appendix IV. This list will get them started and invite further exploration.

Exercises

Telling the ensemble exactly how the play will be rehearsed, or how the class will proceed (and this goes beyond a syllabus) is an incredibly freeing experience. Following the already prescribed rehearsals or classes, I introduce the terminology we will use early in our process. I don't explain the terms in a lecture format. All of the terminology is revealed through work on our feet—through doing. The exercises in this chapter will assist you to introduce the language you can use in class or rehearsal. Establishing this language is akin to establishing rules. I insist, when directing or teaching, that actors talk to me and spy-back using this terminology. It not only establishes common ground, it is an amazing time saver.

In-rehearsal or in-class exercise: Acting with balls!

Introduce the terms through a simple ball game. You will need bean bag juggling balls for the work in this chapter. An excellent source for quality balls is: www.dube.com. The *standard size* comes in various colors. These balls last for many years. Purchase at least 7 balls. Don't just go out and buy "hacky-sacks." You'll find them too small to see and catch.

- Begin, in a circle, by tossing a ball underhand to a member of the ensemble.
- Say *your* name just as the ball leaves your fingers.
- The actor who catches the ball says *his* or *her* name as he or she tosses to someone else.
- After everyone has had a chance to toss and catch several times, offer instructions.

Instructions from the Teacher/Director: *Our actions, or what we are doing, are tossing and catching. (Teaching tip: You can also ask the ensemble what the actions are. I tend to ask more questions than give the answers immediately. You might begin by asking, 'What are we doing?') To toss and catch is what we are doing to get what we want. We will be talking a great deal in rehearsal/class about action. As a director/teacher, part of my job is to observe actors and make certain there is always a clear action being played as I have to make certain the story is clear. Actors, as characters, must be striving toward a goal, an objective. In my training, my teachers always stressed to 'play the objective'. I have come to understand the impossibility of this directive.* (Toss balls, 3–5 minutes.)

Action has been retermed over the years since Stanislavski to suit different methodologists. Many directors and teachers use the word intention instead of action. As teachers, directors, and actors we should deal in precise meanings of words. I don't use intention because it means something we intend, or plan, to do. It precedes action. Once we put into motion our intent, it becomes action. Intention originates in what Michael Chekhov called the thinking center—*in the neck/head area. Action originates in the* feeling center—*from the bottom of the neck to the waist—and is then transferred to the* willing center—*from the waist down. We have a feeling and then we do something about it. The feeling comes from something that happens to us. Once we have a feeling, we perform an action in response and engage the full physical being."* (Toss balls, 3–5 minutes.)

Action can also be called form. *The action/form is what we are physically doing. What we do to get what we want manifests in a form— the posture of the body. The form is the story—how the audience*

ESTABLISHING THE LANGUAGE OF CLASS AND REHEARSAL 57

recognizes what the actor is doing. During this ball game, for instance, if a stranger walked into the studio while we were playing, he or she would immediately recognize we are tossing and catching—the form would be clear. In our acting, we search for clarity of action/form. Crystal clear form, on the stage, is the building block—the foundation—of our work. (Toss balls, 3–5 minutes.)

Teaching Tip: At this point instruct the actors to hold their form throughout each artistic frame. Actor A tosses to Actor B and holds his or her form of tossing until Actor B catches the ball and checks in with Actor A while holding the form of catching. Then, Actor B begins a new artistic frame by making contact with another actor prior to tossing the ball. Actors will forget to hold form or alter it even slightly. Constantly remind students about holding form throughout the entire artistic frame. (Toss balls, 3–5 minutes.)

Before moving on to the next section, have the actors change the text: Actor A says his or her name just prior to tossing and then says the name of the Actor B he or she is tossing to (e.g., "Susan," *toss*, "Mark"). Say the person's name you are tossing to just as the ball leaves your fingers.

At some point, inevitably, someone will *throw* the ball overhanded. Stop the exercise and point out that overhanded is throwing, not tossing. Our action here is to toss, not throw. This reinforces the concept of clear form.

Instructions from the Teacher/Director: The objective *is what I (the character) want(s). (And this is where I respectfully disagree with some of my former teachers.) The definition of want is desire. Desire is not something playable. It is a feeling and Stanislavski teaches us that we cannot play a feeling. (There is a major difference between playing a feeling and fantasizing about it.) What we can do is play an action to try and coax a feeling forth. The objective drives us to do something—action. Again, action is something we do to get what we want.*

What then is our objective? Our objective is to keep the ball in the air. *There will be times when the ball is dropped. Think of this as a metaphor for dropping the ball on the stage. Occasionally, we may drop a line or play in general rather than playing a specific action. The best thing to do is to not fret over it. Simply pick up the ball and move on. Dropping the ball is actually a positive thing because you will feel tension, usually followed by uttering a curse word. The most important lesson here is not to allow tension into the body because it is the actor's worst enemy. Instead, recognize you've dropped the ball, pick it up with a 'feeling of ease in the body', and begin again.* (Toss balls, 3–5 minutes.)

Teaching Tip: Before moving on to the next section, have the actors replace their names with this text: "I toss" and "I catch." Actor A tosses the ball and, just as the ball leaves the finger tips, says his or her text, "I toss." Actor B catches the ball and checks in with his or her partner and says his or her text, "I catch." You can also add more balls to help the game move along and increase the stakes. Adding more balls adds tension. This is a teaching moment in that you can remind the actors to work with ease in their bodies. (Toss balls, 3–5 minutes.)

The quality of action *is how I do what I do to get what I want. Is action the only thing playable? No, there is one other thing and that is the quality of action. The quality of an action is an adverb and follows the action. We may choose to* toss lovingly, *for example. The quality of action exists in the feeling center. Remember, we must coax our feelings in our acting and that we cannot command them. It is the quality of action that helps coax our feelings. Again, the action is the form—the story. The quality of action coaxes the feeling.*

Even though we know there are only two things playable, we must always be aware of our objective. Our objective is to keep the ball in the air. How should we best accomplish our objective? By tossing and catching precisely. *Precisely becomes the quality of action. To do* this we should examine what it takes to toss and catch precisely for the actor—after all we are using the ball exercise as a metaphor for sending and receiving action and quality of action. The ball itself is a physical metaphor for the action. Characters must send and receive and respond to an action. The ball game aids us in solidifying this basic principle of acting. (Toss balls, 3–5 minutes.)

Artistic frames

So, how do we go about tossing and catching precisely? We should reconsider Chekhov's technique of artistic frames. Again, the artistic frame is similar, yet more profound, to Stanislavski's idea of beats. Each frame has a beginning, middle, and ending (B-M-E). The beginning is in the imagination—I prefer the word fantasy—fantasizing a perfect toss to the perfect place and that is to the actor's feeling center in the area of the heart—the Actor's Ideal Center. Fantasizing encompasses more than imagining. In our fantasies we are more involved physically and emotionally than when we imagine. If I ask you to imagine you will probably involve your visual sense only. When I ask you to fantasize you will naturally begin in your feeling center. This is extremely important . . . feel first. Feel the joy of completing the action precisely. (Toss balls, 3–5 minutes.)

Incorporating the imagination

To feel first is something the actor can totally do—in his imagination. We have all experienced joy and we know what that feels like. It is something we can fantasize without putting context to it. We begin with the ball in our hands and fantasize this feeling of joy, the feeling of completing our action precisely. We don't have to act it—we simply fantasize it. Included in our fantasy is: objective, action, and our quality of 'precisely'. This is our beginning. We must take the time to fantasize before we go on to our next step—the middle, which is our physical action—the doing of the form. In our imagination/fantasy, we create the joy, imagine our bodies tossing the ball and our partner catching it in his feeling center, and complete the fantasy by checking-in with our partner and sharing the feeling. Then, we toss the ball and when it reaches our partner and precisely lands in the feeling center of the other we complete the form. We radiate. We radiate the feeling of joy until we can no longer do so. This radiating process is the checking-in through a physical form. Throughout this process we are constantly with our partner and especially in this ending. When the moment of radiation is complete the artistic frame ends and we begin a new frame with another partner. In this exercise it is vital to have a clear B-M-E for each artistic frame. The moment of checking-in is radiation. (Toss balls, 3–5 minutes.)

To summarize

We experience a complete artistic frame that begins with preparation. The beginning section of preparation: Actor A imagines/fantasizes the atmosphere of 'joy/glad' and making the perfect toss to her partner's Ideal Center. Actor B imagines/fantasizes the same atmosphere and making the perfect catch. The middle is the execution/doing section or the action/form: to toss and to catch. The ending section is sustaining or radiation: hold the forms until the height of radiation and then begin a new frame. One artistic frame, in this exercise, consists of: fantasize—feeling Center, do—willing center, radiate—feeling center.

This practice of working on one brief artistic frame of tossing and catching will aid us greatly in creating clear B-M-Es. This practice is important, for all too often on the stage we are off to something else before we finish what we started. It muddies the story for the audience and a moment of the play is lost.

Notice that, in our artistic frame, we have not included our thinking center in the process. There is really nothing to think about. This is a basic principle I am adamant about in rehearsal. Let's first do and then think! As an actor portraying a character, thinking about what you are going to do before actually doing it is less productive than doing something and then thinking about it. Your brain will be involved at all times after you first read the play. The more productive way is to dive in and do and then spy-back on what you did. In this way you can analyze afterward then collaborate with your director if an adjustment need be made.

ESTABLISHING THE LANGUAGE OF CLASS AND REHEARSAL

> *Teaching Tip:* The teacher/director is at his or her best when he or she stays away from offering suggestions of quality of actions. The quality of action, as I have stated, exists in the feeling center of the actor. Instead, I try to lead actors through their actions and encourage them to explore qualities via Michael Chekhov's technique of polarity. While pursuing any objective if you don't get what you want by tossing angrily, try tossing gently. Constantly changing the course of action and/or quality in pursuit of an objective is far more interesting for the actor to play and the audience to watch.

Let's begin the game again. This time toss to a person and say the name of the character they are playing. We will continue to work with the quality of precisely. (Toss balls, 3–5 minutes.)

> *Teaching Tip:* You will notice something will naturally happen in this part of the exercise. New qualities will emerge after a time. At some point the quality of "precisely" goes out the window and relationships, through qualities, begin to emerge. Actors begin to experience the play. The actor playing Theseus may toss the ball lovingly to Hippolyta. Hippolyta may toss the ball angrily to Egeus. Egeus may toss the ball admiringly to Demetrius. Demetrius may toss the ball lovingly or angrily to Hermia. It is a fascinating exercise to watch—the play unfolds. A lot of balls will be dropped and that is a good thing.
>
> After you have played the game for 5 or so minutes using character names, pause and spy-back. Allow the actors to talk about what they did and the changes that occurred. Make sure everyone understands that they began to become engaged in the story through action and qualities and they already know a great deal

> about the play and themselves within it. They did not have to think. By engaging in action and knowing the given circumstances from the first read, qualities come naturally. This will be a revelation to many and is the basic principle of good rehearsal practices.

The two playables

Directors and actors can somewhat rejoice in that there are only two actable things: the action and the quality of the action. Fortunately, these are inseparable.

> ***Teaching Tip:*** I understand there are redundancies in this book concerning terminology. They are purposeful because you can't repeat them too often if you wish to solidify these terms. Human beings tend to want to put things into their own words. This habit is counterproductive in our work. You should be a stickler concerning terms.

Action—What I do to get what I want.
Quality of action—How I do what I do to get what I want.

Now, as a teacher, I must offer my own "train analogy." Imagine a train running on its two tracks. The engine is the character—chugging toward the *objective*. The tracks represent the *action* and the *quality of action*. For the train to remain on the tracks and chugging toward its objective it must have the equal support of both tracks. What would happen to a train whose tracks suddenly became uneven or if one track was lost altogether? It would result in a wreck. That's what happens when the actor begins to play one or the other (action or quality) too heavily to keep the train equal on equal tracks—a wreck—in the sense that the story is not clear—the ball is dropped.

If you tossed the ball angrily, for example, and the toss (action) was so hard and fast that the next actor couldn't catch it, you experienced

ESTABLISHING THE LANGUAGE OF CLASS AND REHEARSAL 63

playing the quality more strongly than the action. This resulted in the objective (to keep the ball in the air) not being accomplished. It is a delicate balance and one of which we must be constantly aware. That's my job as director and teacher—to make sure you are always chugging along on even tracks.

Instruction from the Teacher/Director: *Let's begin again remembering these things: hold your form at the end of the action until the moment of radiation is complete, hold on to the train analogy, and always check-in with your partner. This time as you toss say one of your lines from the play. Don't think about the quality of action before you toss. Allow it to emerge on its own. For instance, if I were Theseus I might toss the ball to Hippolyta and say, 'Now, fair Hippolyta, our nuptial hour draws on apace.' In this exercise the action is always 'to toss.' Allow the quality to emerge from the action and the text. You'll get the ball several times. Use the same line and change the tempo of the action. You'll find yourself inherently adjusting the quality to the form (derived from tempo) to the action.* (Toss balls for 3–5 minutes.)

> *Teaching Tip:* After a proper amount of time, stop the game and spy-back. You'll note the actors may have experienced a freedom they may not have felt before. They may also have lots of questions concerning how to apply this to scenes. Tell them that scenes are built on moment-to-moment exchanges and are made up of many artistic frames. In rehearsals, we explore the play by breaking it into artistic frames just as we did with our ball games. Near the end of this rehearsal, I do a review of what we covered much like a director would review the work of the day with a run through. I've found, as you see in this chapter, that it is good to review often as these terms are new to your actors.

What's left in our language, our terminology for rehearsals? I think it is important to again review before we move on. What have we covered in class/rehearsal? (Note to teacher: Rather than reciting the definitions ask individual actors to define the terms. The answers should be exactly as written.)

> Objective—What I want. (I believe it's important to use "I" rather than what the character wants. You are the character and no one else.)
> Action—What I do to get what I want.
> Quality of action—How I do what I do to get what I want.
> Form—The physical manifestation of action.
> Spy-back—Reviewing what you have done. What was my action? What was my quality of action? Did any quality coax a strong feeling? (*Note to teacher: At first everyone will find this difficult—to identify the verbs and adverbs. It gets easier with practice.*)
> Artistic frame—Beginning, middle, and end. Fantasize, do, radiate. Preparation, execution, sustaining. Artistic frames become longer in scene work; we will address that later on.
> Thinking center—From the neck up; the brain.
> Feeling center—From the shoulders to the waist; the heart center.
> The Actor's Ideal Center—In the area of the heart.

Acting with Balls (https://vimeo.com/188675545)

We have yet to talk about stakes and obstacles. We will during the rehearsal process when we have text to illuminate these ideas. During rehearsals we could talk about the themes and ideas of the play, but we won't. The themes and ideas of the play have already been communicated to you via the production concept. What we must work toward is realizing your objectives, actions, and quality of actions under the umbrella of the concept. In this way we will tell our story clearly.

Our theme, our superobjective, for Midsummer *(Love Conquers All) is our story and I, as your director, will guide you through that theme. Your job, as actors, is to support that theme through our process by the two things playable—actions and qualities. It will be a fun and collaborative process.*

Follow-up

Give your actors time for questions and journaling in the final spy-back of this session. You'll want to make certain the definitions for the terms are written exactly as given and not reinterpreted. This is the only way the language between director/teacher and actors can be clear.

Bring your bean bag balls to rehearsal and class with you every day. Instead of just reading through the text you're working on before you get on your feet, get on your feet and speak the text tossing the balls. Actors will find the separation of artistic frames easily. They will feel action and quality changes.

Further reading

Chekhov, Michael, *On the Technique of Acting*, HarperCollins Publishers, 1991. Preface "Michael Chekhov's Chart for Inspired Acting" by Mala Powers.

5
USING PSYCHOLOGICAL GESTURE AS ACTION

Framework

If your class or cast is unfamiliar with Chekhov's psychological gesture (PG), it is well worthwhile to take time and teach the technique to them. Chekhov teaches us that we can use the PG in several ways: as a physical manifestation for the entire character, as an image behind a single line, for a full speech, for a single moment, for different scenes—different moments within the scenes, and for action, which is what I will concentrate on in this chapter. Establishing work on *action* early in the rehearsal process is vital.

Even the majority of well-seasoned equity actors I've worked with have appreciated beginning rehearsals in an artistic way like using PG. Introducing PG early also aids in creating the ensemble—something we all should be adamant about no matter the level between civic and professional theater.

What is PG? What does it mean? First and foremost the PG is an archetype, a form that is universally known, very much like the work we have done previously on archetypes and essence. One could easily say archetypal gesture (AG) and PG are one and the same as they both reveal essences. This is what we search for in acting—the essence of what we are doing. Yet, there is one major difference between AG and PG.

The AG is the form only. The PG consists of two parts—the form, action, or gesture, and its psychological counterpart—the quality of action. We all know what it is to respond on a "gut level." The gut-level emotion means that whatever caused this response touched the essence of our being—we recognized the archetype and the quality stirred an emotion.

Chekhov addresses archetype and essence through the use of PG. PG, at first, is an expression of the archetype through movement. The movement, from beginning to end, is the form, and the form represents the physical essence. The movement/action coupled with the quality of action is what makes the work psychophysical. The quality of action is the psychological part of the PG.

The PG begins as an impulse in response to a need, for example, a need "to open." The impulse is an inward experience and is expressed outwardly as a form. Think of the first thing humans built to serve as something more comfortable than the ground or a rock to sit upon. Whatever was built, stool or chair, sprang from a need and then an idea emerged. This need led to the idea, which led to the action of "I build" and describes the psychophysical process of the PG—need, idea, and form. In our Chekhov work we say feeling, thinking, and willing/doing. Because all human beings go through this process it is universally recognizable.

It is very important that the actor take time to fully formulate the gesture in the fantasy/imagination prior to physicalizing it. The PG, in the imagination, as in its physical manifestation, is full bodied. Much more than simply visualizing, the actor's first impulse must again spring from a need to express the gesture itself. Therefore, the actor should fantasize a need "to open," "to close," "to embrace," etc. Since "need" is archetypal we can understand it and easily fantasize it. Once the need is present, the actor imagines the gesture in his or her entire body, radiates the gesture into the space, and finally physically produces it and again radiates the need to his or her partner and into the entire space, 360 degrees. Radiating throughout the process should always be stressed.

In the beginning, teach PG and AG as a form only. There is nothing to feel by exploring the form. Actors are always searching for something to feel and in discovering PG for the first time we are simply experiencing the full-bodied form. Feeling something by executing the form will come later when adding a quality of action. It's important to communicate this to the company.

All PGs are not created equally. Although the PG is an archetypal form, a form universally recognized, it is not necessarily exact from person to person. There should be a bit of allowance for creativity.

USING PSYCHOLOGICAL GESTURE AS ACTION

Of course, the PG is a rehearsal tool. The actor cannot go through a performance forming PGs all evening, although it may be really interesting to watch. The actor eventually can incorporate, after repetition, the process all inwardly. The audience may see the gesture, but it is reduced outwardly to a more natural state. The power of the gesture, once the actor has fully invested in the process, remains inward. Actors should invest in full-bodied PGs offstage before entrances or prior to performance. There is a specific order in learning the process.

Pre-class exploration

Staccato-Legato (https://vimeo.com/188675555)
Psychological Gesture — Forms (https://vimeo.com/188675552)
Psychological Gesture — With Text (https://vimeo.com/188675549)
Psychological Gesture — Kata (https://vimeo.com/188675547)

View these on PG. The first video (Staccato-Legato) is the standard exercise of staccato-legato and precedes work on PG. Work along with the actors in the video while watching. Have the forms in your own body before introducing them to others. You should also have a printout of the definitions of PG (see below) for your class or rehearsal. You might also have the actors memorize the two speeches highlighted in this chapter. It will save time. Note: The last video (Psychological Gesture — Kata) is a kata of PGs developed at the Great Lakes Michael Chekhov Consortium. It is meant to be a warm-up in the Chekhov Technique.

In-class exercise: Psychological gesture for action

Teaching the form

- Have the actors form a circle.
- Explain to them that we are working, at first, on getting the forms of PGs into our bodies.
- Go over the rules of creating a strong PG.
- Do each PG several times and move on to the next.

- Repetition will insure muscle memory and will also increase the will power to do the gesture.
- Do each gesture both staccato and legato at least 3 times in both tempos.
- Have the students read aloud the definitions before executing the PG.

Note: Chekhov used the terms staccato/legato and we understand he means between fast and slow. The musical terms of allegro and largo would be more accurate, yet we must adhere to Chekhov's original terms.

Rules of forming the PG

Teaching the form of our list of PGs is straightforward. There are some rules to creating a good PG. The PG should:

- Be clear, simple, and strong.
- Have a beginning, middle, and ending—preparation, execution, sustaining.
- Begin as a fantasy. Fantasize the entire gesture before executing it.
- Begin in the Actor's Ideal Center. The impulse of the gesture should originate here.
- Be full bodied.
- Have a tempo between legato and staccato—slow and fast.
- Begin with the gesture—Open.

PG definitions

Open	Lift	Smash	Close
Embrace	Wring	Push	Pull
Tear or Rip	Penetrate	Throw	

We somewhat take for granted that we know the definitions of words. I adhere to dictionary standards and give actors the definitions below before teaching each gesture.

USING PSYCHOLOGICAL GESTURE AS ACTION

Open: "Spread out or open from a closed or folded state. Afford access to. Ready and willing to receive favorably."

Close: "The concluding time. Make shut, finish, or terminate."

Push: "The act of applying force in order to move something away. An effort to advance."

Pull: "Applying force to move something toward or with you."

Smash: "To break to pieces with violence and often with a crashing sound, as by striking. Letting fall, or dashing against something. Shatter."

Lift: "Giving temporary assistance. Raise from a lower to a higher position."

Embrace: "The state of taking in or encircling. A close and protective acceptance."

Tear: "An opening made forcibly by pulling apart."

Throw: "Propelling something through the air with a movement of the arm and wrist."

Wring: "A twisting squeeze. Twist and compress."

Penetrate: "To pierce or pass into or through."

Instructions from the Teacher/Director: *The PG, just as the forms of tossing and catching in the ball game, begins in the fantasy or imagination of the actor. The impulse must be felt first which may or may not engage the thinking center (we often respond without thinking) and then the actor completes the gesture in a movement—from the willing center. I'm sure science would tell us the thinking center is always engaged. Yet, for our purposes as actors we must search for our work organically, which begins in the feeling center. It is useful for us to remind ourselves to not engage the thinking center too much.*

> *Teaching Tip:* There are two schools of thought on where to begin the gesture. One is to begin from a neutral posture. I've never liked the word neutral. When you put your car in neutral, on a level surface, and press the accelerator, what happens? Nothing, except that the engine revs faster. There is no motion. To me, neutral means nothing. Instead of saying "neutral" say, "Let's begin in a place of readiness and connect to the Actor's Ideal Center."

The other school of thought is to begin the gesture from its polar opposite. If I want to "open," for instance, I'd begin from "close." This is sort of a conundrum in that before we do anything we must connect to the Actor's Ideal Center. I have come to the conclusion that beginning in the place of readiness and moving immediately to "open" is preferable.

When I work as an actor on PG, I have an image of a sun in my chest. A sunburst is constant like a heartbeat yet much stronger. I fantasize that the gesture begins with a burst. The burst may be slow or fast (legato or staccato) depending on the given circumstances. Encourage actors to find their own image. The sunburst connects me to Chekhov's thoughts on "rays."

There is profundity in executing the PG. The actor begins standing upright with his or her feet apart and begins the process as described. The profound gesture changes the space entirely. The movement tells an amazing story with a clear beginning, middle, and ending. The ending of the gesture should radiate into the space. Repeating the gestures multiple times increases the will power and the need will grow. Remember to explore the tempo of the gesture between staccato and legato. Be sure the actors are fully opening with their entire bodies. I'm rather adamant concerning clarity of any gesture. While observing the gesture of "open," for instance, watch that the actors are not leaning their heads too far backward so that the neck is closing and stopping the flow of energy. Also, pay attention especially to the lower body. Legs and feet should spread equally with the arms and hands.

After learning the PG of "open" I suggest you work on "close." It is, of course, exactly the opposite of what the actors just did, reinforcing the concept of polarity. Return each time to the place of readiness. Move on diligently through each of the PGs. The gesture should not require more than one full step to execute. Example: To "throw" might end with the right foot, leg, and arm thrust forward. The left arm and hand would be stretched backward—honoring the back space. I prefer that actors work

> both sides of their bodies with the gestures as they tend to favor a dominant side.
>
> Once all of the gestures are in the muscle memory of the actors, then we can add text. Begin again with the gesture of "open" and add text. The text will be the words: "I open, etc."

In-class/rehearsal exercise: Speaking the PG

- The actor begins in a place of readiness.
- The actor creates an impulse (I Open) from the Actor's Ideal Center.
- The actor executes the gesture.
- The text—"I open" is articulated at the end of the gesture and radiated into the space.

You'll notice a quality will emerge with the text and the quality usually depends on tempo. When the quality is added, the actor may experience an emotional response. This is a good thing. If not, no worries. Emotional connection for an actor may need to include given circumstances. Vary the tempos between the slowest and the fastest possible. The qualities will change with each variance of tempo. Continue through all the PGs utilizing repetition.

> ***Teaching Tip:*** The worth of working on PG as action is that the list of the gestures is brief, yet you can fit any action word into the archetypal list. Test it for yourself. Choose any action verb and it will fall into one of the archetypes. Here are some examples: to plunge = to push or to penetrate, to seduce = to embrace, to grasp = to pull or embrace, etc.

Words excite actors and directors—or at least they should. Starting with archetypal words relieves the pressure of specifically identifying the action at the beginning and aids actors to not begin work in the thinking center. We eventually find a specific verb/action by exploring the PGs in varying rhythms, organically finding just the right word through *repetition*. Finding just the right word from working with the archetype will excite the actor and make his or her willpower grow. Finding just the right word from exploring the PG will ultimately come from the given circumstances.

Don't confuse "willpower" with "willing center." The willing center, in Chekhov's teaching, is from the waist to the feet—from where we move. The willpower is "control of one's impulses and actions or self-control." I think this can be confusing in Chekhov's texts. Sometimes we can control our actions. At other times, we can't. So, we can control our willpower. Our movement, from the willing center, is directly connected to our willpower and how we control it or not.

The gesture becomes specific through an artistic process involving the whole being and is not limited to the thinking center. Therefore the entire body is engaged—so important for the actor. After all, in the theater we are not in a natural environment. It is an elevated environment. There are no close-ups or various camera angles. The audience sees the entire body of the actor at all times. In the theater, the actor's body must always be engaged. It is through the action of the actor—engaging the feeling, thinking, and willing centers that the audience experiences theater at its highest level. To begin to reach this goal, ask each actor to choose a line from the play.

In-class/rehearsal exercise: Addition of written text to the PG

- Have the actors, one at a time and in a circle, go through all steps and create a PG for a single line of text from any play they know or are working on.

USING PSYCHOLOGICAL GESTURE AS ACTION 75

- Drop the name of the PG and insert the text instead.
- Remember to not skip any steps in B-M-E.
- After each actor has created one PG for the line of text, stop and spy-back.
- Begin the spy-back with these words, "How did you come to the conclusion of your chosen PG?"

Instructions from the Director/Teacher: *A wonderful and wondrous thing about using PG as action is that surprising things happen. It is natural for actors and directors to discard certain PGs because we don't think one or the other is correct for the given circumstances. It is a mistake to discard anything in our art because we* think *something may not work. Do before you* think! *Look at the following line*:

Hermia
I do entreat your grace to pardon me.

In Hermia's line, we might discard the PG—smash. We look at the clues: 'entreat', and 'pardon', with no exclamation at the end of the sentence. Our thinking center looks at these clues and negates—to smash. Yet let's consider what happens if the actor smashes—gently or reservedly (with reserve) and with a slow tempo. We must consider Hermia's atmosphere, which is 'mad'. What if she controls her anger? She has everything to lose—her love interest and her life—the highest stakes of all. To smash makes sense in this scenario. Hermia is not necessarily smashing Theseus. She may be smashing the theme of 'male domination' in the play. Through the varying tempos, Hermia may find that smashing gently will aid in achieving her objective. Perhaps Theseus respects her verve of smashing and appreciates her quality of 'gently'. It all depends on how Theseus reacts to the quality of action, and—this is really the thing between actors—are you truthfully listening and responding accordingly? We respond to an action through its quality more than the action itself.

Honestly, most acting is predetermined and not based on what is given from our fellow actors. We often rest until our cues. Using PG as a rehearsal tool forces us to listen and react accordingly.

Look at Hermia's line to Theseus again:

Hermia
I do entreat your grace to pardon me.

- (I smash, gently.)
- The actors begin and follow all the rules of making a good PG.
- This time say the action and quality after creating the gesture in the fantasy.
- Following that, execute the gesture using the tempo of legato, and speak the text.
- The actors, having committed 100 percent to the action and quality, will have an organic experience.
- Because of this investment the feeling is easily coaxed again and again. Commitment is the key to consistency.

As I said earlier, we can't perform PGs on the stage as it is not natural behavior. We can, however, have the inward experience. By working with PGs in rehearsal, the outward experience creates an inward one. The PG, having been created, will remain as does any profound physical experience. We store experiences in our physical being and these experiences are there for us to call upon using this work.

Teaching Tip: Encourage actors to try multiple gestures for any line or speech. Hermia, for instance, could just as easily use "embrace" or "open." Actors will find the appropriate gesture through exploration. They will know when the right gesture has been found.

Working alone

Once the technique is learned, the work can be done individually outside of the rehearsal hall, whether it is a monologue or scene work—the actor's homework.

> **Teaching Tip:** I prefer to work with PG from early scenes of the play—especially those in which the audience is being introduced to relationships. The following two speeches are a good example because they occur at the beginning of the play and Theseus and Hippolyta are preparing for their wedding. They are just getting to know each other and are clearly filled with infatuation. There is a lot to explore here and working with PG early will inform their relationship for the remainder of the play. The director should talk with the actors about atmosphere, both objective and subjective.

In-class/rehearsal exercise

Have two actors do the following speeches facing each other and speaking aloud. No PGs at this time. These are the speeches I suggested earlier that could be memorized.

Theseus
Now, fair Hippolyta, our nuptial hour
Draws on apace; four happy days bring in
Another moon: but, O, methinks, how slow
This old moon wanes! She lingers my desires,
Like to a step-dame or a dowager
Long withering out a young man's revenue.

Hippolyta
Four days will quickly steep themselves in night;
Four nights will quickly dream away the time;
And then the moon, like to a silver bow
New-bent in heaven, shall behold the night
Of our solemnities.

Look at the clues in the lines with your actors. First, read the clues in the lines aloud and then read the lines without the clues.

Theseus
(**Theseus** *compliments* **Hippolyta**.)
Now, fair Hippolyta, our nuptial hour
Draws on apace; four happy days bring in
Another moon:
 (**Theseus** *tells* **Hippolyta** *how happy he is about the upcoming wedding.*)
but, O, methinks, how slow
This old moon wanes!
 (**Theseus** *tells* **Hippolyta** *how anxious he is to finally be married, to get to the wedding day—and wedding night! "Lingers my desires" means that* **Theseus** *is having a difficult time waiting for the event.*)
She lingers my desires, Like to a step-dame or
a dowager
 (*"Withering" is a wonderful word/image considering his state or subjective atmosphere which could be interpreted as more than ready for the consummation of the marriage.*)
Long withering out a young man's revenue.

Hippolyta
(**Hippolyta** *is calming* **Theseus** *down a bit*.)
Four days will quickly steep themselves in night;
Four nights will quickly dream away the time;
And then the moon, like to a silver bow
New-bent in heaven, shall behold the night
Of our solemnities.

(*The new moon will christen the night of their wedding. She may be promising the night of all nights! She is teasing him.*)

Clues to atmosphere

We observe in the clues these subjective atmospheres: Theseus = lust. Hippolyta = love and patience. (Lust, love, and patience fit into the archetypal atmospheres of glad/bad, respectively.) Here is an example of polarity. The objective atmosphere is "glad." The play begins with some conflict and within archetypal atmospheres the audience will immediately recognize. *Midsummer*, among its other themes, is a play that explores sexual relationships. I chose, in my production, to highlight sexuality from the beginning and it can be seen in the following work on PG.

Score of the finished exercise

The following is my observation of the actions and qualities that resulted from work on PG between the actors playing Theseus and Hippolyta in our production. It represents about one hour of rehearsal, which may sound excessive for two short speeches. Regardless, the work bolstered their entire relationship and was crucial in that the same two actors also played Oberon and Titania. We did not need to repeat this work for other scenes. The foundation was built. Following is the score the actors found through their exploration. *Please note the score is not the only way the exchange might happen. It is simply an observation of what did happen in this particular production. There are many other possibilities.* I offer the work at this point as a guide only for teachers and directors. It is best to allow your actors to find their own score. The sequence of the exercise continues after our score.

Theseus
PG = I pull. Specific action = I grab. Quality = Conqueringly. Tempo = Staccato.

Now, fair Hippolyta, our nuptial hour
Draws on apace; four happy days bring in
Another moon:

PG = I embrace. Specific action = I cocoon. Quality = Lustfully. Tempo = Legato.

but, O, methinks, how slow
This old moon wanes! She lingers my desires,
Like to a step-dame or a dowager
Long withering out a young man's revenue.

Hippolyta

PG = I push. Specific action = I separate. Quality = Calmingly. Tempo = Legato.

Four days will quickly steep themselves in night;
Four nights will quickly dream away the time;

PG = I open. Specific action = I tease. Quality = Alluringly. Tempo = Legato.

And then the moon, like to a silver bow
New-bent in heaven, shall behold the night
Of our solemnities.

Exercise continues

Have your actor pair up and do this work together. It doesn't matter about gender if you're in class. The exercise is about finding the form, tempos, and qualities. The PG is the action.

Follow this sequence:

First time through:

Theseus—Fantasize the PG, execute the physical gesture, radiate, and say the name of the gesture using the words "I pull" at the height of radiation, followed by the line of text, and radiate the quality until it begins to dissipate. When the gesture begins to dissipate, return to a place of readiness and begin the process again with the next gesture. Go through both speeches in this sequence and spy-back.

Second time through:

Repeat the above; yet, this time, move from gesture to gesture without returning to a place of readiness. So, at the end of the first line of text, Theseus would radiate while holding the form of "I pull" and begin the process fantasizing the next PG while remaining still in the first gesture.

USING PSYCHOLOGICAL GESTURE AS ACTION

Third time through:
Repeat the above and don't say the name of the gesture.

Fourth time through:
Allow the actor receiving the gesture to respond with his or her own gesture when he or she feels the need to do so. He or she may respond immediately or at any given point during the line. Have him or her hold her form until the next gesture has been executed. It may look like this:

Theseus—Pull "Now fair Hippolyta" (Hippolyta—Push until Theseus—Embrace). Theseus—Embrace "but, O methinks how slow this old moon wanes" (Hippolyta—Embrace and hold until he or she speaks using a new gesture). Continue this give and take throughout both speeches. Repeat this step several times exploring different gestures.

Fifth time through:
Fantasize each gesture thoroughly and do the exercise without physically forming the PGs speaking the dialogue.

Theseus

PG = I pull.

Now, fair Hippolyta, our nuptial hour
Draws on apace; four happy days bring in
Another moon:

PG = I embrace.

but, O, methinks, how slow
This old moon wanes! She lingers my desires,
Like to a step-dame or a dowager
Long withering out a young man's revenue.

Hippolyta

PG = I push.

Four days will quickly steep themselves in night;
Four nights will quickly dream away the time;

PG = I open.

And then the moon, like to a silver bow
New-bent in heaven, shall behold the night
Of our solemnities.

> *Teaching Tip:* Actors tend to move closer and closer to each other during this work. They should allow at least ten feet between themselves throughout. You'll need to constantly remind them of the steps of fantasizing, doing, and radiating. Vary the tempos from gesture to gesture to find polarity and new qualities.
>
> This work on PG should be accomplished before we begin to block the play. It affects the blocking and natural movements. Actually, from this work the blocking will emerge. The director often simply needs to tend to entrances and exits, where the action should take place on the stage, and brief suggestions to create nuance and pictures.

In-class/rehearsal exercise: Blocking emerges from the PGs

Give your actors, upon completion of your work on PGs, some simple guidance on blocking and see what transpires. You'll find the investment of your work on PG will remain and wonderfully organic acting will occur. Here is my observation on what transpired with the blocking after our work on PG for the two speeches:

> *Blocking:* I asked the actors to enter the space with Theseus chasing Hippolyta. She eluded him for a bit and Theseus, finally catching her, pulled her into his arms. Both were somewhat breathless.
>
> **Oberon:**
> *PG = I pull. Specific action = I grab. Quality = Forcefully. Tempo = Staccato.*
>
> Now, fair Hippolyta, our nuptial hour
> Draws on apace; four happy days bring in
> Another moon:

USING PSYCHOLOGICAL GESTURE AS ACTION

Blocking: I asked Theseus to take Hippolyta to the floor.
PG = I embrace. Specific action = I cocoon. Quality = Lustfully. Tempo = Legato.

but, O, methinks, how slow
This old moon wanes! She lingers my desires,
Like to a step-dame or a dowager
Long withering out a young man's revenue.

Blocking: I asked Hippolyta to separate herself from Theseus. They remained on the floor.
Hippolyta:
PG = I push. Specific action = I separate. Quality = Calmingly. Tempo = Legato.

Four days will quickly steep themselves in night;
Four nights will quickly dream away the time;

Blocking: I asked Hippolyta to stand. She slowly stood and gave Theseus a complete turn of her body using the gesture of "open."
PG = I open. Specific action = I tease. Quality = Alluringly. Tempo = Legato.

And then the moon, like to a silver bow
New-bent in heaven, shall behold the night
Of our solemnities.

> *Teaching Tip:* Please remember that the above score was arrived at from the sequence work on PG and it represents the collaboration between actor and director. Once the actors understand how to incorporate PG, we can move onto individual blocks and introduce the director's work of AoA to them. This gives the actors specific parameters within which to explore. It helps them understand that the overall concept must always be adhered to as each AoA fits into the main themes of the play. Following the work on PG, I have found it productive to give the actors rough blocking and afterward introduce the work on AoA which we cover in the next chapter.
>
> Note: I have also begun rehearsals giving actors the AoAs prior to working on PG. It is up to the director to judge individual actors and situations. If time is an enemy, give the actors the AoAs first. If not, allow them to explore PG first. Some directors, as have I, may change the AoA depending on the actor's work.

Follow-up

I urge actors to record their scores in a journal from rehearsal to rehearsal. The work on PGs is organically fruitful and, for the most part, is stored in muscle memory. Yet, if the actor is exploring multiple PGs, as suggested, the score can become long and difficult for the body to recall everything. A quick written reminder is usually all that is necessary. Creating a rehearsal journal is a good habit to adopt because it helps the actor create a process of working. It is as important as musicians playing scales daily.

The director has his or her own score that consists of atmospheres, AoAs, blocks, rhythmical waves, etc. Commonly called "the director's book," in the Chekhov world it is filled with much more information than just blocking and notes. I would suggest to directors to have a double-spaced script, in a three-ring binder, with a blank page between each page of script. Go into the process with a clear plan and be prepared to compromise.

Suggested reading

There are samples of more scores from other plays in Appendix III.

Further reading

Chekhov, Michael, *To the Actor*, Routledge Publishing, 2002. Chapter 5 "The Psychological Gesture."

6
PUTTING IT ALL TOGETHER THUS FAR

Framework

Michael Chekhov gives us a clear path to success in acting and directing. It is not a linear path. It is, rather, a circular one. The path concludes with what he termed as "Inspired Acting." The inspiration comes from layering the production and performance with all the tools we have explored thus far with more to follow. Chekhov tells us to always begin with atmosphere. After first establishing the atmosphere the director can choose, when working with actors, to begin with AoAs, PGs, QoM, or any tool in the Chekhov Technique. Each play is different in this regard. Each cast is different. Each rehearsal or studio class is different. The director/teacher, when experienced with work, will be inspired with regard to the proper tools with which to begin his or her own preparation and the casting process. The teacher, in the studio, learns with experience what tools to use for given situations.

In this chapter you'll find the score of what transpired from our work in our rehearsal process from partial blocks 12–13 of *Midsummer*. It is the same scene as we looked at earlier but includes all the techniques we've explored to this point and is meant to be a guide only. The score is *our result* of the work and is certainly not meant to be the only way it can be performed. Indeed, you shouldn't try to copy it because that will not lead to "Inspired Acting." Realize the score does not include all the dialogues from the scene. If you'd like to work on the entire scene it is from Act II, scene I.

The reader can hopefully see and sense the polarity derived between actions, qualities of action, and QoM. Yet, again, the work must be discovered. The teacher/director should encourage actors to search for polarity, for it is a key element in creating rhythmical waves.

Pre-class/rehearsal exploration

Using this text, or any other you are working with, decide the overall objective atmosphere. From there, divide the script into blocks, decide the artistic frames, and "baptize" (name) the AoAs with themes.

In-class/rehearsal exercise: A possible sequence of putting it all together

When you meet your class, have them divide in their scripts the work you have done in the exploration concerning blocks and artistic frames. (I have found that allowing the actors to do this is more productive than giving them the work beforehand. It instills in them good habits. Don't allow them to ask questions about your work. That instills in them bad habits. The questions will be answered when the actors get on their feet and begin working. In a rehearsal process, I always give the stage manager a hard copy of the script divided into blocks. He or she then will share with the cast and production team.)

Look again at partial blocks 12–13 of *Midsummer*. Along with the added elements you will notice redundancies. Use them as a reminder of previous work. The division of blocks of text is how much text the director wishes to work on in a given time period as described earlier. The division of blocks is completely subjective. Blocks can consist of several artistic frames. Remember that each artistic frame has its own AoA. Note: In Appendix III, I introduce an alternative to naming the AoA.

> *Teaching Tip:* In the last chapter we began work with PG. Following the work on atmosphere, I suggest you experiment by giving the actors the AoA first this time. Have the actors read through the blocks

PUTTING IT ALL TOGETHER THUS FAR

first by speaking the AoA and then the dialogue. Here we are only concentrating on the objective atmosphere and the AoAs. The actors should read the AoA with its inherent quality.

When the actors have completed the work on AoAs have them work on the artistic frames using PG as we did in the last chapter. After each frame the actors should identify the qualities they discovered while working toward naming a specific action from the PG. This will take quite a while, easily an entire studio class of 1 hour and 45 minutes and likely more classes. With practice the time is shortened considerably. After the work on PG, which includes action and qualities, continue work on QoM. There is also the matter of tempo. You'll discover the tempos when working on PGs and QoM. I have recorded all but tempo in the score. As another in-class/rehearsal exercise you can vary the sequence of work on a different scene. Experiment with the order of the Technique.

The atmosphere that is prevalent prior to this scene is "glad." You may consider working on that atmosphere first and then changing it suddenly to "mad."

Teacher/director's work — artistic frame 1

Overall objective atmosphere = Mad. Arc of action = The confrontation.

Clues to AoA = "proud Titania," Titania confronts Oberon who is obviously jealous.

Clues to Atmosphere = "ill met," "jealous Oberon," Titania orders the fairies to leave, "rash wonton," which means a skittish and willful creature.

Note: Artistic frames are enclosed in brackets. Actions, clues, qualities, and QoM are in italics.

Block 12.
Enter, from one side, **Oberon**, *with his train; from the other,* **Titania**, *with hers.*

Oberon

PG = I push. Action = I taunt. Quality = Angrily. QoM = Molding.
[THE CONFRONTATION.

Ill met by moonlight, proud Titania.

Titania

PG = I open. Action = I challenge. Quality = Condescendingly. QoM = Flying.

What, jealous Oberon?

PG = I push. Action = I command. Quality = Authoritatively. QoM = Molding.

Fairies, skip hence:
I have forsworn his bed and company.

Oberon

PG = I embrace. Action = I grab. Quality = Manly. QoM = Molding.

Tarry, rash wanton: am not I thy lord?

Titania

PG = I close. Action = I acquiesce. Quality = Condescendingly. QoM = Flowing.

Then I must be thy lady:

PG = I penetrate. Action = I confront. Quality = Hurtfully. QoM = Molding.

but I know
When thou hast stolen away from fairy land,
And in the shape of Corin sat all day,
Playing on pipes of corn and versing love
To amorous Phillida. Why art thou here,
Come from the farthest step of India. . .?

PG = I wring. Action = I accuse. Quality = Angrily. QoM = Molding.

Oberon

How canst thou thus for shame, Titania,
Glance at my credit with Hippolyta,
Knowing I know thy love to Theseus?]

Teacher/director's work—artistic frame 2

Overall objective atmosphere = Mad. Arc of action = The accusation.

Clues to AoA = Titania is accusing Oberon of being the source or instigator of all of their confrontations for a long time. She is telling the truth from her perspective and we have reason to believe her. It's difficult for him to deny the allegations yet his stubbornness prevails. This is another example of the theme of male dominance in the play.

Titania
PG = I push. Action = I place all my cards on the table. Quality = Angrily. QoM = Molding.
[THE ACCUSATION.
These are the forgeries of jealousy:
And never, since the middle summer's spring,
Met we on hill, in dale, forest or mead,
By paved fountain or by rushy brook,
Or in the beached margent of the sea,
To dance our ringlets to the whistling wind . . .
PG = I lift. Action = I appeal. Quality = Truthfully. QoM = Flowing.
We are their parents and the original.]

Teacher/director's work—artistic frame 3

Overall objective atmosphere = Mad. Arc of action = The challenge.

Clues to AoA = Oberon challenges Titania to give up the boy and says all will be well. Titania refuses and challenges him by saying no. She knows there will be repercussions and yet stands steadfast.

Block 13.
Oberon
PG = I close. Action = I stand firm. Quality = Solidly. QoM = Molding.
[THE CHALLENGE.
Do you amend it then, it lies in you.

PG = I embrace. Action = I soften. Quality = Easily. QoM = Flowing.
Why should Titania cross her Oberon?
I do but beg a little changeling boy,
To be my henchman

Titania

PG = I smash. Action = I kill (the idea). Quality = Definitely. QoM = Molding.

Set your heart at rest:
The fairy land buys not the child of me . . .]

Teacher/director's work—artistic frame 4

Overall objective atmosphere = Mad. Arc of action = The fishing expedition.

Clues to AoA = Oberon needs time to concoct a plan for keeping Titania in the forest. Notice a change of subjective atmosphere in Oberon.

Oberon

PG = I throw. Action = I query. Quality = Baitingly. QoM = Flowing.

[THE FISHING EXPEDITION.
How long within this wood intend you stay?

Titania

PG = I close. Action = I suspect. Quality = Cautiously. QoM = Molding.

Perchance till after Theseus' wedding-day.]

Teacher/director's work—artistic frame 5

Overall objective atmosphere = Mad. Arc of action = The attempt.
Clues to AoA = "patiently," Titania is making an attempt at reconciliation and seeking a solution to the problem.

Titania (continued)

PG = I open. Action = I soften. Quality = Soothingly. QoM = Flowing.

PUTTING IT ALL TOGETHER THUS FAR

[THE ATTEMPT.
If you will patiently dance in our round
And see our moonlight revels, go with us;

PG = I close. Action = I stand firm. Quality = Fixedly. QoM = Molding.

If not, shun me, and I will spare your haunts.

Oberon

PG = I open. Action = I bargain. Quality = Slyly. QoM = Flowing.

Give me that boy, and I will go with thee.]

Teacher/director's work—artistic frame 6

Overall objective atmosphere = Mad. Arc of action = The final word. Clues to AoA = "Not for thy fairy kingdom," or, not for all the world would I do this. "Chide downright" is also a clue. Titania and Oberon are powerful fairies. Oberon has already changed the weather to the detriment of the humans. Imagine if the two really got into a physical/magical confrontation!

Titania

PG = I tear (rip). Action = I finalize. Quality = Wholeheartedly. QoM = Molding.

[THE FINAL WORD.
Not for thy fairy kingdom. Fairies, away!
We shall chide downright, if I longer stay.]

Exit **Titania** *with her train.*

In-class/rehearsal exercise: Speaking the score

For directors and actors, the polarity created through collaboration via our acquired terminology is dynamic. Look at the score of our work without the text. Compare through the ending block and you will see a very dynamic rhythmical wave.

Act the physical score without the text. In other words, speak all the words including the baptisms of the AoAs and execute the sequence and don't include the dialogue. Actors can have their scores on music stands beside them to help remind them of the sequence. This exercise proves how important the work underneath the dialogue truly is. The dialogue and the Technique are equally important. The truth of Inspired Acting cannot exist without the two. Actors can keep their work fresh by simply speaking and executing the score or even doing the score without words at all. As long as all the rules are employed of creating a good PG from the imagination the work will remain organic in performance.

In this exercise follow the suggested order: Speak the theme of the AoA when appropriate. Fantasize and radiate. Speak the PG, speak the QoM, speak and execute the action and quality.

Oberon

Fantasize. Radiate. Speak "THE CONFRONTATION," Speak PG, "I push," Speak QoM, "Molding." Speak and execute action and quality, "I taunt, angrily."

Titania

1. Fantasize. Radiate. Speak PG, "I open," Speak QoM, "flowing." Speak and execute action and quality, "I challenge, condescendingly."

2. Fantasize. Radiate. Speak PG, "I push," Speak QoM, "Molding." Speak and execute action and quality, "I command, authoritatively."

Oberon

Fantasize. Radiate. Speak PG, "I embrace," Speak QoM, "Molding." Speak and execute action and quality, "I grab, manly."

Titania

1. Fantasize. Radiate. Speak PG, "I close," Speak QoM, "Flowing." Speak and execute action and quality, "I acquiesce, condescendingly."

PUTTING IT ALL TOGETHER THUS FAR

   2 Fantasize. Radiate. Speak PG, "I penetrate," Speak QoM, "Molding." Speak and execute action and quality, "I confront, hurtfully."

Oberon
      Fantasize. Radiate. Speak PG, "I wring," Speak QoM, "Molding." Speak and execute action and quality, "I accuse, angrily."

Titania
1. Fantasize. Radiate. Speak "THE ACCUSATION," Speak PG, "I push," Speak QoM, "Molding." Speak and execute action and quality, "I place all my cards on the table, angrily."
2. Fantasize. Radiate. Speak PG, "I lift," Speak QoM, "Flowing." Speak and execute action and quality, "I appeal, truthfully." ***Block 13.***

Oberon
1. Fantasize. Radiate. Speak "THE CHALLENGE," Speak PG, "I lift," Speak QoM, "Molding." Speak and execute action and quality, "I stand firm, solidly."
2. Fantasize. Radiate. Expansion. Speak PG, "I embrace," Speak QoM, "Flowing." Speak and execute action and quality, "I soften, easily."

Titania
      Fantasize. Radiate. Speak PG, "I smash," Speak QoM, "Molding." Speak action and quality, "I kill (the idea), definitely."

Oberon
      Fantasize. Radiate. Speak "THE FISHING EXPEDITION," Speak PG, "I throw," Speak QoM, "Flowing." Speak and execute action and quality, "I query, baitingly."

Titania
1. Fantasize. Radiate. Speak PG, "I close," Speak QoM, "Molding." Speak and execute action and quality, "I suspect, cautiously."

2. Fantasize. Radiate. Speak "THE ATTEMPT," Speak PG, "I open," Speak QoM, "Flowing." Speak and execute action and quality, "I soften, soothingly."
3. Fantasize. Radiate. Speak PG, "I close," Speak QoM, "Molding." Speak and execute action and quality, "I stand firm, fixedly."

Oberon
Fantasize. Radiate. Speak PG, "I open," Speak QoM, "Flowing." Speak and execute action and quality, "I bargain, slyly."

Titania
Fantasize. Radiate. Speak PG, "I tear (rip)," Speak QoM, "Molding." Speak and execute action and quality, "I finalize, wholeheartedly."

> ***Teaching Tip:*** There are several possibilities for this exercise. You can get the actors used to the work by having two other actors read from the script while the physical work is being done. The readers don't necessarily need to read the entire dialogue, just cue lines.
>
> The execution of the action, at first, could be the archetypal PG itself. After a few times through have the actors execute a more natural action.
>
> The process of fantasize and radiate should occur all in the imagination—inwardly. Make certain the actors are taking time and not skipping steps. In the final phase of this work the actors will drop all of the physical doings and act the scene naturalistically where you'll see the fruit of your labors.

Working alone

Once you understand the mechanics of this work it is easily done alone or with a scene partner. This is homework. Most actors will memorize lines for homework and then attend rehearsal. This practice doesn't make you "director proof." As an accomplished actor, you really don't want directors who act through you—or through your work. Sometimes this is inevitable. Yet the more the actor brings to the role, the less the director is likely to get involved as long as the actor is working within the concept.

Follow-up

Acting the score without text can be a revelation. Actors will understand deeply each artistic frame by negating the text and simply incorporating each action, quality, and atmosphere through physicalizing and verbalizing the score only. When you return to the text, you'll find immense clarity in the story.

The artistic frames add to the rhythmical wave of the entire play. The director is prudent to consider the artistic frames for the characters. I admit this is a tremendous amount of work for a director or teacher of a scene study class. Yet, this work is the *art* of directing/teaching. If you want to transcend your work from the norm of responding to a presentation to an artistic realm, consider spending your preparation time breaking the play/scene/monologue into artistic frames and sharing this work with your class or cast.

The rhythmical wave is not only the overall wave that we create for the climaxes. There must be waves within the overall wave as the above score indicates. Like a balloon the play must inflate and deflate, "expansion and contraction," if we are to take the audience on the roller coaster we seek. Musicals and operas do this by mixing ballads and up-tempo numbers. Directors and actors find these moments through action and quality of action, which, to support the journey of the play, should be widely varied with polarity. We will explore "expansion and contraction" in another chapter.

It is joyful to rehearse this way—truly collaborative. The process is not about the actor or director individually. Rather, it is about discovering the text in an artistic way. This is something we may have lost in our theater because of decreased rehearsal time due to economics. In academic theater this kind of rehearsal process is crucial. It is so because the production is our laboratory for testing what we are learning in the studio.

Actors, directors, and designers should be given time to experience a true artistic process before that process must be truncated in the regions or in the commercial world. I have taken criticism over the years because I insist on a longer rehearsal process in the academic institution. In the end, criticism or no, I believe the rehearsal process to be an extension of the studio and it takes time to put into practice what we are learning in our acting, voice, and movement studios. Students deserve the time as do all artists, no matter the level.

Further reading

Chekhov, Michael, *To the Actor*, Routledge Publishing, 2002. Chapter 4 "The Atmosphere and Individual Feelings."

7
CHARACTER RELATIONSHIPS

Framework

We know our characters from the given circumstances of the play—what the playwright gives us and what we can infer from the givens. In acting classes some teachers ask us to create a written "backstory," or a narrative based on the given circumstances that fill in character history before, during, and after the play. I have never found this exercise useful because there is nothing playable in doing it. It is a cerebral exercise and there it sits—in the brain. It is also not very useful to share written backstories with your scene partners as they can often conflict. Rather, we should look for ways to share our backstories with our partners in more organic ways. The solutions are easy, fun, and (a very good thing) gets in the way of too much thinking. Important: I believe that thinking, using the brain, plays an extremely vital role in the actor's process. I also believe that many actors think far too much before actually doing. It is better to do the thinking after doing—remember to spy-back. That's the time to think. *We think about how we feel—we don't feel about how we think.*

This chapter is concerned with creating character relationships through an improvisation exercise called "The Facts," the use of polarity in actions and qualities, atmosphere, and Chekhov's technique of "sensation(s)."

Sensation is a function of the senses. It is awareness through some means of stimulation, like experiencing pain or cold, and immediately affects our feeling center. In the Chekhov Technique, we work on three sensations: rising, balancing, and falling. Like PGs, these are broad, archetypal words and are most useful to actors because we can fit any line or speech into one of these categories. Note: some Chekhov teachers prefer floating, balancing, and falling. It just depends on who studied with whom as to the preference. We will explore rising, balancing, and falling because that is the way it was presented to me by Jack Colvin, an actor/teacher who worked with Chekhov on this final exercise that Chekhov created. Sadly, Jack has passed on. His studio in Los Angeles is still going strong through his pupils. The exercise is lovingly termed "The Three Sisters," I think by Jack, to compliment the technique of Chekhov's "Four Brothers." Jack used the final speeches of Masha, Olga, and Irina from *Three Sisters* to demonstrate this exercise.

Pre-class/rehearsal exploration

Divide the text you are using into artistic frames and label the AoAs. Share this work with your class or cast via email prior to your meeting.

In-class/rehearsal exercise: "The Facts"

- This exercise can be done during or outside of scheduled "block" rehearsals.
- I have often called actors, outside of their blocks with me, with a stage manager or assistant stage manager to do this exercise for 30–45 minutes.
- This seems to be enough time for the exercise and usually prompts actors to do more work on their own.

> **Teaching Tip:** Have the actors, in pairs, stand facing each other, 7–10 feet apart. Actor A states a "fact" from the past concerning the relationship. The fact must be within the parameters of the given circumstances—in other words the fact must be plausible. Actor B accepts the statement as a fact and cannot change it. Actor B then chooses to continue with the theme of the fact or may change the subject altogether.

CHARACTER RELATIONSHIPS

Example: Bottom and Quince

Bottom
When we were six, working in crafts pre-school, I beat you up for banging your hammer on my loom.

Quince
You were always a bully. You pulled my sister's hair and I didn't include you in my first play.

Bottom
I never forgave you for that.

Quince
When I saw you as the lead in our 1st grade play, I thought you were wonderful as Helen of Troy.

Bottom
And you were wonderful as first spear carrier from stage right. I wore a dress well and your helmet was too big. At least it covered your huge nose.

Quince
Okay, okay, enough with the insults. You were really wonderful in your first real role—Hercules and the Sabine women. You've gained some weight since then but you were a stunning leading man.

Bottom
And I think you are a fine playwright. What was your first play? Oh, yes, Mars and Venus.

Etc. for 30–45 minutes.

Teaching Tip: The above exchange is based on some direction I gave to the actors playing Bottom and Quince and the direction is crucial to how the improvisation proceeded. It is a director's job to guide the actors toward the specific story that he or she envisions. In this production, I saw Bottom and Quince as rivals and I cast it that way purposefully. If Bottom and Quince are best of friends then there is no conflict between these two most important rude mechanicals. If there is no conflict there can be no journey toward resolution. There is a great pay-off in the play within the play if we set up conflict between Bottom and Quince and there is a definite journey between the two, once the conflict is established in their first scene. Bottom is the "great actor" and Quince is the "great playwright." At least they see themselves that way. Of course, Quince is also the director. There is much conflict to be mined here. In this production the actors playing these two roles truly enjoyed the journey they discovered from rivals to great friends. During the rehearsal period the actors developed a conflicting and meaningful relationship that culminated in complete joy and love with their collaborative success near the end of the play. Without specific guidance toward "love conquers all" and if not for this exercise this journey may not have happened.

With some side coaching, the actors playing Bottom and Quince built a journey from being rivals to reconciliation and then bonded with a close friendship. The director should help the actors in the improvisation to discover the journey envisioned.

This exercise can also be done in groups quite effectively. In this production, I had all the fairies create their backstory this way as well as Egeus, Hermia, the lovers, etc. Again, it is imperative to provide basic direction toward the overall superobjective. Another lovely moment occurred that I've never seen in a production of this play between Egeus and Hermia—Egeus initiated reconciliation between himself and his daughter just before the play within the play. This is another example of the actors really understanding the theme for which we were striving and put a nice button on the production illuminating its main theme.

Creating relationships using polarity

The use of polarity is a most productive way of establishing relationships and creating a multidimensional character no matter the size of the role. What is polarity exactly? It is an opposite. For instance if your action is to attack and your quality of action is "forcefully," you may choose to continue to attack but change your quality to "reservedly." I love that qualities can be any verb ending with a "ly." One of my favorites is "piss-offedly." Another is "fuck-youedly." We all know the feeling of these adverbs.

In-class exercise

Read aloud this speech from *Midsummer* and then see the score we arrived at in the production. Read slowly to discover the changes in the text. Make note of where the changes occur. Don't be concerned, in the first read, about having actors identify or label anything. Spyback on where you think the transitions of action or qualities might be. The teacher/director can offer artistic frames and AoAs after the initial reading. (Note: I didn't identify the AoAs for you this time. Use this speech to practice that exercise.)

Egeus

Full of vexation come I, with complaint
Against my child, my daughter Hermia.
Stand forth, Demetrius. My noble lord,
This man hath my consent to marry her.
Stand forth, Lysander. And my gracious duke,
This man hath bewitch'd the bosom of my child;
Thou, thou, Lysander, thou hast given her rhymes,
And interchanged love-tokens with my child:
Thou hast by moonlight at her window sung,
With feigning voice verses of feigning love,
And stolen the impression of her fantasy.
With cunning hast thou filch'd my daughter's heart,
Turn'd her obedience, which is due to me,
To stubborn harshness: and, my gracious duke,
Be it so she will not here before your grace
Consent to marry with Demetrius,
I beg the ancient privilege of Athens,
As she is mine, I may dispose of her:
Which shall be either to this gentleman,
Or to her death, according to our law
Immediately provided in that case.

Teaching Tip: Many actors and directors look at this speech as an angry rant. Egeus is of course angry at Hermia and is demanding his right as her father. Egeus appears only at the beginning and ending of the play. So, how does the actor playing the role navigate toward making the character more than one-dimensional? It is well for the director to remember that Egeus and Hermia represent a major theme of the play—Feminism and Male Dominance. As I stated earlier, there is a great pay-off at the end of the play with the reconciliation of father and daughter. (I have always found it interesting and brilliant on Shakespeare's part that Egeus and Hermia are the only representations of family in the play. This serves to heighten this particular theme. Fathers are constantly referred to, yet not manifest in a character other than Egeus. Therefore he is very important.)

As a director one must decide if the audience is to hate Egeus or to understand his frustration. It is far more interesting to have Egeus present his argument—within historical parameters—and, while the audience may not agree with the argument, they should understand his point of view. The conflict becomes more complicated and interesting. You might think of the audience here as your "grand jury." The goal is to have them hand down an indictment. With this direction let's look at how Egeus might create this experience for the audience. Note that the action precedes the text and this is important from a physical standpoint. Again the reader should read aloud with the actions and qualities as stated. Also, remember these actions and qualities were arrived through collaboration. It is tempting for actors to bring this work into class or rehearsal having arrived at the score over a cup of coffee—with pencil in hand and head in the script. I can't state enough how important it is to find this work reading aloud and on the feet. While the following score is what we, director and actor, ultimately agreed upon, you can read this speech, articulating actions and qualities, to gain understanding of the process and then navigate your own score.

In-class exercise

Once you have read through and worked on the specificity of the written score, another good exercise is to find the PG of the specific action. While this may be somewhat of a backward process, it is nonetheless another way to work in class with certain speeches in this book. I would also encourage you to explore the score as written and then create a new one with different actions and qualities. There are many opportunities for interpretation. Working in this way will instill in your actors not to settle on a single interpretation too early. You can create several different and progressive exercises in working in this manner—all worthwhile.

Note: Remember to use the specific action to discover the root PG.

Egeus
(Action = To complain. Quality = Vehemently.)
Note: Remember to identify the AoAs.

Full of vexation come I, with complaint
Against my child, my daughter Hermia.

(Action = To introduce. Quality = Proudly)
Stand forth, Demetrius. My noble lord,
This man hath my consent to marry her.

(Action = To introduce. Quality = Angrily)
Stand forth, Lysander.

(Action = To suck up. Quality = Respectfully)
And my gracious duke,

(Action = To reveal. Quality = Mournfully)
This man hath bewitch'd the bosom of my child;

(Action = To accuse. Quality = Angrily)
Thou, thou, Lysander, thou hast given her rhymes,
And interchanged love-tokens with my child:

(Action = To accuse. Quality = Tearfully)
Thou hast by moonlight at her window sung,
With feigning voice verses of feigning love,

And stolen the impression of her fantasy.

(Action = To accuse. Quality = Angrily)
With cunning hast thou filch'd my daughter's heart,
Turn'd her obedience,

(Action = To proclaim. Quality = Rightfully)
which is due to me,
To stubborn harshness:

(Action = To claim. Quality = Respectfully)
and, my gracious duke,
Be it so she will not here before your grace
Consent to marry with Demetrius,
I beg the ancient privilege of Athens,
As she is mine, I may dispose of her:

(Action = To demand. Quality = Lawfully)
Which shall be either to this gentleman,
Or to her death, according to our law
Immediately provided in that case.

How did we arrive at the "score" of this speech? Again, there is a temptation for the actor to sit down with the script and think through the score before putting it on its feet. That is exactly the wrong approach. If done this way the speech will stay in the thinking center and it is difficult to then get into the feeling center. Instead, the actor must act first and then spy-back on what he or she did. The speech must be discovered organically, and we can do this through polarity and artistic frames.

The director should study the text and identify the artistic frames and record the clues. The clues are a good place to begin a discussion with actors. He or she shouldn't score the qualities because that is what we want the actor to do—discover organically and with careful guidance. Guide the actors to action by first working on PGs. There are many clues in the speech that we can draw on.

Egeus
Artistic frame 1.

Action = To complain. Quality = Vehemently.
Full of vexation come I, with complaint
Against my child, my daughter Hermia.

CHARACTER RELATIONSHIPS

Clues for 1: "Vexation" means annoyed or irritated. Shakespeare gives us the action with the word "complaint." The word "full" can be interpreted as completely. Egeus is completely irritated with his daughter. This means he is irritated in all three centers.

Artistic frame 2.

Action = To introduce. Quality = Proudly.
Stand forth, Demetrius. My noble lord,
This man hath my consent to marry her.

Clues for 2: "Stand forth" is the introduction—the action. Demetrius is the preferred suitor as he has "consent" from Egeus. The father should be proud of his choice—"consent" leads to the quality of proudly.

Artistic frame 3

Action = To introduce. Quality = Angrily.
Stand forth, Lysander.

Clues for 3: Lysander is abhorred by Egeus because Hermia is fighting her father's authority. Putting this in historical context, what Hermia is doing is unheard of and raises the stakes enormously.

Artistic frame 4.

Action = To suck up. Quality = Respectfully.
And my gracious duke

Clues for 4: The word "gracious" is key. Egeus turns his attention back to the duke and away from his own anger. In other words he remembers his objective.

Artistic frame 5.

Action = To reveal. Quality = Mournfully.
This man hath bewitch'd the bosom of my child

Clues for 5: "My child"—Egeus considers Hermia as a child and may play upon the duke's sympathy—given the law of the land and the father's privilege.

Artistic frame 6.

Action = To accuse. Quality = Angrily.
Thou, thou, Lysander, thou hast given her rhymes,
And interchanged love-tokens with my child

Clues for 6: The real clue here is polarity. In artistic frame 5, Egeus is talking directly to the duke. He is better off, to reach his objective, to play on sympathy. In artistic frame 6, Egeus is talking directly to Lysander—the source of his anger.

Artistic frame 7.

Action = To accuse. Quality = Tearfully.
Thou hast by moonlight at her window sung,
With feigning voice verses of feigning love,
And stolen the impression of her fantasy.

Clues for 7: Egeus begins to wax poetic. This is a drastic difference from his earlier dialogue. Thinking of polarity—the tenor of the words between artistic frames 6 and 7 demands a new quality and again may play upon the duke's sympathy and honor.

Artistic frame 8.

Action = To accuse. Quality = Angrily.
With cunning hast thou filch'd my daughter's heart,
Turn'd her obedience

Clues for 8: "Filch'd" is stolen; also "obedience," both strong and angry words in this context.

Artistic frame 9.

Action = To proclaim. Quality = Rightfully.
which is due to me, To stubborn harshness

Clues for 9: Here, Egeus reminds the duke of the laws of Athens.

Artistic frame 10.

Action = To claim. Quality = Respectfully.
And, my gracious duke,
Be it so she will not here before your grace
Consent to marry with Demetrius,
I beg the ancient privilege of Athens,
As she is mine, I may dispose of her

Clues for 10: Egeus repeats the word "gracious." He "begs."

Artistic frame 11.

Action = To demand. Quality = Lawfully.
Which shall be either to this gentleman,
Or to her death, according to our law

Immediately provided in that case.

Clues for 11: "According to our law"—Egeus has presented a knowledgeable and shrewd case before the person who will ultimately decide the case and has done so with a great variety of actions and qualities. Theseus, and most importantly the audience, must listen.

NOTE TO DIRECTOR/TEACHER

Notice we haven't talked about the objective. There is worth in not talking about the objective until the above work is done. If you ask the actor about the objective prior to her actually acting the artistic frames he or she will inevitably state something complex and from the thinking center. Instead, ask the actor after this work and the objective will be simply stated and come from having had an experience generated from "doing." The statement will be adamant and brief. You will get an answer with conviction—from the feeling center. Chekhov said, "We must come to know the objective." We come to know the objective through discovering actions and qualities. When we discover our objective in this way, it appears in all of our three centers more deeply than working via dry analysis. Discovering the objective should not be an exercise initiated from the thinking center.

NOTE TO ACTORS

This work does not all need be done in rehearsal. Actors should be responsible for finding the artistic frames. (I do maintain it is a more fruitful rehearsal process if the director/teacher guides actors using the technique of artistic frames. Just don't count on it.) The actor should get on his or her feet and act. If the actor looks carefully at the clues in the text first, the action becomes rather easy. Shakespeare, especially, often gives us the action as in examples from the above speech. The best way to rehearse I've found is to work on one artistic frame at a time until you can spy-back and identify the action and quality. Rehearse the first artistic frame and identify what you did.

If you can't, then do it again. Rehearse it until you can label the action and quality. Many times when you can't label the action or quality it has to do with commitment. You must be 100 percent committed to both action and quality (remember the train analogy) before the verb and adverb reveal themselves. Don't rely on the director to do this work for you or even with you. I tell actors this: don't ask directors questions unless it's absolutely necessary. When an actor asks me a question about the character, an objective, an action, or quality, I feel I must provide an answer. Once I give that answer, because I am the director and have an ego, the answer is final. There is no room for growth. Actors should work out artistic frames for themselves. That includes beginning, middle, ending, action, quality of action, and objective. This is part of the actor's craft.

Once you have identified the action and quality for the first frame, move on to the second frame and repeat the process. After you have completed the work of the second frame, do not move on to the third. Instead, go back and put one and two together. When you feel you have two complete frames, move on to three. After you have three frames completed, put frames one, two, and three together. In this way you are rehearsing the most important B-M-E and you will not tend to skip your endings before moving on to the next frame—a mistake many actors make. Repetition strengthens willpower.

Another marvelous thing about working this way is that it is easier to remember polarity and it's the best way to actually learn your lines. Let's just make a list of actions and qualities from the above speech.

In-class/rehearsal exercise

Speak the action and quality aloud:

Action = To complain. Quality = Vehemently
Action = To introduce. Quality = Proudly
Action = To introduce. Quality = Angrily
Action = To suck up. Quality = Respectfully
Action = To reveal. Quality = Mournfully
Action = To accuse. Quality = Angrily

CHARACTER RELATIONSHIPS

Action = To accuse. Quality = Tearfully
Action = To accuse. Quality = Angrily
Action = To proclaim. Quality = Rightfully
Action = To claim. Quality = Respectfully
Action = To demand. Quality = Lawfully

Look at the polarity especially in qualities! Also, notice it is not necessary to change action each time you change quality. This gives the character much dimension and takes the audience on the journey of the rhythmical wave. If the speech is done as an angry rant, then there is only a flat line created with occasional upward "blips." The score looks like an EKG. The roller coaster is much more fun for both actor and audience. Working on one frame at a time gives you the opportunity to discover opposites (polarity) in the next frame.

How does this work help in establishing character relationships? It is because of polarity. Have a look at whom Egeus is referring to in each artistic frame.

In-class/rehearsal exercise

Speak the name of the character followed by the action and quality:

Action = To complain. Quality = Vehemently.	To Theseus.
Action = To introduce. Quality = Proudly.	To Demetrius.
Action = To introduce. Quality = Angrily.	To Lysander.
Action = To suck up. Quality = Respectfully.	To Theseus.
Action = To reveal. Quality = Mournfully.	To Theseus.
Action = To accuse. Quality = Angrily.	To Lysander.
Action = To accuse. Quality = Tearfully.	To Lysander.
Action = To accuse. Quality = Angrily.	To Lysander.
Action = To proclaim. Quality = Rightfully.	To Theseus.
Action = To claim. Quality = Respectfully.	To Theseus.
Action = To demand. Quality = Lawfully.	To Theseus.

In one brief speech, Egeus (through the use of polarity in actions and qualities) provides the audience with a tremendous amount of character relationship. Some would call this speech and opening scene, exposition, and that is a fine academic word. There is nothing actable about it, however. Should the actor playing Egeus choose to rant throughout the speech, the audience will most likely miss the story. It is wise to remember that human beings watch the action and listen to the quality of action. We tend to tune out of angry rants and purging. Take the audience on a listening tour of the play with a wide variety of actions and qualities and they will listen and watch intently.

In-class exercise

- Use the score of actions and qualities above without text.
- Speak the action using a PG that is most germane to the specified action and allow the quality to emerge.
- Work on one frame at a time until the actor is committed 100 percent to both and then move on to the next frame.
- When the second frame is clear, go back and put frames one and two together.
- Follow this pattern through to the end.
- Afterward, add the text and imagine the PG without physicalizing it.
- Finally, perform the speech without imagining the PG. The work will be ingrained in the body.

In-class/rehearsal exercise

- Using the information in the follow-up, cast Egeus, Theseus, Hippolyta, Demetrius, Hermia, and Lysander.
- Have the actor playing Egeus do the speech several times and vary the qualities.
- Watch closely how the other characters react to these changes and side-coach them to listen carefully to the qualities.

CHARACTER RELATIONSHIPS

> *Teaching Tip:* We have not talked about obstacles and stakes though they have been mentioned previously. They are important to identify in our work, yet there is nothing playable here. The obstacles and stakes are there to live in the fantasy life. The actor simply has to commit to them as the character.

To continue and review our common language, we define the terms as:

Score: The actor's map of objectives, actions (PGs,) qualities, obstacles, stakes, and atmospheres. It is a chronicle of discoveries that is repeatable.

Polarity: Finding opposite words in action and quality, an aid for creating rhythmical waves. Also, polarity in composition is the opposite from beginning to end—the journey.

Obstacles: What is in the way of what I want. (Helps motivate action/quality of action.)

Stakes: What I stand to lose if I don't get what I want. (Helps motivate action/quality of action.)

Action and quality of action: I must stress again the importance of committing 100 percent to both of these components of the methodology as they are the only playable things for the actor. The director should concentrate her efforts, when working artistic frames with actors, on making certain the action and quality are clear and committed within the AoA of each frame.

In-class/rehearsal exercise: Atmosphere

We now leave *Midsummer* for a bit and turn our exploration to Anton Chekhov's *Three Sisters*. Let's begin by reading, aloud and on our feet, these final three speeches of the play thinking only of atmosphere. I have inserted a slash where you may consider a change. Remember that the essences of atmospheres are: glad, mad, sad, bad, and fear. At the end of the play the three sisters have been through their individual difficulties and are experiencing a reunion of familial ties and realities of their changing world. In these final moments the themes of family, individualism, love, and change are all tied nicely into three short speeches. In your reading, try to discover the atmospheres and record them. In the next exercise, I have included the atmospheres we discovered in our production.

Masha
Oh, but listen to the band! /They're leaving us. /One has left us altogether—left us forever. We shall remain behind, on our own, to start our life again. /We have to live. . . . We have to live.

Irina
A time will come when people will understand what it was all for, what the purpose was of all this suffering, and what was hidden from us will be hidden no more. /In the meantime, though, we have to live . . . we have to work, that's all, we have to work! /Tomorrow, I shall go on my way alone. I shall take up my teaching post, and devote my life to those who may have some use for it. /It's autumn now. Soon winter will come and bring the first falls of snow, and I shall be working, I shall be working.

Olga
The band plays so bravely you feel you want to live! /Merciful God! Time will pass, and we shall depart forever. We shall be forgotten—our faces, our voices, even how many of us there were. /But our sufferings will turn to joy for those who live after us. Peace and happiness will dwell on earth, and people living now will be blessed and spoken well of. Dear sisters, our life is not ended yet. We shall live! /And the band plays so bravely, so joyfully—another moment, you feel, and we shall know why we live and why we suffer. . . . If only we could know, if only we could know!

In-class/rehearsal exercise

Let's now look at each speech with an atmosphere assigned to each suggested change. Take time to imagine/fantasize the atmosphere prior

CHARACTER RELATIONSHIPS

to speaking just as in our previous work. You can also have the actors explore each atmosphere prior to speaking the text as described earlier in the book.

Masha

(*Glad*) Oh, but listen to the band! (*Sad*) They're leaving us. One has left us altogether—left us forever. We shall remain behind, on our own, to start this life again. (*Mad-Determined*) We have to live.... We have to live.

Irina

(*Sad*) A time will come when people will understand what it was all for, what the purpose was of all this suffering, and what was hidden from us will be hidden no more. (*Mad-Determined*) In the meantime, though, we have to live . . . we have to work, that's all, we have to work! (*Fear*) Tomorrow, I shall go on my way alone. I shall take up my teaching post, and devote my life to those who may have some use for it. (*Glad-Determined*) It's autumn now. Soon winter will come and bring the first falls of snow, and I shall be working, I shall be working.

Olga

(*Glad*) The band plays so bravely you feel you want to live! (*Sad*) Merciful God! Time will pass, and we shall depart forever. We shall be forgotten—our faces, our voices, even how many of us there were. (*Glad*) But our sufferings will turn to joy for those who live after us. Peace and happiness will dwell on earth, and people living now will be blessed and spoken well of. Dear sisters, our life is not ended yet. We shall live! (*Glad-reinvest in the archetype*) And the band plays so bravely, so joyfully—another moment, you feel, and we shall know why we live and why we suffer. . . . If only we could know, if only we could know!

Teaching Tip: When working with actors on these three speeches in class, have them spy-back at this point. What did they feel at the changes? Be certain the actors are taking the time necessary to imagine the atmospheres. Once you have explored the scene using atmosphere, move on to the technique of sensations.

In-class/rehearsal exercise: Sensations—rising, falling, balancing

Before we move on and add sensations to the text, we should experience the exercise for itself. As in the majority of the Technique the exercises are simple yet profound. There are two parts to sensations. The first is the anticipation of the feeling and the second is the feeling itself. Imagine riding a roller coaster and making the climb up the long hill (rising). That is the anticipation of what is to come (falling). There is also a time on the ride where one is suspended briefly. We can consider this (balancing). Take care to experience the anticipation and the sensation.

Teaching rising

Rising can be described as weightlessness, suspension, buoyancy, as well as the action or motion of moving upward. Some rising idioms are: to get a rise out of someone, head in the clouds, spaced out, airhead, my heart lifted, you raise me up, walking on air.

- Have the actors break into groups of eight.
- One actor lies flat on the floor.
- Six actors will serve as "lifters," while another actor acts as the "spotter."
- The actor being lifted will naturally anticipate the lift.
- The lifters are stationed at the lower legs, center, and shoulders of the person to be lifted.
- The spotter will count to 3.
- On 3, the actors slowly lift the person on the floor to a comfortable height.
- The spotter is stationed at the head of the actor being lifted.
- The spotter will then instruct the lifters to lower the person lifted to the floor.
- Do this at least three times legato.

- After everyone is comfortable, perform the lift staccato three or more times.
- Eventually, take a walk with the actor in the air following the spotter.
- Finally, have the actor being lifted to take the text above, or other text you're working with, and explore it while being lifted in various tempos.
- Raise and lower the actor throughout the speech.

Other ways to experience rising is jumping, climbing stairs, climbing or jumping a rope. You can also have participants take turns sitting in a chair and being lifted by the others to experience the sensation of rising.

Teaching falling

Falling can be tension filled or it can be a release of tension, or surrender, such as when you raise an arm up and then allow it to fall. Falling can be in any direction, such as falling up a flight of stairs, but it generally seems to move in a downward direction. We can also think about falling idioms, such as to fall to pieces, fall asleep, fall into bed, fall in love, fall into a trap, fall behind, or fall into ruin.

- Have the actors stand in a circle.
- Instruct them to lean backward on their heels and catch themselves just before actually falling.
- Once you have done this several times allow them to use text.
- The "fall" should precede the text.
- The sensation of falling will linger throughout quite a bit of dialogue.
- When the actor needs the physical sensation again, he or she should repeat the action followed by text.

Another good way to experience the sensation of falling is to have the actors form a tight circle around a single person. The actor in the center leans backward until literally falling into the arms of other actors who support the weight of the person falling. This is an old exercise based on trust, yet is excellent for experiencing this sensation. The actors who catch the falling person "pass" her around the circle— falling forward and backward. Add text after the actor has experienced the sensation.

Teaching balancing

Balancing is the easiest sensation to accomplish. The sensation of a person attempting to balance is, in essence, struggling between rising or falling. Most characters are not written in a balanced state—if they were, they would be without conflict. Rather, characters are constantly searching for balance.

Think of these idioms: hanging in the balance, on the edge, the balance of power, going back and forth over an issue, tug of war.

- You can have actors stand on one leg while another actor pushes them slightly off-balance.
- Have actors stand on their tiptoes on a chair, with others spotting them.
- Have them do handstands—or anything to do with balancing.
- Add text after the actor has experienced the sensation.

In-class/rehearsal exercise: Sensations and relationships

Let's look at the speeches from *Three Sisters* again and insert possible sensations coupled with atmospheres:

Masha
(Glad-Rising) Oh, but listen to the band! *(Sad-Falling)* They're leaving us. One has left us altogether—left us forever. We shall remain behind, on our own, to start this life again. *(Mad-Determined-Rising)* We have to live. . . . We have to live.

CHARACTER RELATIONSHIPS

Irina
(Sad-Falling) A time will come when people will understand what it was all for, what the purpose was of all this suffering, and what was hidden from us will be hidden no more. *(Mad-Determined-Balancing)* In the meantime, though, we have to live . . . we have to work, that's all, we have to work! *(Fear-Falling)* Tomorrow, I shall go on my way alone. I shall take up my teaching post, and devote my life to those who may have some use for it. *(Glad-Determined-Rising)* It's autumn now. Soon winter will come and bring the first falls of snow, and I shall be working, I shall be working.

Olga
(Glad-Rising) The band plays so bravely you feel you want to live! *(Sad-Falling)* Merciful God! Time will pass, and we shall depart forever. We shall be forgotten—our faces, our voices, even how many of us there were. *(Glad-Rising)* But our sufferings will turn to joy for those who live after us. Peace and happiness will dwell on earth, and people living now will be blessed and spoken well of. Dear sisters, our life is not ended yet. We shall live! *(Glad-reinvest in the sensation of rising).* And the band plays so bravely, so joyfully—another moment, you feel, and we shall know why we live and why we suffer . . If only we could know, if only we could know!

In-class/rehearsal exercise

Using these speeches, or others you are working on and scored as above, have your actors speak the text while actually doing the sensations. In this example of *Three Sisters*, have all three actors work on the sensation the other is experiencing at the time. For example, in Masha's opening line, "Oh, but listen to the band!" *(Glad-Rising)*, have the actors doing Olga and Irina rising as well.

There is also the counterpoint that can be most interesting as well. For example, in Masha's opening line, have Olga falling and Irina balancing. Consider all combinations. Eventually, you will come to an exciting collaboration. Like PG, the actual doing of sensations becomes an inward process. Regardless, to be true the play, Olga's final speech is rising for all three sisters. In our production, the play ended hopefully, in the atmosphere of glad, and in the sensation of rising.

Once the actors have experienced the sensations they need only imagine it and, after a time, they no longer even need to imagine. It is ingrained through the psychophysical way of working in the Technique. These speeches tell us a lot about the characters of Masha, Olga, and Irina. Just as QoM gives us inclinations toward character, so do sensations. Is Masha basically a rising, balancing, or falling character? Certainly, Masha, as do Olga and Irina, experiences all three sensations during her journey. Yet, we could make an argument that Masha is primarily a rising character. Olga, for me, is a balancing character. Irina is a falling character. I say this about the entire play and not necessarily these three speeches. Just exploring the technique of sensation(s) creates a tremendous amount of conflict and contrast between the sisters and reveals deep character relationships. It is, or can be, a beautiful moment in the end to see them all "rise" together.

Follow-up

Once again, the actor should get into the habit of recording his or her findings in a rehearsal journal. When working on actions and qualities, as in the Egeus speech, the actor will find several different actions and qualities for each frame and may not recall them all unless he or she has recorded them. (The facts from the same exercise should be written down as well.) Usually, there will be more different qualities than actions for a given frame and this is very productive for helping actors understand how to listen on stage. I encourage actors, in rehearsal, to vary their qualities while working with others. Human beings respond to the quality of the voice more than anything else. If I play "to penetrate, aggressively," one time through and "to penetrate, slyly," the second time through, the actor I am working with will have different reactions depending on the quality. If the response is the same to different qualities, the actor is not listening. We listen to the quality first and the content second. Some directors demand that actors' performances be concrete in action and quality throughout a run. Others, like me, allow actors to work with their score of qualities from frame to frame. I do insist on consistent action derived from our collaboration. The practice of varying qualities keeps actors "on their toes" and gives them the opportunity to truly listen from performance to performance.

Encourage actors to work with sensations on their own. Once an actor has practiced the three sensations using text, it is an easy matter to recover the sensation through the imagination. Just as in our work on PG, actors must consciously radiate the sensation he or she is working with. Remind actors to radiate in a 360-degree radius.

Further reading

Petit, Lenard, *The Michael Chekhov Handbook*, Routledge, 2010. Chapter 5 "Application," 8 "Sensation," pp. 126–35.

8
WORK ON SOLILOQUIES

Framework

In Shakespeare there are important soliloquies that support main themes and we must pay particular attention to them. These are often long speeches and the actor and director have a unique problem to solve. How do we keep an audience engaged that is used to visual stimulation through technology rather than a chiefly auditory experience? In Shakespeare's day audiences were used to an auditory experience and listened intently. Not so much in modern theater. Audiences have become used to all the visual explosions that Broadway and film can muster. We must discover how to keep the soliloquy vocally and visually active to make certain the audience receives the necessary information. This can be accomplished with atmosphere, tempo/rhythm, actions, and qualities. It involves the entire production team.

This chapter explores the unique problems the soliloquy in Shakespeare presents us and also explores the tools Chekhov gives us to solve those problems. I also introduce a new technique here, *expansion and contraction*. This technique can be applied to all the previous work. It's just best exemplified in soliloquies.

The majority of soliloquies begin with a thesis statement:

Hamlet: "To be, or not to be, that is the question":
Macbeth: "If it were done, when 'tis done, then 'twere well it were done quickly."
Edmund: "Thou, Nature, art my goddess, to thy law my services are bound."
Helena: "How happy some o'er other some can be!"

In these examples, and many more, the character presents a problem to the audience and goes on for many lines attempting to solve the problem. I firmly believe in the actor involving the audience during soliloquies. I always have actors break the "fourth wall" in these speeches. The character, in these situations, is appealing to the audience for help. The audience becomes the character's therapist and sounding board. By exploring the problem aloud and with the audience the character usually comes to a conclusion. Another benefit is the audience begins to side with the characters' discoveries and decisions simply by being included in a "private session." So, let's begin to solve Helena's most famous speech from *Midsummer*.

Pre-class exploration

Go to www.markmonday.com and view the photo of Helena performing her soliloquy. It can be found in the *Midsummer* file and is easily recognized. There are photographs from other productions referenced in this book on this site as well. Also, print out or email her speech to your actors.

Note that the actress playing Helena has been placed on a secluded part of the stage, which helps narrow the focus for the audience. This is the beginning of her speech: "How happy some o'er other some can be. . . ." She is in a follow spot—something I believe in during important speeches in Shakespeare. The lighting around her is subdued or dimmed to focus the audience's attention—making them unable to view the entire set.

Also note the contrast in color between costume and scenery and especially the commitment of the actor's body to the opening of the soliloquy as her entire physical being is involved in her action/form. We can see her plead to the audience. We don't need to hear the words to know her action. This is an archetypal action, a PG. We can also guess her subjective atmosphere from the picture—Helena is "mad." Just from viewing the form we know a lot about what is going on. We don't need the text to understand the visual story. The text provides the argument of her plea and reveals her objective and qualities. Helena wants the audience to be on her side of the argument. If Helena can get the audience to root for her it will increase her will to succeed. The audience gives her hope as well.

In-class/rehearsal exercise: Expansion and contraction

Characters, and we in real life, are always in some state between expansion and contraction. Do you remember reading your name for the first time on a cast list? That feeling was a complete state of expansion. Do you remember not being cast after what you thought was a great callback? That was a complete state of contraction. We are, indeed, like hot air balloons in that we are always expanding and contracting due to our circumstances. This is an image we can work with. Not only is it an inward image, it is an outward manifestation of form as well. We sometimes inflate or deflate slowly. At other times the air is popped out of our emotional balloon instantly. It all depends on the circumstances. In the score of Helena's speech I've noted the expansion and contraction moments. Actors can imagine, within themselves, a balloon that is constantly expanding and contracting. Through imagination/fantasy a physical form will appear naturally. Read aloud the speech first just paying attention to expansion and contraction. Work with the image of a balloon inwardly and allow the body to expand and contract accordingly.

Work with the text in the same way we work on PG. In the first line of Helena's speech she begins in complete expansion, or from a fully open position. She contracts slowly until she experiences a fully closed position. It's important for the actor to note how he or she experiences the work inwardly, so spy-back afterward. Did he or she find qualities of action during the movement? Did he or she remember to radiate fully in all directions? Did he or she remember to breathe? You'll find more leading questions as you continue your work.

Block 9.

Helena

(Begin contraction from complete expansion) How happy some o'er other some can be!

Through Athens I am thought as fair as she.
But what of that? Demetrius thinks not so;
He will not know what all but he do know:
And as he errs, doting on Hermia's eyes,
So I, admiring of his qualities: *(Take note to use the entire part of the speech to contract.)*
(begin expansion slowly) Things base and vile, holding no quantity,
Love can transpose to form and dignity:
Love looks not with the eyes, but with the mind,
And therefore is wing'd Cupid painted blind:
(begin contraction slowly) Nor hath Love's mind of any judgement taste;
Wings and no eyes figure unheedy haste.
And therefore is Love said to be a child,
Because in choice he is so oft beguil'd.
As waggish boys in game themselves forswear,
So the boy Love is perjured everywhere:
(expansion) For ere Demetrius look'd on Hermia's eyne,
He hail'd down oaths that he was only mine;
(contraction) And when this hail some heat from Hermia felt,
So he dissolved, and showers of oaths did melt.
(expansion) I will go tell him of fair Hermia's flight:
Then to the wood will he to-morrow night
Pursue her; and for this intelligence
If I have thanks, it is a dear expense.
But herein mean I to enrich my pain,
To have his sight thither and back again.
Exit

How did we arrive at the choices of when to expand and contract? First, we go back to our technique of polarity. We understand that expansion and contraction helps create polarity, simply by working with the balloon image. Beginning with expansion and contraction also helps us find the artistic frames. Yet mostly, we find where to expand and contract through clues in the text and given circumstances.

Breaking this speech down into artistic frames, expansion and contraction, atmospheres, actions, and qualities using the textual clues created the following score at the end of the rehearsal period. I urge you, once again, to create a completely new score after working on this one.

Note: If the atmosphere, action, etc. do not change I have not noted it in the next artistic frame. Use the score to baptize your own AoAs for each frame and note where and which sensations could be used.

In-class/rehearsal exercise: Acting the score with the addition of expansion and contraction

Block 9.

Helena

Artistic frame 1.
Subjective Atmosphere = Mad.
Action = To plead (to the audience). Quality = Angrily.
Contraction.
Clue = Punctuation (!) and jealously in second line. A contraction of
  physicality and emotion. Contraction does not necessarily mean
  devoid of emotion.

How happy some o'er other some can be! (*The "problem" Helena
  presents to the audience.*)
Through Athens I am thought as fair as she.

Artistic frame 2.
Subjective Atmosphere = Sad.
Quality = Deflatedly.
Contraction.
Clue = Further contraction physically and emotionally from her plea
  evident in her first line, "Demetrius thinks not so"; her intended
  love doesn't think she is as attractive as Hermia.

But what of that? Demetrius thinks not so; (*The problem continues to unfold with a different quality*)
He will not know what all but he do know:
And as he errs, doting on Hermia's eyes,
So I, admiring of his qualities:

Artistic frame 3.
Atmosphere = Glad.
Action = To realize. Quality = Wowly.
Beginning of a slow expansion.
Note: As director I will often ask an actor to say the quality of action before the line. In this instance I asked the actor to say "Wow" prior to the line, articulating the quality with the word, and to maintain the quality throughout. We used the word "wow" because each time Helena says the word, she makes a discovery. This is a rehearsal tool only.

(*Wow!*) Things base and vile, holding no quantity,
Love can transpose to form and dignity:

Quality = Confidently.

(*Wow!*) Love looks not with the eyes, but with the mind,
And therefore is wing'd Cupid painted blind:
Nor hath Love's mind of any judgement taste;
Wings and no eyes figure unheedy haste.

Artistic frame 4.
Action = To conclude. Quality = Sadly.
Slow contraction.
Clues = This is a new discovery and Helena has found something profound to share with the audience who feels sorry not only for her but for the truth in what she says.

(*Wow!*) And therefore is Love said to be a child,
Because in choice he is so oft beguil'd.
As waggish boys in game themselves forswear,
So the boy Love is perjured everywhere:
(*Bit of Expansion*) For ere Demetrius look'd on Hermia's eyne,
He hail'd down oaths that he was only mine;

(*Contraction*) And when this hail some heat from Hermia felt,
So he dissolved, and showers of oaths did melt.

Artistic frame 5.
Atmosphere = Glad.
Action = To plan. Quality = Excitedly.
Expansion. (This is the largest expansion of the speech.)
Clue = A plan occurs to her.

(*Wow!*) I will go tell him of fair Hermia's flight:
Then to the wood will he to-morrow night
Pursue her; and for this intelligence
If I have thanks, it is a dear expense.
But herein mean I to enrich my pain,
To have his sight thither and back again.

Exit

Teaching Tip: The artistic frames of this speech, including the varied actions and qualities, etc. help keep it visually alive for the audience. Helena is constantly working out her problem and imploring the audience to go along on the ride with her. She is making discoveries utilizing the audience. In Shakespearean soliloquies, I tend to allow the actor to move into the audience—making contact with them, if we are playing on a stage where the audience is accessible. The actor, pleading to the audience to be on her side of the problem, derives thoughts and ideas from them. By including the audience on a personal level the actor receives a new thought. I think of it as "spring boarding" from discovery to discovery. The character takes a jump on a diving board and, while up in the air, presents the problem to the audience. The character lands briefly on the board again and a new thought occurs. This analogy represents talking to the audience directly while in the air and the landing or new thought propels the character to a new and more profound place. The stakes rise with each new leap. This is another visual image of expansion and contraction.

Helena's speech is a perfect example of the "spring boarding" concept.

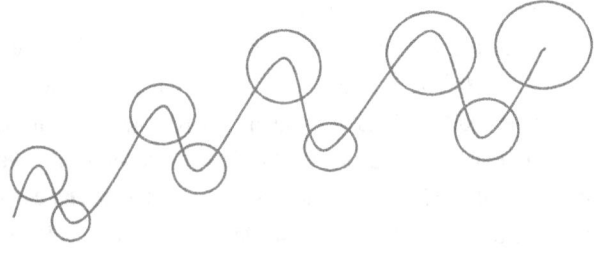

Artistic Frames

One   Two   Three   Four   Five

This is an example of a rhythmical wave that helps develop the overall wave for the play. You can easily see how the audience is taken on a ride that is exciting because it is filled with varying tempos, actions and qualities, expansion and contraction, rising, falling, and balancing.

Follow-up

In the world of Michael Chekhov we can imagine ourselves expanding and contracting as necessary. For rehearsal purposes we can create an image to work with. I have already mentioned a balloon and diving board as images. Because our imaginations can be so strong, we can create any image that is useful to us. It is time, maybe past time, to note that in Chekhov's Technique we don't use memories from our past to serve us in a given moment on the stage. That kind of work doesn't exist in the imagination and therefore is not repeatable over the long term. Most important, our personal memories don't truly aid us in reaching the essences we seek. Instead, we train and rely on our imagination and connect to our Higher Ego through fantasizing. Audiences relate to the essence—the archetype.

> **Teaching Tip:** It is also good to remember that text breathes. Text inherently expands and contracts if you look at it that way. Ponder this piece of text from *As You Like It*:
>
> All the world's a stage,
> And all the men and women merely players:
>
> One can hear, in his or her imagination, that Jacques may take a huge breath before expounding his thesis that "All the world's a stage." This is expansion. We take our clue concerning contraction from the word, "merely." The actor playing Jacques should consider how to negotiate his breath from the inherent action and the technique of expansion and contraction. There exists the possibility in this line to inhale and expand with volume on "All the world's a stage," and begin contraction, which includes how to use the breath and volume through the end of the line. Expansion and contraction is totally connected to breathing. Use the punctuation as clues.

There comes a time in rehearsal when we no longer need to use tools such as expansion/contraction. When we get to performance we do not have to use our tools on the stage. Because we have built our work in an organic way we will have the sensations of the exercise and will be free to act moment to moment living in the world of the play. At any time during a run an actor can reinvest in an exercise offstage or in the studio.

I mentioned earlier that Helena's objective is to get the audience on her side. She is seeking support from the audience for her journey through the play—supporting her quest. In playing actions and qualities to achieve an objective the actor often believes that he or she must change the mind of the other character from which he or she wants something—not really. What humans do when we want something and the person from whom we want it is uncooperative is to try to change how they *feel* about giving us what we want. When we can change the way the other feels then their mind will change. This is human psychology and good information for the actor.

When Helena moves among the audience she befriends them. She sorts out her thoughts among them. In this production the actress sat on the lap of a patron for an artistic frame which truly endeared her to all the men in the audience. She cajoled, thanked, and appreciated the audience. By the end of her speech the atmosphere of the audience was changed from the previous scene and they were completely on her side. Her objective was accomplished by changing how the audience felt from experiencing the atmosphere created from the previous scene.

In Chekhov terminology we are trying to change the subjective atmosphere of the other. The actor is wise to construct actions and qualities that play upon the feelings of others. Even the action of "to reason" with another person is meant to have a calming effect and appeals to the feeling center. We know, for instance, when we lose our temper we rarely get what we want and if we do there is usually a price to pay. There are given circumstances in plays and in life that we do lose our temper. It is always best to curb the temper on- and off-stage. A character may have the atmosphere of rage within and choose to play actions and qualities that are counterpoint to that rage. The audience sees the actor's action yet feels the rage. It is always more interesting and brings us to the idea of inner and outer tempo. Tempos are directly related to expansion and contraction.

Inner and outer tempos are fascinating to observe on stage. In Helena's speech to the audience, we can observe it working. She begins the speech with a subjective atmosphere of anger (mad) and mad is most often a fast tempo. She is smart enough to know she will not accomplish her objective by raging at the audience. So, Helena goes about her business by playing actions and qualities that are polar opposite from her inner atmosphere. Outwardly, she at times appears to be pursuing her course logically, calmly—a slow tempo. Inwardly, she is just as angry for most of the speech. She controls her feelings by attempting to solve her problem. By the end, her own atmosphere has changed. She goes from mad to glad because she feels an answer to her dilemma is found. The audience feels good because, on some level, they understand they have helped. It's a win-win situation for the actor.

Inner and outer tempos can match or be the opposite of each other. The actor, as her character, can also consciously choose to match or choose the opposite tempo of her scene partner. Carefully observing another's inner tempo is extremely useful. Controlling your own tempo to match another can be a powerful tool in aiding to fulfill an objective on the stage and in real life as well. Use it wisely.

Further practice exercises

Create a score for the speeches of Edmund, Macbeth, and Hamlet found in Appendix IV using all the tools we've explored.

Further reading

Chekhov, Michael, *On the Technique of Acting*, HarperCollins, 1991. Chapter 7 "From Script to Rehearsal Hall."

9
CHARACTERIZATION

Framework

As part of the premise of this book is collaboration between actor and director, I believe it is important to address how the director is involved in the process of character development. In most professional theaters in which I have been involved, the director rarely addresses character development. Perhaps there is little time to do so for the director, or he or she may feel the character has been cast, or he or she may leave that aspect of the work up to the actor. It truly is the actor's craft that should include the tools concerning developing a character.

Experience teaches me that actor training in America often does not include this work in studio classes. Teachers want, more and more, to train actors to play themselves in their work onstage. The industry seems to rely more on casting "types" than hiring actors capable of creating a fully engaged physical character that includes what the playwright has written concerning that character. Michael Chekhov would think this trend is terribly unfortunate. There is an alternative to help find our "Ideal Theater."

The best way I've found to help actors create a character with physical attributes other than themselves is to give them the time and opportunity to do so—with a bit of guidance. The work begins, once again, with archetypes and progresses from there with other techniques.

The material in this chapter is concerned with how the director/teacher can guide actors toward a physical characterization. Characters that actors play are never the exact replica of the actors portraying them. Movie stars are often an exception to this as producers want to cast the name more than a person who can create a character beyond "self."

Note: I think Johnny Depp is an exception in his film work and provides us with an excellent example of creating physical characterization for actors. Mr. Depp uses the Chekhov Technique in his work.

In-class exercise

- Look again at the archetypes of Hippolyta/Titania: queen, warrior, lover, and mother.
- Use the following speeches to work on the centers suggested.
- We look and listen for the actions and qualities to emerge from each specific center.
- It is highly useful to consider the synonyms of archetypes.

Synonyms of Archetypes for Hippolyta/Titania:

Queen—aristocrat, regal, sovereign, dignified, noble, stately, imposing, grand, statuesque, majestic.
Warrior—fighter, competitor, militarist, mercenary, volunteer, gladiator.
Lover—admirer, friend, desirer, supporter, suitor, wooer, partner.
Mother—originator, producer, protector, creator, caregiver.

Of course using these definitions for characterization is dependent on the given circumstances of the play and the moments in the play in which they present themselves. In the case of Titania, I believe most of the definitions are useful, but we need to determine which are most useful. The next step is to consider the center—thinking, feeling, or willing—in which the definitions exist and to reduce the list on the basis of the given circumstances. Identifying the center, derived from the givens, is a good way of beginning to develop a character of many dimensions.

Remind actors to engage the imagination to work from the suggested centers. It may help to walk about the space connecting/moving from each center before speaking. You can also direct actors to give themselves an image of what the center may look like. It could be anything the fantasy might conjure. For instance, Titania might imagine a jeweled crown above her head for the first part of her speech.

CHARACTERIZATION

Remember, a center can exist outside of our bodies as well. Have the actors walk about the space fantasizing a crown above their heads and initiate their movements from there. Also, remember to radiate movements into the space before actually moving.

> ***Teaching Tip:*** Assign archetypes and centers to each speech. You may find more than one center in the speeches. If so, take the time to instruct your actors to work on the center prior to speaking.

Thinking center — Queen (Sovereign)

Titania
Come, now a roundel and a fairy song;
Then, for the third part of a minute, hence:
Some to kill cankers in the musk-rose buds,
Some war with reremice for their leathern wings,
To make my small elves coats, and some keep back
The clamorous owl that nightly hoots and wonders
At our quaint spirits. Sing me now asleep;
Then to your offices and let me rest.

(Next Speech: remember to create an image first and walk the space again. Each definition of an archetype may lead to a new image.)

Feeling center — Fighter

Titania
Out of this wood do not desire to go:
Thou shalt remain here, whether thou wilt or no.

(Next Speech)

Willing center — Competitor

Hippolyta
I was with Hercules and Cadmus once,
When in a wood of Crete they bay'd the bear

With hounds of Sparta: never did I hear
Such gallant chiding; for, besides the groves,
The skies, the fountains, every region near
Seem'd all one mutual cry; I never heard
So musical a discord, such sweet thunder.

(Next Speech)

Feeling center—Friend

Titania
If you will patiently dance in our round
And see our moonlight revels, go with us. . . .

(Next Speech)

Feeling center—Desirer

Titania
I pray thee, gentle mortal, sing again:
Mine ear is much enamour'd of thy note;
So is mine eye enthralled to thy shape;
And thy fair virtue's force perforce doth move me
On the first view to say, to swear, I love thee.

Analysis of the work

The above work comes from script analysis and is done throughout the rehearsal process as characters develop with time. Regardless, I like to talk with actors about character archetypes and their definitions in the first few rehearsals. We need a mechanism to physicalize all of our analysis or it is of little use to us. We can begin by simply adopting these essences and reading the speech. Qualities will emerge because we are working with a universal thing. Yet the analysis is still not in our bodies.

Again, using walking exercises is a good start. Actors begin by walking in the space engaged from their Actor's Ideal Center. Having scripts in hand is fine at this point. We have already determined in which center the speech exists. Before we begin reading, the actors, having engaged their Actor's Ideal Center, should shift to the center in which

CHARACTERIZATION

the speech lives. We are capable of moving our centers to any area of the body we wish. At first, we place the center in the general regions of thinking, feeling, and willing. We can get more specific later. It is inevitable the actors will move in straight lines when beginning to walk. Instead, we should move in all directions with highly varied movements and tempos as long as the movements generate and radiate from the particular center. Eventually, allow the words to spring from the movement.

As I said earlier, centers do not need to reside exclusively in the body. Our fantasy/imagination allows us to place a center outside of our body. We can also create an image for the center and that can be anything that serves us. I often give the example of Joan of Arc. Joan, I believe, is primarily a feeling-centered person. Yet, saying she is driven by her heart is too simplistic and small for the actor's purpose. Instead, I will say that it is easy to fantasize Joan's heart leading her—outside of her body. To put it above everyday life and into the realm of art, I imagine the beating heart of the Virgin Mary guiding Joan and all her movements. It is not Joan's heart but Mary's and it is visible, for Joan, outside of her chest. It can change in size, color, and the number of beats per minute depending on the situation and what the actor needs from the image. This simple exercise changes the movements of the actor playing Joan dramatically. Why is this even important?

The simple answer is because we make art, not mirror everyday life. To raise the performance to an artistic level requires the actor to use tools that involve the fantasy/imagination. To be truly involved with a character, the words of the play, and the vision of a particular production, the actor's imagination must be constantly "tuned-in" to the Higher Ego. The use of centers is an excellent way to accomplish this.

Human beings, and characters, have a dominant center. This doesn't mean we don't use all of our three centers. It simply means we have a preference. Some of us, when confronted with anger respond with anger—from our feeling center. Others may respond with reason—from our thinking center. Still others may respond with action—from our willing center. Regardless, movements begin and radiate from a particular center. It depends on the archetypes of the person and the circumstances. This information is crucial to characterization.

Getting back to the walking exercises, there will come a point when the actor has a desire to make the image of the center more specific as in the example of Joan of Arc. There obviously has to be a dialogue between the director and actor for this thought to occur to the actor. Don't rush the process. Art takes time. Actors should be encouraged to find the character's center, both general and specific, in their own time. If the director gives the actor time to "play," incredible results will occur. The rehearsal time is well worth the effort.

In-class/rehearsal exercise

Another exciting exercise for characterization is Michael Chekhov's "Imaginary Body." We teach this exercise in the Great Lakes Michael Chekhov Consortium, in the following manner.[1]

Instructions from Teacher/Director: *Lie down on your backs and close your eyes. Beginning at the feet we are going to erase our bodies. This is not only a visual image we are working toward. It must also be something you feel. You should feel yourself being erased using your imagination/fantasy. It doesn't have to be painful. In fact, fantasize how pleasant it feels. Imagine yourself above you with an eraser. Take the real time necessary to erase your right foot. (Time elapses.) That done, moving up the right side of your body, erase your leg up to the knee. Then erase your knee to your pelvis. Next, erase from your pelvis to your shoulder. Then erase your arm and hand. You now have half a body with the neck and head intact. Now, begin at your left foot and repeat the process. Finally, erase your neck and head. You are standing now above an empty space ready to create the physical character of whom you are portraying.*

Begin to create the character by asking yourself some questions. What are my character's archetypes? What do my feet look like in the archetype of 'warrior'? How long are my legs? What is the shape of my legs? Are they enticing, muscular? Create them. Create from the bottom. What about my thighs? Are they plump or hardened from my archetypal clues? Are my hips voluptuous or small? Are my abs hardened or have I consumed too much ale?

---

[1] There is an alternative way to teach Imaginary Body in Appendix IV contributed by my valued colleague Melissa Owens.

> *Teaching Tip:* These are samples of leading questions the director can propose and they are important to characterization. You can include everything from the shape of the toes to length, texture, and color of the hair.
>
> Again, don't rush the process. Once the actors, in their imaginations, have completed work on the Imaginary Body, have them rise and begin to walk and move in the space. Then, have them read or recite a few of their speeches. You will observe a remarkable difference in physicality that may inform an entire characterization. It is imperative to have the actors in this process consider the character's primary center. Where does the character live the majority of his or her life? From which center does the character normally respond to outside stimuli? The clues to characterization are all in the text. The text creates the archetypes. The archetypes determine the conflict between characters and the physicality of the characters (form) tells the story.
>
> If every character the actor plays is identical to the actor in voice and body, then it can only be concluded that the actor has not elevated his or her craft to art. The voice, especially, should be of concern in the Imaginary Body exercise. As I have said, the human voice is capable of many different tones, volumes, rhythms, and tempos. Once the body is erased so is the voice. Explore the voice of the character. The voice can be altered through range, tempo, and rhythm, all according to the archetypes and given circumstance. The actor is hired to play the character. The character is not hired to play the actor.

Follow-up for the actor

Creating a character, especially the physical character, is only limited by one's imagination. Movement classes, in most academic institutions, consist of Stage Combat, Alexander Technique, Viewpoints, Laban, Mask, Dance, Suzuki, Margolis, etc. All of these are fine techniques in and of themselves and have an important place in actor training. Yet, how many of these techniques actually connect to the actor's imagination and aid in creating a physical characterization based on the text of the play?

In *To the Actor* Chekhov states, "First and foremost is extreme sensitivity of body to the psychological creative impulses. . . . The body of an actor must absorb psychological qualities, must be filled and permeated with them so that they will convert it into a sensitive membrane, a kind of receiver and conveyor of the subtlest images, feelings, emotions and will impulses."

While the body must be in a physical condition for the demands placed on actors, it must also be trained to accept the psychological aspect of acting. In other words, the body must respond to the impulses of giving and receiving. The body literally tells the audience the story of the moment and the entire play. We cannot then afford to separate the psychology from the physical. They must be in harmony. Chekhov teaches us how to do this.

The aforementioned techniques train the physical being and touch on the psychological but do not approach a true psychophysical process. Chekhov's Technique blends the psychophysical like no other.

The actor is wise who brings the work in this chapter to rehearsals — not working on it during so. Bring these techniques into rehearsals and allow the director to comment. Most directors appreciate the work, yet are too busy with other aspects of the production to compliment actors on the good work they bring to rehearsal. Take this as being in control of the craft of acting — the job of the actor. Also, don't count on the director to applaud or even recognize the work of the actor. That is not the director's job. Instead, embrace the craft of the actor. The fewer notes from the director the better!

Further reading

Chekhov, Michael, *To the Actor*, Routledge, 2002. Chapter 6 "Character and Characterization."

10
SCENES AND BLOCKS WITH MULTIPLE CHARACTERS

Framework

Rehearsing multiple character scenes in the block format requires disciplined preparation from the director. The director schedules X amount of time for a block and must stick to that time to keep the remainder of the rehearsal blocks from falling behind.

Once the rehearsal begins the actors have the opportunity to create choices within the AoA the director has introduced within the allotted amount of time. In any given rehearsal we have the urge to keep going after the allotted time especially in group scenes when the actors are improvising and creating at a high level. Indeed, if the director sets up the rehearsal properly the actors have an excellent opportunity to create at such a level. It is always best to stop at a point which leaves everyone feeling accomplished and anxious for the next rehearsal.

In beginning rehearsals, give the actors a guide for the scene with the use of AoA and objective atmosphere. Instruct the actors to act under the umbrella of the director's vision and then allow them to create. Doing this reinforces the collaborative process we seek. In early rehearsals we are painting with broad strokes. The real beauty of the process happens when actors begin to add actions and qualities to the work of AoAs within the artistic frames. The director must allow time for the actors to explore those choices. The umbrella of the AoA guides choices of action and quality of actions.

The director should come into rehearsal with a score of the scene to be worked on in each block. In this chapter I break down a multicharacter scene into artistic frames. My initial direction to the actors is outlined in "Director's Note (To Actors)." I keep my direction to a minimum, at first, to leave lots of room for improvisation and interpretation.

You will also find in this score something I like to call "director's secrets." I reveal these secrets in subtle ways and when necessary, as when actors aren't quite following the AoA of each artistic frame. Often, actors discover actions and qualities that are different from the secrets I have discovered, and this is a very good thing. Some secrets are best kept to ourselves so we can allow room for actors to discover organically.

Pre-class exploration

Determine the "mechanicals" archetypes prior to class.

In-class exercise

- Rehearse this scene as scored (certainly not the ideal way but just as an experiment).
- Following that, develop your own vision and rehearse with the new parameters.
- Rehearse one artistic frame at a time spying-back after each frame.
- Keep the actors working within the AoA.

Score of the scene

Scene II. Athens. Quince's house.

Block 10.
Artistic frame 1.
AoA = The greeting. Objective atmosphere = Glad.
Enter **Quince, Snug, Bottom, Flute, Snout,** *and* **Starveling**

SCENES AND BLOCKS WITH MULTIPLE CHARACTERS

> **DIRECTOR'S NOTE (TO ACTORS)**
>
> The mechanicals enter the front of Quince's house separately with Quince entering first. There should be happy music accompanying the entrance. Each greeting should have a beginning, middle, and ending. Perhaps Snug and Snout could enter together. This is a very joyful reunion with genuine excitement anticipating the announcement of the new play and which role each mechanical will be playing in it. We should learn a lot about each character's archetypes in this improvised greeting. It would be good practice to do this work after having done "The Facts" exercise.

In this production Bottom was a large, heavyset man with a massive bass voice. Quince was a small-framed man with a tenor voice. Flute was also a large man and had what I would call, in the best way, a baby face. Starveling was a very lean man capable of being just a bit effeminate. Snug, the lion in the play within the play, was another large man and muscular. He was capable of being extremely shy and cowardly. Snout was the smallest of the mechanicals. Snug literally made two of Snout. Snug and Snout, as characters, struck up a wonderful friendship from the first rehearsal of artistic frame 1. Snout protected Snug throughout the play and the two truly endeared themselves to the audience. This would not have happened had we not worked on "The Greeting" as its own frame following "The Facts" exercise.

> *Teaching Tip:* "Cast" your class in variety of ways concerning the gender, shapes, and sizes of actors. You'll find that relationships change depending on casting. In the spy-back session of each artistic frame have the actors report on how they felt, moment to moment, working under the umbrella of the AoA. After several rehearsals of each frame, you can begin to narrow and define actions and qualities.

Artistic frame 2.
AoA = The anticipation. Objective atmosphere = Fear.

> **DIRECTOR'S NOTE (TO ACTORS)**

"The Greeting" dies down and there is an awkward moment as everyone realizes Bottom is not present. He is always late as divas often are. Bottom is above, on the bridge, watching the action below waiting for his solo entrance. The mechanicals do not notice him. (*Secret: Quince must make a choice of either knowing that Bottom is present or not. Try it both ways.*)

Quince
Is all our company here?

Artistic frame 3.
AoA = The grand entrance. Objective atmosphere = Glad.

> **DIRECTOR'S NOTE (TO ACTORS)**

Everyone is thrilled and/or relieved Bottom has arrived. Quince is the playwright and director of the play. As director, he should make a choice about Bottom's lateness. The first words from Bottom's mouth are to tell Quince what to do. How does Quince feel about that?

Bottom
You were best to call them generally, man by man, according to the scrip.

Artistic frame 4.
AoA = The duel. Objective atmosphere = Mad.

> **DIRECTOR'S NOTE (TO ACTORS)**

While the atmosphere is in the world of "mad" it doesn't mean that Quince and Bottom are angry at each other. We want to establish a relationship of rivalry, which can exist in the world of "mad." Each wants to be in charge. The other mechanicals recognize the rivalry. The next four speeches should build in intensity toward the end based on the AoA.

SCENES AND BLOCKS WITH MULTIPLE CHARACTERS

Quince
Here is the scroll of every man's name, which is
thought fit, through all Athens, to play in our
interlude before the Duke and the Duchess, on his
wedding-day at night. (*Secret: Quince has chosen the best of the best. There should be a sense of pride from all.*)

Bottom
First, good Peter Quince, say what the play treats
on, then read the names of the actors, and so grow
to a point. (*Secret: Bottom is usurping Quince as director.*)

Quince
Marry, our play is "The most lamentable comedy, and
most cruel death of Pyramus and Thisbe." (*Secret: Quince's initial response until the title of the play may be gruff. Have Quince constantly search for polarity.*)

Bottom
A very good piece of work, I assure you, and a
merry. (*Secret: How does Bottom know this is good work? He hasn't read the play.*)
Now, good Peter Quince, call forth your
actors by the scroll. Masters, spread yourselves.

Artistic frame 5.
AoA = The performance. Objective atmosphere = Glad.

DIRECTOR'S NOTE (TO ACTORS)

Bottom performs for the mechanicals in the first two minutes of taking the stage. Bottom loves to act—lives to act. He should take great joy in it. The other mechanicals, save Quince, are waiting for this moment. They know it is coming and they revel in it.

Quince
Answer as I call you. Nick Bottom, the weaver. (*Secret: Even though Quince is director and author, he knows where his bread is buttered and calls Bottom first.*)

Bottom
Ready. Name what part I am for, and proceed.

Quince
You, Nick Bottom, are set down for Pyramus.

Bottom
What is Pyramus? A lover, or a tyrant?

Quince
A lover, that kills himself most gallant for love.

Bottom
That will ask some tears in the true performing of
it. If I do it, let the audience look to their eyes (*Secret: The word "If" may be an operative word.*)
I will move storms (*Secret: Polarity.*) I will condole in some measure. To the rest—yet my chief humour is for a
tyrant:
    The raging rocks
    And shivering shocks
    Shall break the locks
    Of prison gates;
    And Phibbus' car
    Shall shine from far
    And make and mar
    The foolish Fates.
This was lofty! Now name the rest of the players.
This is Ercles' vein, a tyrant's vein; a lover is
more condoling. (*Secret: Huge positive reaction from the other Mechanicals.*)

Teaching Tip: Coax these "secrets" from your cast and don't simply dictate. Ask more questions in your direction than giving mandates. Actors love to discover!

Artistic frame 6.
AoA = The director. Objective atmosphere = Glad.

SCENES AND BLOCKS WITH MULTIPLE CHARACTERS

DIRECTOR'S NOTE (TO ACTORS)

This is Quince's time. Bottom has performed and Quince takes his place in the spotlight. The mechanicals do not know which roles they will be playing so they are very excited for their assignments.

Quince
Francis Flute, the bellows-mender.

Flute
Here, Peter Quince.

Quince
Flute, you must take Thisbe on you.

Flute
What is Thisbe? A wandering knight?

Quince
It is the lady that Pyramus must love. (*Secret: Quince knows this may be difficult for Flute.*)

Flute
Nay, faith, let me not play a woman: I have a beard coming. (*Secret: Reaction from others at this statement.*)

Quince
That's all one: you shall play it in a mask, and
you may speak as small as you will. (*Secret: Does this pacify Flute?*)

Artistic frame 7.
AoA = The interruption. Objective atmosphere = Glad.

DIRECTOR'S NOTE (TO ACTORS)

Bottom is so enthusiastic and full of himself that he thinks he can play all the roles. Quince must find a way to continually placate him. Quince has the task of keeping the diva Bottom happy and content with the role of Pyramus.

Bottom
An I may hide my face, let me play Thisbe too, I'll speak in a monstrous little voice: "Thisne, Thisne!" — "Ah, Pyramus, lover dear! Thy Thisbe dear, and lady dear!"

Quince
No, no; you must play Pyramus: and, Flute, you Thisbe.

Bottom
Well, proceed.

Artistic frame 8.
AoA = The director continues. Objective atmosphere = Glad.

DIRECTOR'S NOTE (TO ACTORS)

Quince is trying his best to get through the casting of the play before Bottom interrupts again. It's important to give Snug time to establish his archetypes. We must love him as the lion.

Quince
Robin Starveling, the tailor.

Starveling
Here, Peter Quince.

Quince
Robin Starveling, you must play Thisbe's mother. Tom Snout, the tinker.

Snout
Here, Peter Quince.

Quince
You, Pyramus' father: myself, Thisbe's father: Snug, the joiner; you, the lion's part: and, I hope, here is a play fitted.

Snug
Have you the lion's part written? Pray you, if it be, give it me, for I am slow of study.

SCENES AND BLOCKS WITH MULTIPLE CHARACTERS

Quince
You may do it extempore, for it is nothing but roaring.

Artistic frame 9.
AoA = The resolution. Objective atmosphere = Glad.

DIRECTOR'S NOTE (TO ACTORS)

This is a long frame and the arc is driven by Quince. Quince's actions and qualities must be varied and sufficient to appease Bottom. Quince knows that Bottom must be won over if all the other mechanicals are to be onboard. It is Quince who takes us on a journey and he should look to polarity for answers.

NOTE TO READER

In this next section I have included the actions and qualities I observed after the initial improvised rehearsals. As an exercise, try to discover for yourself the secrets that led us to the score.

> ***Teaching Tip:*** You might find it helpful to briefly explore the atmospheres of each frame prior to adding the dialogue. Add the time for this into your schedule. Also, have the actors articulate aloud the action (A), PG, and Quality (Q) prior to speaking the dialogue. Physicalize the PG before speaking the quality.

Bottom
(A = To announce. PG = Open. Q = Boastfully)
Let me play the lion too: I will roar, that I will do any man's heart good to hear me; I will roar, that I will make the Duke say "Let him roar again, let him roar again."

Quince
(A = To pacify. PG = Embrace. Q = Calmly)
An you should do it too terribly, you would fright the Duchess and the ladies, that they would shriek; and that were enough to hang us all.

All

(A = To agree. PG = Close. Q = Fearfully)
That would hang us, every mother's son.

Bottom

(A = To agree. PG = Lift. Q = Easily)
I grant you, friends, if that you should fright the
ladies out of their wits, they would have no more discretion but to hang us:

(A = To assure. PG = Open. Q = Lovingly)
but I will aggravate my voice so that I will roar you as gently as any sucking dove; I will roar you an 'twere any nightingale.

Quince

(A = To throttle. PG = Strike. Q = Heatedly)
You can play no part but Pyramus:

(A = To suck up. PG = Embrace. Q = Sweetly)
for Pyramus is a sweet-faced man; a proper man, as one shall see in a summer's day; a most lovely gentleman-like man: therefore you must needs play Pyramus.

Bottom

(A = To agree. PG = Embrace. Q = You're right [edly])
Well, I will undertake it.

(A = To get direction. PG = Close. Q = Pompously)
What beard were I best to play it in?

Quince

(A = To get direction. PG = Close. Q = Pompously)
Why, what you will.

Bottom

(A = To seek [a decision]. PG = Pull. Q = Importantly)
I will discharge it in either your
straw-colour beard, your orange-tawny beard, your purple-in-grain beard, or your French-crown-colour beard, your perfect yellow.

Quince

(A = To appeal [to Bottom's vanity]. PG = Pull. Q = Baitingly)
Some of your French crowns have no hair at all, and then you will play bare-faced.

(A = To complete. PG = Close. Q = Quickly)

SCENES AND BLOCKS WITH MULTIPLE CHARACTERS

But, masters, here
are your parts: and I am to entreat you, request
you and desire you, to con them by to-morrow night;
and meet me in the palace wood, a mile without the
town, by moonlight; there will we rehearse, for if
we meet in the city, we shall be dogged with
company, and our devices known. In the meantime I
will draw a bill of properties, such as our play
wants. I pray you, fail me not.

Bottom
(A = To one-up. PG = Embrace. Q = Flourishly)
We will meet; and there we may rehearse most
obscenely and courageously. Take pains; be perfect: adieu.

Quince
(A = To get the last word. PG = Close. Q = Authoritatively)
At the Duke's oak we meet.

Bottom
(A = To one-up. PG = Push. Q = More authoritatively)
Enough; hold or cut bow-strings.

Exeunt

Note: There is the exit yet to stage, which should be frenetic and comical. I would consider the exit to exist in frame nine.

Hopefully, you can compare the AoA, atmospheres, actions, and qualities with the rhythmical wave below and get a visual understanding of the wonderful journey we discovered in this scene.

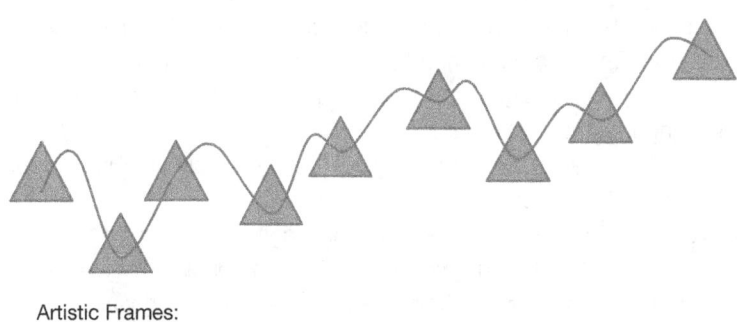

Artistic Frames:

1   2   3   4   5   6   7   8   9

This is the rhythmical wave the AoAs in this scene should create. The director's task is to help the actors stay securely under the umbrella of AoAs and artistic frames. It is helpful for actors to see the curve. Most actors are able to visualize easily. Seeing the diagram and understanding the frames help them, and the director, create the rhythmical wave. It is also useful for the actors to see that these diagrams and notes are in the director's journal.

Recall from an earlier chapter that rhythmical waves exist within the overall wave of the play. Actors and directors must build these waves carefully. This is an example of how just a few frames must be structured to provide us with a journey where there is no major climax. These blocks represent the introduction of the mechanicals and is exposition leading us to a subplot.

Many actors I've worked with want to copy my diagrams into their own rehearsal journal. This reinforces the "feeling of the whole" and supports the superobjective. It also gently suggests that actors should keep a rehearsal journal.

In this production the actors were highly receptive to the concept of creating the rhythmical wave and understood how, to take the audience on the journey, we had to create the highs and lows that constitute that journey. It can't be all high or all low. To find a truthful journey, the acting, no matter how broad or absurd, must be grounded in reality. That reality creates a true wave and forms the journey between highs and lows.

The play within the play allows the actors to be as broad and as outlandish as possible if they have established their relationships properly and invest wholeheartedly in their actions and qualities. These actors invested in relationships (in that they were true friends) so deeply and believed in the given circumstances (in that this was the most important event in their lives) so vehemently that by the time the play within the play happened the audience roared with laughter and, most important, was genuinely invested in its success. This proved true throughout the run.

Yet, this could not have happened had the actors not understood that collaboration between themselves and the director is paramount. It is a matter of give and take—really listening to each other, not just for cues but also for content, which is identified through quality of action and willingness to play and improvise. Indeed, for a long while no two rehearsals were the same with these actors. Even in tech rehearsals they were playing—playing as children play—never settling for repetition. Of course, we eventually agreed on the performances. Because the process was so free, the mechanicals always made the work seem as if it was the first time ever happening.

Follow-up

In my work as a director, I always keep a separate journal for the rehearsal process that I call my "Director's Book of Secrets." I keep the journal separate from my "Director's Book" because I don't want anyone else to have access to it. The secrets contained in the journal are derived from my own fantasy and are admittedly very specific. It would be easy to direct a play completely from the secrets. I don't because the play would become more like a one-person puppet show than a collaboration of actor and director. The secrets are there to act as a guide for the director to help the actors discover on their own. Yes, sometimes the actors don't discover the specificity involved in moment-to-moment acting at which point the director can introduce the secrets. Just please be sure to introduce them in subtle ways.

It is extremely easy to get too attached to the secrets in the journal. Actors will most of the time respond to the AoA and atmospheres and discover things about the play beyond what even the director has found. This is truly the goal and the worth of a good director—to help the actors "go beyond the play." Whatever the actors find, however, must be viable within each artistic frame and AoA. In our manner of working the director simply keeps talented actors creating within a specific vision.

It may seem to the reader that this idea of a Director's Book of Secrets is introduced very late in this book. This has been purposeful because of the vast amount of information I believe is important to comprehend before considering this concept. Now, you can return to earlier chapters and create your own book of secrets with the text contained therein. There is also other material in the appendices to work with. Of course, you can choose any material you wish to apply all of the principles in this book, and I hope you will.

11
TEMPO/RHYTHM AND ATMOSPHERE

Application to all genres

Framework

We know that tempo and rhythm in music are two different yet related things. In Shakespeare, when dealing with iambic pentameter, we use the terms similarly. As iambic pentameter is generally written with ten syllables per line, making five iambic feet, there is a basic rhythm established.

In contemporary theater there may not appear to be such an established rhythm as in Shakespeare. I believe there is a rhythm to be discovered in much of modern theater. Think of the works of Tennessee Williams and David Mamet and Samuel Beckett's play *Waiting for Godot*. Rhythm definitely exists in these texts and is distinctive to geography and demographics. Surely, tempo is partially controlled, as you by now know, by action and qualities of action. The material in this chapter can be applied to all genres. There is also material in the appendices that addresses rhythm and tempo for work on contemporary pieces.

Many actors and directors are musically inclined and have often studied music. I find adding music terminology to the actor's score can aid actors in helping create the proper tempo/rhythm. Indeed, singers and actors who have studied music interpret music terminology as atmosphere. The terms are as palpable to singers atmospherically as the work on atmosphere is to Chekhov actors. Atmosphere, both objective and subjective, certainly affects rhythm/tempo.

I have worked with musical theater students in higher education for many years. Often, they are so concerned with their voices and dance abilities that they place their acting studies lower on the priority list. We must help them understand that the vast number of their competition in auditions sing just as well or better and dance just as well or better.

What distinguishes an audition is the acting. When directing musical theater students, I have found that adhering to the concepts in this book is vital to the success of their acting in a production. As a director, I don't pay a lot of attention to their singing voices or dancing. The musical director and choreographer are my strong collaborators in those areas. I trust them. What I do as a director in songs and dances is to make certain everyone is doing so according to the stated atmosphere and as an individual character. Every member of the ensemble, including chorus members, must have "acting chops."

We have explored tempo using staccato and legato. Yet, between those two extremes there exist many options. Using music terminology is simply another tool at our disposal.

Many singers from around the globe have come to study the Chekhov Technique with us at the Great Lakes Michael Chekhov Consortium. I have learned to help them understand atmosphere through their own use of musical terms. Therefore, I have included various appropriate terms in the example below.

In this chapter, we will continue with some Shakespeare, adding music terminology, and look at a song using our new and previously used tools of the Technique.

In-class exercise: Titania's speech

Here is Titania's speech again with rhythm and tempo included. I have also included the divisions of iambic pentameter and the operative words, which are in italics. Determining the operative words will reveal a great deal in all of our work concerning clarity of meaning. Stressing the operative words is extremely important in tempo and rhythm. The action (A), PG, quality (Q), and musical terms and tempos appear in italics and are enclosed within brackets.

TEMPO/RHYTHM AND ATMOSPHERE

> **Teaching Tip:** As always read aloud and include the AoA, atmosphere, etc. Following the first read-thru, work on PGs alone as the next step in the exercise.

Arc of Action = The truth. Atmosphere = Mad.
Titania
(A = To attack. PG = Smash. Q = Angrily. Musical term = Abandon: free, unrestrained, passionate. Tempo = Staccato, fast, abandon.)
These are/ the *for/geries/* of *jea/lousy*:

In-class exercise: Scoring on your own

Work on the above line until the actor(s) have the technique in their bodies. The beginning of the next section can still be done with spirit, in the atmosphere of "mad," just with more control.

In the world of Michael Chekhov, we call this "veiling." To veil is to hide or control one's subjective atmosphere. Veiling must be initiated from the feeling center and quickly synapses to the thinking center. The actor first feels that his or her objective is not being successfully accomplished. Following that feeling the actor makes a conscious decision to veil—control—his or her emotions to reach the goal. Even though veiling is controlled from the thinking center, the impulse to veil comes from the feeling center. Remember, we feel, we think, we do.

Allow the speech to ebb and flow in intensity through the last line of the artistic frame. Note that all of the above musical terms can also become qualities of action: freely, unrestrainedly, and passionately. They are all in the family of the quality that we have baptized as the chief quality of each frame. We are adding other elements to our work—rhythm and tempo. By using the musical terms as qualities, you can have several rehearsals and change qualities for variance.

Tempo aids in creating the rhythmical wave that is so important to our craft. Within the artistic frames are nuances that musical terms describe perfectly. The director might consider having a list of musical terms handy at all times—along with a thesaurus of course. This is a long artistic frame. Use all of the words, as qualities, to create polarity. Score the next speech with all of the work from the first line.

Each art strives to resemble music.

W. Paret

Begin scoring this part of the speech. It is within the same artistic frame as stated above. Titania is still angry, yet she changes her actions and qualities to reach her objective. She controls her subjective atmosphere and therefore the tempo and rhythm changes.

And nev/er, since/ the mid/dle sum/mer's spring,
Met we/ on hill,/ in dale,/ forest/ or mead,
By pav/ed foun/tain or by rush/y brook,
Or in /the beach/ed mar/gent of/ the sea,
To dance/ our ring/lets to/ the whist/ling wind,
But with/ thy *brawls*/ thou hast/ disturbed/ our sport.

> **Teaching Tip:** We rarely get what we want using the quality of angrily. As I have stated before, humans respond to qualities more than to action. It is the tone (quality) of the spoken word that guides our reactions. Titania is wise enough to understand she can never get anything from Oberon by attacking him.
>
> Hopefully, she understands this from Oberon's reaction to her attack with the quality of angrily. She changes her action and her qualities to get what she wants. In the next section she becomes more vulnerable and appeals to his heart. She alters her tempo with veiling, action, and qualities of action.

TEMPO/RHYTHM AND ATMOSPHERE

Here is the next part of the speech scored for you. Your score of the previous part of the speech should be similar.

(A = To educate. PG = Open. Q = Sensibly. Musical term = Lentando: gradual slowing and softening.)
Therefore/ the *winds*/, piping/ to us/ in *vain*,
As in/ *revenge*,/ have *suck'd*/ up from/ the *sea*
Conta/gious *fogs*; /which fall/ing in/ the *land*
Have eve/ry pelting *riv/er* made/ so *proud*
That they/ have *ov/er borne* their/ *continents*:

Teaching Tip: Remember to explore each section several times with varying qualities. Take the term "lentando" to heart. Have the actor gradually slow the speech. The tendency for most actors is to begin fast and slow down immediately maintaining the slow tempo for four lines. Instead, each ensuing line should be slightly slower. Look carefully at quality changes to slow down each line. It is a good thing to find quality changes existing in the same family. Even subtle differences make an impact on the actor and the audience. Use your thesaurus.

(A = To illuminate. PG = Penetrate. Q = Sadly. Musical term = Con dolore: with sadness.)
The *ox*/ hath there/fore *stretch'd*/ his yoke /in *vain*,
The *plough/man* lost/ his *sweat*,/ and the/ green *corn*
Hath *rott/ed* ere his/ *youth* attain'd/ a *beard*;
The *fold*/ stands *emp/ty* in/ the drown/ed *field*,
And *crows*/ are *fatt/ed* with/ the mur/rion *flock*;
The nine/ *men's* mor/ris is/ *fill'd* up/ with *mud*,
And the/ quaint *ma/zes* in /the wan/ton *green*
For *lack*/ of *tread*/ are *un/disting/uishable*:

> **Teaching Tip:** In the above eight lines the actor simply cannot afford to speak all with the quality of sadly. Following every two lines find qualities within the same family of sadly to add nuance.

(A = To nail (to drive home the point). PG = Smash. Q = Sternly.
   Musical term = Obbligato: required, indispensable.)
The hu/man *mo/rtals* want/ their win/ter *here*;
No *night/* is now/ with *hymn/* or ca/rol *blest*:

> **Teaching Tip:** When you encounter a colon, look for a change in action and/or quality of action.

(A = To solidify. PG = Pull. Q = Reasonably.)
Therefore/ the *moon*, the *gov/ernes/* of *floods*,
Pale in/ her *an/ger*, *wash/es* all/ the *air*,
That rheum/atic *di/seas/es* do/ *abound*:
And thor/ough this/ *dis/temp/erature/* we *see*
The *sea/sons al/ter*: the/ spring, the/ summer,
The child/ing *au/tumn*, angry win/ter, *change*
Their wont/ed *liv/eries,/* and the/ mazed *world*,
By their/ *increase,/* now *knows/* not which/ is *which*:

(A= To plead. PG = Lift. Q = Honestly. Musical term = Deciso: decisively.)
And this/ same *pro/gen/y* of *e/vils* comes
From our/ *debate/*, from our/ *dissent/sion*;
We are/ their *par/ents* and/ *orig/inal*.

> **Teaching Tip:** Operative words are negotiable. Stress is relative to each measure. In other words there are degrees of stress. In the following line I suggest stressing three words. Even though all three may be operative words they are not equal in importance. We

TEMPO/RHYTHM AND ATMOSPHERE

> can create a scale of 1–5 with five being the most important and therefore receives the most stress:
>
>   2   3   4
>
> By their/ *increase,*/ now *knows*/ not which/ is *which*:
>
> Stress is not always volume. Stress can also be pitch, rate, rhythm, and flow. Also, the numerical scale is not fixed from line to line. The value of 5 in line 10 might not have the same stress as value 5 in line 25. Keeping this in mind will add variety to the rhythm and tempo. The human voice is capable of reproducing an incredible range of sound. Any numerical scale may not do the voice justice and would, in a way, reduce our work to math and not art. It is much more organic to keep the numerical scale brief and discover the infinite number of qualities available instead. Regardless, the numbers are important for the meaning of each line.
>
> Using this technique in every genre clarifies meaning for the actor and the audience. It is imperative in music lyrics.

It will take a good amount of time for your actors to incorporate all of this work. In my studio, I have found that taking the time to truly ingrain the Technique into one monologue or one scene is more important than moving on to other material. Teach slowly and your actors will grow.

Study of atmospheres: Affecting rhythm/tempo

I mentioned earlier that atmosphere affects rhythm and tempo. Examine the first three scenes again from *Midsummer*. Scene I begins with Theseus and Hippolyta pledging their love for each other. The opening of the play is light and somewhat lusty. An atmosphere of "glad" is interrupted by the entrance of Egeus and his train. The quick tempo suddenly changes because the atmosphere changes. As I have identified before, this scene in which Egeus is pleading his case causes an atmosphere of "fear." The pace becomes more deliberate. We can see the rhythmical wave already forming. Within this same scene, following the exit of Egeus, Theseus, and Hippolyta, the atmosphere changes once again when Lysander proposes to Hermia. The tempo quickens with the atmosphere of "glad." Lysander devises a plan to flee Athens and its cruel laws. The young couple is elated with the promise of happiness as Helena enters. Her presence reveals yet another atmosphere—"mad." The colliding atmospheres of "glad" and "sad" create conflict. Michael Chekhov states that two conflicting atmospheres can only be maintained for a given period of time. One atmosphere must give way to the other. This can happen in various ways. Perhaps one person acquiesces to the other. In this case Hermia decides to leave the environment. While Hermia remains happy for the opportunity to be with Lysander, she genuinely feels bad for her best friend, Helena. Hermia's atmosphere has altered. She can only cope by leaving. Helena then delivers a speech we have already examined. It begins in an atmosphere of "mad" and ends in an atmosphere of "hope" or "glad." The constant conflict of atmosphere creates a natural tempo/rhythm. From the end of this scene, featuring all of the nobility of Athens in the play, we move to the entrance of the rude mechanicals.

While scene I certainly ends with the atmosphere of "glad," scene II begins with the same atmosphere but on steroids. The working men of Athens are contemplating the possibility of performing a play before the duke on his wedding night. The stakes are high as they will become "made men" should they be chosen to entertain. Yet within the scene is the opportunity for many atmosphere and tempo changes. Look at part of the same scene covered in Chapter 10 but with added tempo/rhythm and atmosphere notes. Scene III, in the forest, follows, scored with atmosphere and tempo/rhythm.

In-class exercise: Read aloud while imagining the atmospheres and working with tempos

Work on the atmospheres as previously described prior to the reading. Score the scenes with music terminology.

TEMPO/RHYTHM AND ATMOSPHERE

> *Teaching Tip:* Use the following teaching tips as your direction to the actors to assist in creating the score.

Scene II. Athens. Quince's house.

Block 10.
Enter **Quince, Snug, Bottom, Flute, Snout,** *and* **Starveling**
Quince:
Is all our company here?

> *Teaching Tip:* Atmosphere = Glad (ecstatic, circus, chaos). Quince will have a hard time controlling the atmosphere. He is the playwright and director and constantly strives to take charge of the meeting as Bottom steps in immediately with a suggestion. This should threaten Quince. We observe conflicting atmospheres from the onset. One can imagine the conflict escalating between Bottom and Quince in the next few speeches. This will drive the tempo faster as the atmosphere changes from "glad" to "mad." The director, via study of the personal atmospheres, controls the tempo and creates a strong rhythmical wave within the scene.

Bottom
You were best to call them generally, man by man, according to the scrip.

Quince
Here is the scroll of every man's name, which is thought fit, through all Athens, to play in our interlude before the Duke and the Duchess, on his wedding-day at night.

Bottom
First, good Peter Quince, say what the play treats

on, then read the names of the actors, and so grow to a point.

Quince
Marry, our play is "The most lamentable comedy, and most cruel death of Pyramus and Thisbe."

Bottom
A very good piece of work, I assure you, and a merry. Now, good Peter Quince, call forth your actors by the scroll. Masters, spread yourselves.

Teaching Tip: At this point Bottom has the final direction and Quince immediately takes charge. This is first ending of the conflict between the two and the height of the first artistic frame. Therefore the rhythmical wave drops with the next line and begins to climb again indicating a new change in tempo.

Quince
Answer as I call you. Nick Bottom, the weaver.

Bottom
Ready. Name what part I am for, and proceed.

Quince
You, Nick Bottom, are set down for Pyramus.

Bottom
What is Pyramus? A lover, or a tyrant?

Quince
A lover, that kills himself most gallant for love.

Bottom
That will ask some tears in the true performing of it. If I do it, let the audience look to their eyes: I will move storms, I will condole in some

TEMPO/RHYTHM AND ATMOSPHERE

measure. To the rest—yet my chief humour is for a tyrant:

> **Teaching Tip:** The following speech changes the tempo once again because of Bottom's subjective atmosphere. He is now performing and the stakes rise dramatically. It is overacting at its best and should be played with much bravado.

    The raging rocks
    And shivering shocks
    Shall break the locks
    Of prison gates;
    And Phibbus' car
    Shall shine from far
    And make and mar
    The foolish Fates.
This was lofty! Now name the rest of the players.
This is Ercles' vein, a tyrant's vein; a lover is more condoling.

> ***Teaching Tip:*** This speech from Bottom tests the resolve of Quince yet again. Rather than confront Bottom, Quince decides to proceed to the rest of the company. This is revealing concerning the archetypes of Quince and contrasts him beautifully with the archetypes of Bottom.

Quince
Francis Flute, the bellows-mender.
Flute
Here, Peter Quince.
Quince
Flute, you must take Thisbe on you.

Flute
What is Thisbe? A wandering knight?
Quince
It is the lady that Pyramus must love.
Flute
Nay, faith, let me not play a woman: I have a beard coming.
Quince
That's all one: you shall play it in a mask, and you may speak as small as you will.

> *Teaching Tip:* Here, Quince shows the archetype of politician. This is also an atmospheric change and slows the tempo—which Bottom immediately changes.

Bottom
An I may hide my face, let me play Thisbe too, I'll speak in a monstrous little voice: "Thisne, Thisne!"—"Ah, Pyramus, lover dear! Thy Thisbe dear, and lady dear!"
Quince
No, no; you must play Pyramus: and, Flute, you Thisbe.

> *Teaching Tip:* Quince responds rather vehemently with an atmosphere of "mad" and interestingly, Bottom acquiesces. There is an atmospheric spike here and a good opportunity for a pause. We observe one atmosphere giving way to another. Bottom, who is very energetic—"glad"—ready to play both Pyramus and Thisbe, gives in to Quince's "mad."

Bottom:
Well, proceed.

Quince
Robin Starveling, the tailor.

Starveling
Here, Peter Quince.

Quince
Robin Starveling, you must play Thisbe's mother.
Tom Snout, the tinker.

Snout
Here, Peter Quince.

Quince
You, Pyramus' father: myself, Thisbe's father:
Snug, the joiner; you, the lion's part: and, I
hope, here is a play fitted.

Snug
Have you the lion's part written? Pray you, if it
be, give it me, for I am slow of study.

Quince
You may do it extempore, for it is nothing but roaring.

It has gone well for Quince for a few speeches and his atmosphere has brightened. That is until Bottom speaks next.

Bottom
Let me play the lion too: I will roar, that I will
do any man's heart good to hear me; I will roar,
that I will make the Duke say "Let him roar again,
let him roar again."

Quince
An you should do it too terribly, you would fright
the Duchess and the ladies, that they would shriek;
and that were enough to hang us all.

Teaching Tip: In Quince's speech above we see him fight his inner atmosphere of "mad." He controls his anger and outwardly appeals to Bottom's ego. There is another change of tempo here. For a time

> the proceedings have been going along smoothly. Quince could choose to answer Bottom's plea with the same quality with which Bottom delivers his speech—vigorously. Using polarity, Quince is wise to choose a different approach—admiringly. The tempo alters with the device of polarity.
>
> At the end of scene II the mechanicals exit in the same glad, chaotic, exhilarated atmosphere in which they entered. There is a magical transition from the broad comedy of the mechanicals into scene III—the first time we are introduced to the forest world of the fairy king/queendom. If Athens is a hot, dry, and somewhat austere environment, the forest is opposite—cool, dark, mysterious, and lush. The atmosphere changes immediately.

Before moving on to the next scene, return to Chapter 10 and combine the work contained there with the atmosphere and tempo work in this chapter. It's a lot of work!

In-class exercise

Following your work with the mechanicals, proceed in the same manner with atmospheres and tempo with the next scene in the play. Score the scene as in the way we have been working.

Note: In the forest we discover a fairy gathering flowers for her queen—Titania. The fairy is observed by the playful character of the hobgoblin Puck. In this production the fairy was dancing on the moon achieved by a projection on the floor from above, which enhanced the atmosphere dramatically.

Puck
How now, spirit! Whither wander you?

TEMPO/RHYTHM AND ATMOSPHERE

> ***Teaching Tip:*** The atmosphere of mystery (fear, as we are all afraid of the mysterious) can be enhanced if Puck doesn't fully reveal himself for a bit. This is supported by the text in the fairy's second speech, "Either I mistake your shape and making quite. . . ." Puck, being the mischievous character he is, is teasing and taunting the fairy. If the fairy is startled by Puck, then he or she can begin his or her first speech in a tentative tempo. He or she obviously doesn't recognize Puck at first and we can interpret this meeting as Puck and the fairy not knowing each other at all.

Fairy
Over hill, over dale,
Thorough bush, thorough brier,
Over park, over pale,
Thorough flood, thorough fire,
I do wander everywhere,
Swifter than the moon's sphere;
And I serve the fairy queen,
To dew her orbs upon the green.
The cowslips tall her pensioners be:
In their gold coats spots you see;
Those be rubies, fairy favours,
In those freckles live their savours:
I must go seek some dewdrops here
And hang a pearl in every cowslip's ear.
Farewell, thou lob of spirits; I'll be gone:
Our queen and all our elves come here anon.

> ***Teaching Tip:*** Should the actor playing the fairy begin in a tentative atmosphere, it is clear he or she gains more confidence as the speech progresses. He or she is proud to serve Titania and brags about it.
> He or she calls Puck a "lob of spirits." Lob means "country lout." It's clear the fairy gains confidence in the speech, which drives the tempo quicker. The other clue for tempo is that Titania and her train are expected soon. The atmosphere becomes tense which also increases the tempo.

Puck
The king doth keep his revels here to-night:

> ***Teaching Tip:*** Puck has listened carefully to the fairy and now reveals that he or she serves the king of the fairies. This creates conflict between the two and Puck raises his status above the fairy. There is even more tension, which affects the tempo/rhythm. The colon at the end of the first line suggests a pause and we can imagine a stand-off between the characters. Following the pause the tempo should decrease. This is important exposition for the audience must know why Titania and Oberon are fighting with each other. Puck may be issuing a warning and is a clue to the tempo.

Puck *continued*
Take heed the queen come not within his sight;
For Oberon is passing fell and wrath,
Because that she as her attendant hath
A lovely boy, stolen from an Indian king;
She never had so sweet a changeling;
And jealous Oberon would have the child
Knight of his train, to trace the forests wild;
But she perforce withholds the loved boy,
Crowns him with flowers and makes him all her joy:
And now they never meet in grove or green,
By fountain clear, or spangled starlight sheen,
But, they do square, that all their elves for fear
Creep into acorn-cups and hide them there.
Fairy
Either I mistake your shape and making quite,
Or else you are that shrewd and knavish sprite
Call'd Robin Goodfellow: are not you he
That frights the maidens of the villagery;
Skim milk, and sometimes labour in the quern
And bootless make the breathless housewife churn;

And sometime make the drink to bear no barm;
Mislead night-wanderers, laughing at their harm?
Those that Hobgoblin call you and sweet Puck,
You do their work, and they shall have good luck:
Are not you he?

> ***Teaching Tip:*** There is an interesting actor choice to be made here. Does the fairy chide Puck for his mischief or does he or she use the quality of "admiringly" in his or her action? If we use polarity in this situation we can create a very interesting rhythmical wave for the scene. Should the actor playing the fairy choose to use "admiringly" as the quality of action, the relationship changes dramatically and becomes very playful. The tempo increases, polar from the two previous speeches, and can become highly physical between the two. The atmosphere is changed from the beginning of the scene and is interrupted by the entrance of Titania. Upon her entrance the atmosphere changes once again. Both Puck and the fairy abruptly adjust from frolicking into a serious mood.

Puck
Thou speak'st aright;
I am that merry wanderer of the night.
I jest to Oberon and make him smile
When I a fat and bean-fed horse beguile,
Neighing in likeness of a filly foal:
And sometime lurk I in a gossip's bowl,
In very likeness of a roasted crab,
And when she drinks, against her lips I bob
And on her wither'd dewlap pour the ale.
The wisest aunt, telling the saddest tale,
Sometime for three-foot stool mistaketh me;
Then slip I from her bum, down topples she,
And "tailor" cries, and falls into a cough;
And then the whole quire hold their hips and laugh,

And waxen in their mirth and neeze and swear
A merrier hour was never wasted there.
But, room, fairy! Here comes Oberon.

Fairy
And here my mistress. Would that he were gone!

Teaching Tip: The tendency for the actor playing Puck is to rush the speech. Remember that this is our first glimpse into the world of the fairies. Both the actors and the audience should take time to enjoy this world of magic. Remind the actors of "The Palace" exercise where their imaginations were engaged. The tempo of this scene should be joyous, yet somewhat indulged. Puck and the Fairy, serving different masters, have a duty and at the same time have a kindred relationship because of their servitude. These given circumstances create a world of possibilities for actions and qualities. This is a good scene for "The Facts" exercise.

Application to other genres

We leave Shakespeare now to apply the Technique to another genre and style. Michael Chekhov did not set out to develop his technique to be exclusive to classic works. The Technique is applicable to all styles. If each style in the theater world required its own acting technique, we would need several lifetimes to master them all.

The word "style" is used when differentiating periods of theater or creating academic curricula such as: realism, absurdism, Shakespeare, musical theater, etc. Sure, there are differences in each style the actor must master. In Shakespeare the actor must adhere to the rules of iambic pentameter when working with verse. When working on Moliere, the actor must conquer period movement and rhyming couplets. In musical theater the actor must have music and dance education. Each style has its own challenge, which is what makes it a style in the first place.

TEMPO/RHYTHM AND ATMOSPHERE

Now, here is the biggest question concerning styles in acting: Is there a change in acting technique from genre to genre? I think the correct answer is only in the sense stated above. All characters in all genres must be grounded in the truth of the story. This is true from the Greeks to Gilbert and Sullivan to Odets to Ruhl. In any genre, no matter how broad or absurd the character, the actor must be believable. The surest road to believability is to apply solid actor technique to character.

It's a fact that in music theater, characters are not as often "fleshed out" as in a piece such as *A View from the Bridge*. (I use the term music theater to include musical theater, opera, and operetta.) The journey of an individual character is often lessened in music theater because of time. A lot of time is used in this genre to create spectacle, which does not give the librettist the luxury of writing as much dialogue and delving as deeply into a character as does Tennessee Williams. Of course, duets and solos further the character journey yet not in the same way as straight plays.

What is the chief difference between *Les Miserables* and *Three Sisters*? One is sung through and one is not. *Les Mis* certainly deals with change, major themes in both works, and in a more epic manner than *Three Sisters*. Still, the similarities are striking: love, death, and social upheaval. Many of the characters in each of these works experience the same life journey. Therefore, once again, we should begin our course with archetypes in creating the characters. The same rules apply in our Technique to both works—and in all works in theater. Our acting technique is the same; our approach is the same, even though *Les Mis* is more elevated than *Three Sisters*. No matter how elevated above everyday life a work of art is, it must be solidly grounded in reality to be believable.

Let's now look at a song I believe every music theater person should study to apply our Technique. I've scored it to my own liking. Feel free to get out your pencil and disagree. That's what this book is about—to create your own score!

It's not necessarily because of patriotism I choose this song. It is chiefly because everyone knows it and it can be done without an accompanist. (At least everyone thinks they know it. Most people over sing it. It has many nuances that our Technique can illuminate.)

Pre-class exploration

E-mail your class the lyrics to at least the first two verses of "The Star-Spangled Banner" by Francis Scott Key. Be prepared to share with the class your scoring of the first verse.

Operative words

>Oh, say, can you *see*? By the *dawn's* early light
>What so proudly we *hailed* at the *twilight's* last gleaming;
>Whose broad *stripes* and bright *stars*, through the perilous *fight*,
>O'er the ramparts we *watched* were so gallantly *streaming*.
>And the rocket's red *glare*, the bombs *bursting* in air.
>Gave *proof* through the night that our flag was still *there*:
>Oh, say, does that star-spangled *banner* yet *wave*?
>O'er the land of the *free* and the home of the *brave*?

In-class exercise

Have one of the actors speak or sing through the lyrics of the first verse and then spy-back. Ask first about atmosphere. Have the actor narrow the atmosphere to our archetypal group of five. When you agree on the atmosphere, work on it with the entire group in the same way as in the past. Once you have established the atmosphere, have the same actor do the piece again and give him or her a printout of the verse with the operative words.

After this rehearsal, the next step in the exercise is to speak or sing the operative words only. Point out to the actors the various ways to stress the operatives. Finally, speak or sing the lyrics, in entirety, again using atmosphere and operative words. Be certain to spy-back.

In-class exercise

Have your actors choose their own operative words for the next verse and repeat the exercise above.

TEMPO/RHYTHM AND ATMOSPHERE

On the shore dimly seen through the mists of the deep
Where the foe's haughty host in dread silence reposes,
What is that which the breeze, o'er the towering steep,
As it fitfully blows, half conceals, half discloses?
Now it catches the gleam of the morning's first beam,
In full glory reflected now shines in the stream,
'Tis the star-spangled banner—O long may it wave
O'er the land of the free and the home of the brave!

In-class exercise

Here is the first verse again with the division of artistic frames, musical terms, PGs, actions, qualities, and atmospheres. Use this pattern to create a score for the second verse. Resist doing this exercise from the thinking center. In other words, don't allow your actors to sit down and "script" the score. The score must be found working with the Technique, on their feet, to truly be organic and therefore repeatable. Work on one aspect of the Technique at a time and eventually put it altogether. Note: Artistic frames are divided by parentheses.

Work on atmospheres first, followed by PGs. Note that the overall PG for the score is "open." There are most likely more you can find on your own for each frame. Don't be content with one quality of action, explore others and search for polarity. By varying the tempo of the PG, you will find a tremendous number of qualities.

Atmosphere = Proud = Joy = Glad

> **Teaching Tip:** Note how, again, the qualities of action can vary using the words of atmosphere: proudly, joyfully, gladly.

Baptism/Artistic frame = The moment of pride
   PG = Open. Action = To glorify. Overall quality of action = Proudly.
   Musical term = Moderato (yet there is so much more here than straight tempo). Consider the qualities and music terms in braces ({ }).

({Joyfully} {Declamando = Solemn, expressive, impassioned}Oh, say, can you *see*? By the *dawn's* early light {Proudly}What so proudly we *hailed* at the *twilight's* last gleaming; {Gracefully}Whose broad *stripes* and bright *stars*, through the perilous *fight*,
{Gladly}O'er the ramparts we *watched* {Gallantly} were so gallantly *streaming*).

({Proudly} {Con fuoco = With fire}And the rocket's red *glare*, the bombs *bursting* in air.

Gave *proof* through the night that our flag was still *there*):

({Joyfully} {Durezza = hardness, toughness}Oh, say, does that star-spangled *banner* yet *wave*)?

({Proudly} {Deciso = Decisive, decisively}O'er the land of the *free* and the home of the *brave*)?

Teaching Tip: "The Star-Spangled Banner" is a wonderful song to explore QoM. Do this with your cast or class using an excellent recording. The proper recording will take some time to find if you want to hear all of our work incorporated in it.

Teaching Tip: Actors will, in their scoring of operative words, often stress the adverb over the verb. Allow them to do so. Then, point out that the verb is always more important. We will hear the description of the verb if the verb is stressed. In the lyric of, "perilous fight," which word is more important? We must hear "fight" as the operative, otherwise we know something was perilous yet we don't really hear what was perilous.

Follow-up

To me, Shakespeare and musical theater/opera share so many similarities that it simply makes sense to pair them as I have done in this chapter. One can see how the work applies to any opera or musical theater piece by using the tools we have incorporated in our national anthem. Shakespeare, musical theater, opera, and Brecht and epic theater, along with Greek tragedy, comes to mind when I think of the most elevated forms of our theater art. I hope I have given the reader and practitioner enough information to understand that the Technique works for our highest forms and for all other genres and styles as well.

We already know that Michael Chekhov is our only major methodologist who worked extensively with Stanislavski. His Technique, therefore, was born in realistic drama and under the tutelage of the father of modern acting concepts. Should you delve into the work in this book in the way I hope you will, you will find the Technique will work for any production you take on.

With the utilization of operative words, atmosphere, a thorough study of the given circumstances, actions, qualities, and polarity, the actors and director can build dynamic tempo/rhythm in each scene and block that creates the overall rhythmical wave of the play.

We always search for the conflict in plays, yet conflict is a broad term. What we really need to discover is polarity and atmosphere from character to character. Doing this unveils the minor and major conflicts inherent in the play and dictates the tempo/rhythm from scene to scene, speech to speech, and line to line. Most important, this work reveals the depth of the play and the characters within.

While this book is not meant to be a comprehensive work on musical theater, I believe incorporating our Technique into the rigors of musical theater training will elevate the actor above the norm. To be a true "triple threat," the musical theater performer must have as much mastery in his or her acting as in dance or singing. I don't know how long the average life of an ensemble member lasts in musical theater. I do know a career can be extended with outstanding acting technique. In other words, there are so many possibilities in our industry. I certainly never thought I would write a book. Artists need to continually train and expand their horizons.

Further reading

Deer, Joe and Dal Vera, Rocco, *Acting in Musical Theatre*, Routledge, 2008.

12
SPY-BACK

Framework

This final chapter is meant to be a spy-back over our work, with important reminders, and to add material that I have not yet covered and that you may find useful in various situations.

There is a lot to be said about commitment in any art form. We must commit to our art fully and with passion and I don't mean exclusively in the business sense. There is a wonderful exercise I have not yet mentioned called "Crossing the Threshold." It is an excellent exercise to begin a class or rehearsal because it reminds everyone that commitment in our work means going beyond that of everyday life and placing oneself in the Higher Ego—that place where art is made.

In-class/rehearsal exercise

- Form a circle and have the ensemble simply connect with each other.
- Ask them, after the connection, to take one step backward.
- Next, they should silently ask themselves about what is going on in their daily lives and how those events are affecting them at the moment.
- After taking inventory, the ensemble, as individuals, decides to commit to the Higher Ego. In this place the daily life is left behind and each person commits fully to the work at hand,

vowing through the imagination to invest in the function of Higher Ego.
- Each person, in her own time, takes a step forward.
- Eventually, all will cross the threshold into the creative world of Higher Ego where we can have a productive class or rehearsal far above mundane everyday activity.

There is something I tell actors prior to "Crossing the Threshold" and that is about my 300 percent solution. The formula is: 100 percent commitment 100 percent of the time will equal 100 percent payback. It is unrealistic to believe that all human beings, in all rehearsals or classes, can operate at 100 percent capacity. There might be illness or other issues simply out of our control. So, I ask each actor to contribute 100 percent of their capacity, whatever that is, to the work of the day. If an actor is only capable of 50 percent of her capacity for that day, I ask all of that percentage to our task. Folks seem to appreciate this concept and usually give all they have. It is really all we can ask. I am also quick to point out when actors are not working at full capacity or have not committed to the Higher Ego. I think I do it in a professional manner.

In-class exercise

While there is a link to a video of staccato-legato included in this book, I'd like to speak a bit about the exercise itself. Upon first encounter with the exercise it seems to actors as if it is simply a physical warm-up. Once introduced to other aspects of the Technique and practiced daily, most of us find that the entire Technique can be experienced in this exercise.

The exercise of staccato-legato contains all of the attributes we have explored: radiation, PG, atmosphere, ensemble, actions, qualities of action, Actor's Ideal Center, and much more. It is often taught first in the Technique and I understand why. Beginning with staccato-legato and then working through the Technique brings the actor to a full circle of understanding. Yet, I tend to teach the exercise after some immersion in the work. I'd simply rather not ask actors to trust me that the Technique is all in this one exercise. I'd much prefer they experience it for themselves. That said there is worth in experimenting with both ways of introducing the exercise. View the video and listen to the actor's spy-back. Draw your own conclusions through experimentation. This is the way of the Chekhov Technique.

Maintaining status for directors and teachers through collaboration

Working in the most collaborative manner as a director or teacher and maintaining leadership status is an interesting endeavor. In this Technique, we work so hard to create a "feeling of the whole," yet teachers, especially, are placed upon a pedestal above the ensemble. Professional directors are often looked upon with wariness from professional actors. It is a conundrum from any view.

I maintain that creating a true ensemble from the beginning is the key to creating the best production possible. Still, the director and teacher must maintain status as the final person who says "yes" or "no." It really all comes down to trust. The teacher/director must gain the trust of the class or cast immediately and it often happens in a matter of minutes during the first meeting. How do we develop the trust between actor and teacher/director and maintain status?

First of all, as the director/teacher, one must be willing to give and to receive. The giving part is not all from the brain—the intellect. This part should be more from the feeling center and then the whole being. (Remember, we feel, we think, we do.) Therefore, it is a very good thing to listen to actors from the heart first. Ask yourself, when teaching or directing, when a question arises or a problem occurs, "What did I just feel and why did I feel that way?" There are times when our own stubborn convictions get in the way of making great art. Allow your thinking center, your brain, to respond from your feelings—after you've contemplated for some time. This process will go a long way in placing the teacher/director within the ensemble and gaining trust with actors.

Directors and teachers sometimes feel we must have all the answers. It is much more fruitful to guide actors to a conclusion by using the Technique. Find the right tools from the Technique for actors to discover for themselves. In this manner, we are not conceding our status; we are aiding artists toward an organic journey. Sometimes the teacher/director doesn't know the answer, yet we feel we must provide one. Resist providing an immediate answer and explore that answer through the fundamentals of the Technique. In reality, there are only a handful of things for us to consider when solving acting problems.

The director/teacher, to be successful, must be attuned especially to the atmosphere of the ensemble. As the company leader, we must enter the space and maintain leadership. Yet, we must also be acutely aware of what the company is feeling, as a whole, on any particular day or rehearsal. It is an easy task to change the atmosphere of the company by reminding them to commit to the Higher Ego.

If you are in academia and your ensemble comes to a class or rehearsal and has just taken an impossible exam from an egocentric theater history professor and they are not as prepared as you would like, it is counterproductive to talk about their lack of preparation. We all know why they have only cursorily worked on their acting assignment. It is more productive to ask them to commit to the day's work and encourage them to understand that all assignments, from all teachers, should have equal consideration in future.

This can also happen in professional or civic theater when a world event occurs that can affect our atmosphere of humanity. The very best we can do is remind ourselves that we have an obligation to the world and an obligation to our art. When an event such as described descends upon us, we should commit even more to our Higher Ego for the work at hand. Art can help elevate us to transcend terrible things.

In cases like these, begin with an atmosphere exercise that changes from what is current to joy—and that is taking joy in the work. After this, you can "cross the threshold." Remind actors what is most important—creation in the Higher Ego. Always be attuned to whatever might be negative and remember there are tools in the Technique to affect positive change.

Art establishes the basic human truths which must serve as the touchstones of our judgement. . . . I look forward to an America which will readily raise the standards of artistic accomplishment and which will steadily enlarge cultural opportunities for all of our citizens.

John F. Kennedy

A bit more on atmospheric spikes

We have talked about atmospheric spikes from a director's point of view. (Chekhov calls them "accents" and I admittedly take a bit of liberty here.) What does the term mean from the actor's view? An atmospheric spike (accent) is a moment in the text when a character is reminded of the objective or his or her own subjective atmosphere. He or she feels a punch in the stomach, so to speak, and responds accordingly. Look at this example from *King Lear* in a brief exchange between Regan and Goneril:

Regan
Such unconstant starts are we like to have from
him as this of Kent's banishment.

Goneril
There is further compliment of leavetaking
between France and him. Pray you, let's hit
together: if our father carry authority with
such dispositions as he bears, this last
surrender of his will but offend us.

Regan
We shall further think on't. (*The punch in the stomach*)

Goneril
We must *do* something, and i' the heat.

In this exchange between the elder sisters, we observe them forming an alliance to deal with the unforeseen circumstances caused by Lear's wrath. The overriding atmosphere must be fear. Then, Regan suggests they pause and "think on't." She is appealing to reason. Goneril responds by saying, "We must do something, an i' the heat." Goneril experiences an atmospheric spike of anger and Act I, scene I ends abruptly. Goneril is reacting from her feeling center and, as the eldest sibling, orders a course of action to begin now. This exchange tells us a lot about the hierarchy of the family and about Goneril's main archetype. The example also perfectly describes the collision of two atmospheres. The gauntlet has been thrown and there is nothing left to say. The two must part and the scene must end.

Humans learn to deal with, or live within, our atmospheres on various levels, comfortability, or justification. In other words, while living in our own subjective atmospheres, we are either content with our lives, we justify our actions (good or bad), or we deny our misery. Our character attributes are often revealed through atmospheric spikes.

Auditioning using the Chekhov Technique (for directors and actors)

Auditioning, like putting in golf, is a whole different game than being in a full-length play or arriving on the green. In golf, we have a bag full of tools to use to arrive on the green and only one tool to use while putting. In auditioning, the actor has basically a minute or so to "sink the putt." So, we really should choose our auditioning tools carefully.

The actor, in an audition, is wise to choose a monologue that has a clear objective (revealed in the first few lines), beginning, middle, and ending, and at least two action and quality changes. If the actor can manage these parts of the Technique in the audition he or she will "sink the putt." It doesn't necessarily mean he or she will get a callback. It does mean he or she will have a successful audition, which never goes unnoticed.

Casting directors usually ask for two contrasting monologues. This doesn't necessarily mean comedy and tragedy although that is a viable course for actors to choose. Consider that this criterion means contrasting characters. If you are doing Helena from *Midsummer*, you might look at Roberta from *Danny and the Deep Blue Sea* as a companion piece. Look for large contrasts.

In most medium-to-large markets several companies audition together and cast for the entire season. In these cases you need to show range and knowledge of the season you're auditioning for. If you're auditioning for your university program, you are not simply auditioning for a single production. The director may not think you're right for his or her play right now, yet rest assured a good audition will put you in good stead for future.

At some point in the actor's career, he or she will be asked to do cold readings. Usually, you are given about 5 minutes to look over the material. There is only one thing to do in this situation and it is not learning the lines. It is finding action and quality changes. Make bold choices in actions and qualities and definitely look for polarity. It doesn't matter if the choices end up being totally foreign to the play as a whole. What matters is that the actor makes choices.

The director is wise to look for the above attributes in the actor. Too often, an actor doesn't show enough range in an audition or is a "one note Nelly." Directors should look for smart actors who have researched the season or the individual play and planned the audition accordingly. Beyond that, directors must know if the actor is capable of making choices that create a rhythmical wave. When a director sees that actor, he or she knows it is a person who understands the value of the basic fundamentals of playmaking. The director, if interested in the actor, should always give him or her an adjustment in action and/or quality. Only then will the director truly know the collaborative nature of the actor and of these basic principles. The actor should always be prepared to make an adjustment.

The actor must also remember that he or she is trying to make a change in his or her imaginary partner and that change involves a journey based on action and quality. He or she is trying to change how the other feels about something. If this is not the premise of the monologue it is not a good piece for an audition and should be discarded. Change the other's subjective atmosphere and you will change his or her mind. Build a journey toward this goal and directors will take notice. Even if the director is not familiar with our Technique, he or she will undoubtedly feel the journey and be interested in the actor's work. Well, that is the way it should be. If not, perhaps not working for a particular director is actually a good thing. There is nothing worse than going through a dictatorial rehearsal process.

I'll never forget the words of Malcolm Morrison, spoken to me in college, "It's your ass on the stage, baby." As actors, we must adhere to direction. In our Technique, we can use our tools to give the director what he or she wants and maintain our own integrity. I think this is what Malcolm was talking about. Just do this quietly and go about the actor's business.

Final words

Michael Chekhov made me realize that truth as naturalism was far from the truth. In him I witnessed exciting theatrical form with no loss of content, and I know I wanted that too.

SANFORD MEISNER

It is a shame that the Second World War prevented Michael Chekhov (see Appendix V) from becoming a teacher of acting as recognized as those among his peers of Meisner, Strasburg, Alder, and others. It has only been in the last twenty years or so that we have discovered what Chekhov has to offer. Chekhov taught actors of great renown: Gregory Peck, Yul Brenner, Marilyn Monroe, Jack Palance, and many more. It is a good thing to ponder that Chekhov was the only major methodologist to have worked with Stanislavski and yet his work is still not ensconced in most academic curricula. Had Chekhov entered the world of the Group Theater that existed years prior to the Second World War, our training landscape for actors and directors may indeed be quite different.

While I believe that our major methodologists have much to offer, I don't believe they are equal to the depth of what Chekhov offers us. Chekhov gives us a complete method of training in the mind, body, and spirit. Most training in America is of an eclectic nature. It is a smattering of this and that. I'm not convinced that an eclectic training in acting or directing is our best approach. This conventional approach is accepted because it is what most teachers have been taught. Quite frankly, a specific approach, like the Chekhov Technique or Meisner's, can intimidate those who teach in an eclectic manner.

Several years ago, Cherry Jones was addressing actors I was teaching at the time and was asked by a student to articulate her approach to acting. She said, "I don't have a particular technique, I think actors should be able to pull from many sources." All eyes in the room turned toward me. As Ms. Jones continued to speak for the next hour it was clear she did have a particular approach. She simply did not have a comprehensive terminology to articulate it. And there's the rub.

Actors and directors really should have a terminology that we all agree upon. Every other occupation that I can think of has common terms that make working lives efficient. You don't hand a hammer to a person who asks for a level. Terminology is what makes dance and music so much more efficient to rehearse than acting.

The Michael Chekhov Technique derives its terminology directly from the work of Stanislavski. One wonders why our terms vary so from methodologist to methodologist. I can only surmise that each teacher needed to clarify for his or her students a point he or she was trying to make and came up with a synonym. Or, as we can only imagine the egos involved, each main teacher in the golden era of professing Stanislavski in this country simply wanted to make the work her own. Strasburg, for example, is so drastically different than Meisner in his approach. Students can easily get confused when their teachers attempt to blend the theories of our major methodologists into an eclectic approach. It is no surprise Cherry Jones, one of America's prized actors, said what she said.

So, it begs the question why, if an actor such as Ms. Jones can be so successful with an eclectic method, should we study a single approach? As I listened to Ms. Jones, I realized she came to her own conclusions after many years of trial and error having been taught eclectically at Carnegie Mellon University. This is the crux of the issue—we don't necessarily need to put ourselves through many years of trial and error to solidify and be able to articulate our craft. This is true in acting and directing.

In most theater training programs in America, one acting teacher is lucky to see the same students for three different classes in the course of a four-year education. Acting classes usually meet twice per week for sixteen weeks for one hour and 40 minutes. That is roughly forty-five hours of studio time spread among sixteen to twenty students—less than three hours of individual time over the entire semester! Add the little amount of time to the fact that each class places new and different demands, such as those that occur in Moliere and Shakespeare, and we can readily see what an impossible task exists in our training.

Given this scenario it has made sense to me that getting into students as much of one specific technique as possible over the number of classes in which we see them is a logical path to follow. Students are going to be trained somewhat eclectically regardless since they will be exposed to other teachers along their educational journey.

I suppose the chief point I wish to make here is that we must not only train our artists to be able to do their craft, it is equally important to train them to articulate how they do their work. When one can talk about the how, one doesn't need to struggle for years to find the way that works for them. This is why the Michael Chekhov Technique, for me, soars above others. The work is the most Stanislavski based of all, is simple, clear, easily articulated, and is immediately applicable to any text of any genre.

I know if an artist works with the tools in this book, he or she will find the way of working artistically fruitful. As I said in the beginning of the book, I am drawn to the feeling of community, and community is established through collaboration. Use the tools and you will find a collaborative journey on a level you may have never experienced.

Regardless of the methodology you choose for your personal journey, choose the journey of collaboration and help our larger theater community reach the goal of Chekhov's Ideal Theater.

APPENDIX I: LINKS TO WORKBOOK VIDEOS

To view a particular video, please visit its URL below, or go to http://vimeo.com/channels/directingwithmct/

1 Archetypes   https://vimeo.com/188675546
2 Qualities of Movement   https://vimeo.com/188813894
3 Acting with Balls!   https://vimeo.com/188675545
4 Staccato-Legato   https://vimeo.com/188675555
5 Psychological Gesture—Forms   https://vimeo.com/188675552
6 Psychological Gesture—With Text   https://vimeo.com/188675549
7 Psychological Gesture—Kata   https://vimeo.com/188675547

APPENDIX II: CONCEPT STATEMENTS AND CASTING FROM OTHER PLAYS

CONCEPT STATEMENT: JOHN STEINBECK'S *THE GRAPES OF WRATH* BY FRANK GALATI DIRECTED BY MARK MONDAY

The epic story, and the origins, of *The Grapes of Wrath* is not all that well known any longer. Yes, the history of the "dust bowl" is taught briefly in high school history courses and the novel is still occasionally assigned as required reading. It is, therefore, important in our production to educate our mostly college-age patron not only of the importance of the story in history but to reveal the relevancy of its themes to current events.

The majors themes of the play we will explore in this production are: greed (man's inhumanity to man), rebirth, dignity, and family. From these themes, the growth and rebirth of Tom Joad, and from the quote at the top of the page, I believe we can name, or baptize, the superobjective of the play as hope.

In the period of a three-year drought in the 1930s during the Great Depression, tens of thousands of people left the Great Plains region of our country seeking work and a better life for their families. These folks became migrant workers, seeking employment mostly on farms, especially in California. Act I of the play depicts the journey across the Great Plains to California and we must find a way to depict the arduous and dangerous journey on our thrust stage. In Act I, we experience the theme of family and hope when Tom arrives home unexpectedly with Jim Casy, a preacher. The biblical overtones are apparent as this is where the "exodus" begins.

Scenically, there should be multiple levels as there are many locales inherent in the play. Some of the platforming making up these levels should be on casters so that the actors can move them from locale to locale easily. I see, during the "exodus" scene of Act I, a choreographed move of the platforms with actors riding on them. The move will be brisk as it will be staged during the up-tempo song "Sixty-Six is the Path of the People in Flight."

I'm not sure if the Joad's truck falls into the category of scenery or props. Regardless, it is an important element and should hold up to eight people. The truck should be easily maneuverable. It will be the focal point of the migration and all other platforms will be choreographed around it. The song has two verses so the "exodus" will take up to two and a half minutes. We should have at least three movable platforms in addition to the truck.

At the end of the first leg of the journey, Grampa Joad dies. The family must bury Grampa and this should happen onstage. We should make use of one of our traps in the stage and place his wrapped body into the "ground." This brings me to a very important element of the play, which is the narration.

I want to create a character who does all of the narration and I wish to call her "Angel." Our Angel will be ever present in the play. She will provide, for example, a hymn over the dialogue when Grampa is buried. Angel will also play characters within the play. In other words, Angel will be a guide, symbolizing a religious aspect of the play of a "higher guidance." For example, she will take the corpse of Rose of Sharon's baby from John and place it in the flowing river while singing under the dialogue.

Water is an important element scenically. We should have two troughs with hinged lids placed downstage right and left. This will serve as the baths for the characters, the storm near the end of the play, and for other purposes/blocking when the lids are closed. Placing the corpse of the baby into the water is such an important symbol as it calls up the image of Moses being placed in the reeds and the theme of rebirth.

As we are working in a thrust configuration with a raked audience the floor treatment becomes a chief element of the design. The treatment could be, should be, earthy with a possible wind-blown texture.

Yet another important scenic element in the play is canvas tarps. In almost every image of the migration one views in books or online is the presence of canvas, which serves as covering for the vehicles and makeshift tents. We can use canvas pieces surrounding the stage as projection surfaces. I believe projections from the period are paramount in aiding our audience to truly feel a sense of what transpired in this era. I see characters standing in the projections themselves creating a feeling of being in the turmoil of the journey. I assume projections fall in the category of lighting design.

Speaking of lighting, Act I should have an overall sepia tone, look, and feel, which can become denser as the act progresses. Sepia tones will allow us a hazy look, giving us a gloomy atmosphere, which will allow the positive themes of the play to be more prevalent when represented. The designer can possibly incorporate subtle, brighter colors in these moments.

At the end of Act I, the migrants arrive in California. The lighting should be drastically different as the weary travelers first gaze on the fertile fields from a distance. Here, we must have a feeling of hope.

The remainder of the play takes place in various locations and the lighting should suggest these specific changes. Most important is the storm scene and the end of the play. The storm is the highest climax in the play. We must find a balance between the sounds of thunder, lightning, and actually hearing the dialogue.

The end of the play certainly gives us hope for humanity as Rose of Sharon breastfeeds a dying man, a stranger. The lighting here is extremely important as we do not really wish to observe the actual deed. Lighting should reveal the theme of hope, yet be subtle, so as not to illuminate bare breasts on stage. We can also address this with costuming and staging.

Costuming should reflect the period and be distressed accordingly, especially as the journey progresses. One concern is the point in the play where the bathing in the troughs occurs. As the troughs are downstage

APPENDIX II

and the actors will be totally immersed in water, there may be a long exit which, of course, will leave water on the floor treatment. We can quickly mop the stage utilizing characters in the action, yet the floor may still be rather slick for a few scenes. The changes in costumes should be minimal concerning the main characters. That said, the ensemble will be playing several characters each. We will deal with that when the play is cast.

Sound is of import in that most of the music will be live and will be played from various locations on the stage. Hopefully, we can find a balance without amplification. Regardless, it will be a challenge in this space since sound is absorbed dramatically.

Otherwise, there will be music under some dialogue that will need to be recorded. The music will be period, so the sound designer will need to communicate with the director concerning the mood of each. The underscoring should be instrumental.

Props are numerous in that the migrants take only essentials on the journey. The essentials consist of pots and pans, minimal clothing, canvas shelters, all without traditional luggage. So, everything should be wrapped in makeshift carriers with perhaps an occasional small trunk. Actors will have their own instruments including guitars, banjos, harmonicas, etc. Without altering their own instruments permanently, they should look period.

Before the first production meeting, I would like to touch base with each designer and receive reactions concerning this concept statement. At the first production meeting, I would like for each designer to present thoughts and even images in response to our individual initial discussions.

A major point, during our initial discussions, concerns where the major and auxiliary climaxes occur and how each design area will address these climaxes. This is imperative because it is in these climaxes that the major and minor themes are revealed.

M. Monday

Casting the Main Characters of *The Grapes of Wrath* Using Archetypes

Tom Joad

Archetypes = Wounded child, rebel, victim, dreamer.

Tom exemplifies the wounded child archetype not by mistreatment from his family but circumstances growing up in the tumultuous period of the late 1920s and 1930s in the Great Plains of America. Before the play begins, we can imagine the harshness of young Tom's daily life and it leaves a scar on him we can sense as the play begins.

Tom spends four years in prison and we first encounter him on his journey home where we learn he has become a rebel. His philosophy, early in the play, is to seize every moment and to never shy away from a fight.

As the victim, Tom exhibits this archetype at almost every turn. His four-year sentence in prison is harsh to say the least. He becomes the leader of the family across the country almost by default as Pa, his father, cannot seem to cope or make decisions. Tom is greeted numerous times with the theme of greed from the wealthy landowners only willing to pay the barest minimum possible to the migrants.

After meeting Jim Casy, a former preacher, Tom begins his journey toward uniting humanity toward a common good. His personal philosophy changes dramatically and he becomes a dreamer.

From these archetypes, I would first consider that Tom is tall, built well from hard work, and in his thirties. I consider him so because he looks like he could carry the weight of the world on his shoulders. The actor playing Tom might also be ruggedly handsome as he attracts the attention of everyone he meets. The attraction from others must also come from the archetype of rebel and yet we should believe he is sensitive. In other words, there is a rugged exterior about Tom, yet he has a "kind soul" when necessary. The exterior comes from the archetypes of wounded child and victim. The journey of Tom Joad generates the theme of rebirth, which manifests in him and symbolizes a hopeful rebirth of the philosophy of the country.

APPENDIX II

Casting the actor to play Tom is crucial to the success of the production. He must be able to connect with his family members, serve as the patriarch, be capable of quick temperament, and truly listen to the actor playing Jim Casy as Jim changes the fiery exterior of Tom to a more gentle and contemplative person. Without an actor who can incorporate all of these archetypes, we really have no story, no play. So, in a callback, I would have the actors vying for Tom read from the script that reveals all of the aforementioned archetypes. That would include reading with Casy, Ma, and Pa in different scenes.

Ma Joad

Archetypes = Child divine, disciple, matriarch.

Ma is perhaps the most strong-willed character in the play. She, above all, represents the theme of family and togetherness. She never wavers from the archetype of disciple as she exemplifies faith and determination.

With an unwavering strong exterior, we see Ma's emotions rarely on the outside: one is Tom's homecoming, another is the passing of Granma, and finally at the end when she directs Rose of Sharon to breastfeed the dying man.

Interestingly, we know she loves her children and yet she really shows no affection to Pa and other adults. She has a deep love for Tom like no other in the family. While some might think this to be a flaw in her character, I believe Ma sees that Tom might be the only person who can keep the family together following her. She, therefore, invests more of her emotional self into Tom. We can feel her heart breaking when Tom must leave near the end of the play. In Tom, however, we see the true traits of Ma emerge and blossom.

From these facts, I would look for an actor with an exterior of a woman who has worked hard all her life. She must be strong physically and mentally. The actor must be capable of the perception of an impenetrable exterior, yet we must sense her inward feelings. She must be able to "veil" her emotions and engage her "thinking center" immediately.

I would have her, in callbacks, read from passages that reveal the above facts. She should read with Pa, Rose of Sharon, and Tom.

Pa Joad

Archetypes = Dependent child, patriarch, dreamer.

The beginning of the play depicts Pa as the leader of the family as he works hard to make the dream of moving to California a reality. At first, the family is dependent upon him to organize the trip and assume his role as patriarch.

As the play progresses, Pa loses touch with his dreamer and patriarch archetypes because of the hardships the family encounters. He becomes more inward and dependent on Ma and Tom. He increasingly takes on the archetype of dependent child. The character of Pa makes us realize the darker side of dreamer in that "dreams don't always come true."

From these given circumstances, I would look for an actor who is capable of making this vast transition in a brief period. I would work with the actor, in adjustments, on polarity in actions and especially qualities. Tom gets his dreamer archetype from Pa, yet they are not close—much like many father and son relationships. It is important for the actor playing Pa to note that his dreamer dissipates and Tom's increases. Somehow, Pa must embrace this transition and that all lies in his choices of actions and qualities of action.

Jim Casy

Archetypes = Child divine, savior, teacher.

In the character of Jim, we see all of the themes of the play come together. His appearance early in the play, when meeting Tom and espousing his philosophy, truly helps us realize immediately what an impact Casy will have on the entire story.

Jim Casy shares the initials of another famous savior and we must not overlook that. Eventually, Tom becomes a disciple as Casy is first in embracing the migrants and tries to organize their efforts. Casy, like Jesus, is willing to give his life to his cause. Tom comes to this cause of humanity through Casy.

In casting this important role, I would look for an actor with passion, yet his passion should be an internal one—a passion so deep it does not have to be seen externally. Jim is a teacher. His words ring true without forcing an issue. I would look for an actor who listens actively. He must process what he hears quickly and his responses should be thoughtful, based on life experiences and his belief in a "common good for all." The actor who auditions and eventually is cast for Jim must be likable—as if he is a long-lost friend.

Rose of Sharon

Archetypes = Orphan child, dreamer, rebel, virgin.

Rose of Sharon somehow does not seem to fit into the family theme for most of the play. She dreams of things beyond her means, like an iron and a car. Certainly, she is naïve and from that I consider her orphan child archetype—being so far mentally apart from the realities of the Joad family. These attributes also make her a dreamer.

Rose of Sharon is very much like Tom as she shares her rebel archetype with him. She and Tom are distant from the family in that they share a kinship of vision. She overcomes her selfishness, like Tom, as her life journey progresses. Hers might be the largest personal journey in the play. She literally begins as a rebellious teenager to a woman who makes a decision to breastfeed a starving man. She is much like the Virgin Mary in that her decision is a symbol to save mankind.

To cast this role, I would first look for a very sensitive actor in her initial audition. The actor, in callbacks, would read from the beginning, middle, and ending of the play. I would ask her to embrace the "maturity" of her journey. Maturity translates to qualities of action. In the beginning of the play, Rose of Sharon should be able to make quality choices like brashly, selfishly, regardlessly, and shamelessly. At the end of the play, she should be making quality choices such as selflessly and lovingly.

Of course casting a family is always challenging and should be taken into consideration. I believe the chief element, in this play, is gathering a cast that can be viewed as hardworking and simple people. Certainly this can be accomplished with costuming and a bit of makeup. Still, it is a good point to keep in mind.

CONCEPT STATEMENT: *THREE SISTERS* BY ANTON CHEKHOV

TRANSLATED FROM THE RUSSIAN BY MICHAEL FRAYN DIRECTED BY MARK MONDAY

A time will come when people will understand what it was all for, what the purpose was for all this suffering, and what was hidden from us will be hidden no more.

Irina Prozorov

Time heals all wounds.

Chaucer

You may delay, but time will not.

Benjamin Franklin

If you can look into the seeds of time, and say which grain will grow and which will not, speak then unto me.

William Shakespeare

As you may discern from the above quotes, our production of *Three Sisters* will concern time and the many ways it affects the lives of the characters in the play and, through them, our own lives as well.

We learn, at the beginning of the play, that the Prozorov family has been transplanted from Moscow to a provincial town because their father was a general and stationed there. The sisters, Olga, Masha, Irina, and their younger brother, Andrei, still live in the home where their father died. We discover, in the opening monologue, that the father died one year ago to the day. Time has stood still for the sisters since their father's death and each longs to return to Moscow. For all the sisters, and for different reasons, there is really no future for them in the province. Time is an enemy for the three sisters and yet all they seem to do is talk about a change but do very little about it. We have all experienced this sort of helplessness with the passing of time.

Still, things change with time and often not for the better. When Andrei, the younger brother, marries Natasha, life at home changes dramatically. This time, life has played a cruel trick on the sisters. Natasha, who at first appears meek and not really worthy of Andrei's affection, turns out to be a disruptive beast, especially for Olga who has served as the matriarch of the family.

Masha's life seems stalled in time. She is in a difficult marriage with seemingly no future happiness. When Vershinin enters Masha's life, there is a glimmer of hope for her. Yet, it is short lived.

In Irina, the youngest sister, we observe the most hope within the family in that she dreams of finding love and happiness when moving to Moscow. As for most young people, time seems to pass very slowly as dreams are always in the future.

While there are other themes to explore in the play such as hope, loneliness, love, and isolationism, they are all influenced by time. I believe, in our production if we focus on the theme of time, all other themes will be revealed.

This brings me to our main scenic element. In the theater where our play is being staged, because of our thrust configuration and raked audience, the floor treatment can be our strongest thematic image. I envision the face of a clock with roman numerals. On the outside of the circle of the clock, there should be written the four seasons. Most of the furniture should be placed on and surrounding the clock. Upstage should be the area where the large dining room table in Acts I and II can be situated. It should be a separate area from the downstage playing space. It will also serve as other locales of the estate as the play progresses. Acts I and II take place in the living room. Act III is set in Olga's and Irina's room. Act IV is an old garden on the estate. We will take intermission after Act II. The running crew will need to be in costumes to change the scenery between III and IV.

Another important scenic element is the presence of the fir trees on the estate. There should be many of them and they should intrude into the home. I would like to see them from floor to grid—extending out of sight of the audience. Trees represent growth and somehow a sense of timelessness.

As the play takes place over several years, lighting will need to address the seasonal changes and especially the difference between inside and outside. We may even wish to make use of the seasons which are written on the floor to identify changes. The designer and I should have early discussions on lighting various individual areas that I plan to utilize frequently. Another important lighting concern is that I want to make use of the walkway above the stage as I plan to actually stage the duel there. I realize the difficulty in lighting the area in that it is somewhat close to the grid. The duel will take place among the trees and occur during the dialogue on the stage. The lighting, therefore, should be quite subdued and shadowy, which should pose less of a problem with angles.

Costuming should be of the period of early 1900s Russia. We should remember that the family is from an aristocratic background and is expected to dress accordingly even in the provinces. There is a definite class structure. Costume colors should be coordinated between the various love interests. They should complement each other. There is also the military aspect in many of the men's costumes. I expect these will be rented and I would like to be in the loop concerning choices.

Natasha's costumes are very important. When we see her in Act I, we see a girl of the province, one who doesn't fit into the world of the Prozorovs. It would be interesting to see, between Acts I and II, Natasha being dressed by servants while we experience the time change, as it is after her wedding to Andrei, and we learn immediately that the hierarchy of the household has changed. In fact, there is a new arrival—the child of Natasha and Andrei. Perhaps the costume in this change should be the most elaborate in the play.

Properties are of major concern as the Prozorov home should be elaborately decorated. The furniture should be carefully coordinated and not look piecemeal. There should be, in prominent display, a grandfather clock and perhaps another small clock on a piece of furniture.

Thinking of props brings me to another important aspect of our production. Our production of the play is not about "Russianness." We will not be concerned about Russian culture under the Tsar for it really means nothing to our modern audience in America. In many productions of this play the presentation of the samovar is likened to the second coming of Christ. We must have a samovar but its appearance will be just a part of life—a common occurrence. We will concentrate on the humanity of the play—the struggle of the characters. That will make our production universal.

APPENDIX II

Three Sisters is a play about the day-to-day life of any family. I believe that audiences who come to see these types of plays are interested in how characters deal with the same struggles as they have. The choices the characters make are the most important aspect this production will concentrate on. We will find the humor, tragedy, pathos, and the struggle of human existence in our exploration of the play.

Exercise

Using your source of archetypes, and from the examples of concept statements, create an archetypal casting list for Three Sisters. The main characters are: Olga, Masha, Irina, Andrei, Vershinin, Tuzenbach, and Chebutykin.

APPENDIX III: SAMPLE SCORES FROM OTHER PLAYS

Does the Michael Chekhov Technique work for every style and genre of plays? I have addressed this question earlier in the book, yet I feel I should expand on my opinion here. (And I may place myself on a soapbox among directors and teachers of acting with what I am about to say. I'm comfortable with that.)

If you are a director, do you use the techniques of Strasburg for Arthur Miller, Meisner for Ibsen, or Adler for Shakespeare simply because you feel you need different techniques for different playwrights? The same question applies to teachers and actors. The answer is obvious.

The majority of acting teachers in America use what they call an eclectic technique. What does this mean? It means that the eclectic teacher of acting teaches his or her own technique derived from many others. It gets passed on to actors and directors. Honestly, it turns out to be an eclectic mess in which no one is truly able to communicate clearly and makes a rehearsal process or class less efficient than needs to be. Many times, we have to make our best guess concerning a given instruction from those in charge.

Even in writing this book, I was asked from my publisher and reviewers to address if the Chekhov Technique works for all genres. I really didn't, and still don't, understand why this question continues to surface. Does any teacher, actor, or director not base their approach on Stanislavski's teaching? Well, there may be a few but they are in the vast minority. Remember that Michael Chekhov was Stanislavski's "most brilliant pupil." All the rest based their methodologies on certain aspects of Stanislavski's work and never worked directly with him. Chekhov evolved the Technique and Stanislavski, in several important areas of his work, acquiesced to Chekhov.

APPENDIX III

I am not suggesting other methods don't work. They surely do, as I have worked with many talented actors who have studied other methods. I do wish we could come to a collective terminology for directors and actors as I am often jealous of the specificity of terminology used in music and dance.

Exercise

To aid in helping the reader understand that the Chekhov Technique works for all genres, I offer some excerpts from contemporary works. Following is an excerpt from the opening scene of *Family Portrait* by H. G. Clarkson. Clarkson is a California-based playwright and actor. Read the scene aloud and record any first impressions. You should also score the scene according to the way we have already explored. Afterward, you can compare your score to mine.

In my score, I introduce a new way of naming the AoAs. Some of my students have found this way useful. Remember that the director's work of scoring is subjective. We may not agree on certain things in our scores and that is not a bad thing.

Family Portrait

Lights come up on a hospital waiting area. **Marsha** *sits on one of the brightly upholstered chairs. She is a plump woman in her early forties, once quite beautiful, but beginning to rapidly fade. She is dressed quite fashionably. Her make-up and hair is done quite youthfully, almost as an attempt to hide her age. There is a tension to her mouth—as though she has trouble smiling. She is flipping through a magazine, but not really reading it. She looks uncomfortable and anxious, and keeps glancing off stage right and then looking at her watch. She looks at the clock on the wall comparing the time with her watch; there's no difference.*

Marsha
(Under her breath)
Where the hell is he?

(She stands up and straightens her skirt. She puts the magazine down on a small table, and picks up a different one, returns to her chair and sits down again. **George** enters from upstage right without **Marsha** seeing him. He is in his late thirties and quite distinguished looking. He carries a leather briefcase and wears a three-piece pin-striped suit.)

George
(Crossing down to where **Marsha** sits)
Sorry I'm late.

Marsha
Where have you been?

George
I came straight from the office.

Marsha
You said you'd be here by six.

George
Traffic was congested.

Marsha
It's six-thirty.

George
I can tell time. I said I was sorry.
(Pause)
How was your flight?

Marsha
Expensive . . . and tiresome.

George
Mom will be glad you came.

Marsha
I hope so.

George
I see you got here on your own.
Where's your suitcase?

Marsha
I dropped it off at the hotel, then I took a taxi over.

George
You know you could have stayed with us.

Marsha
You never offered.

George
Well, I'm offering now.

Marsha
After I've already paid for the hotel room. . . .
(Pause)
Besides, I don't think Sarah likes me.

George
You've never been very nice to her.

Marsha
That's not true.

George
Marsha.

Marsha
I've always tried to be nice to her.

George
Your idea of trying baffles me.

Marsha
What's that supposed to mean?

George
Never mind.

Marsha
She's never liked me.

George
Well, *she* thinks you don't like her.

Marsha
(Irritated)
Well, it doesn't matter. I'm staying at the Fairmont.
(Pause)

George
How's Jim?

Marsha
I don't know.

George
What do you mean?

Marsha
Exactly what I said.

George
You don't know?

Marsha
No. I don't know how Jim is.

George
I thought you guys were seeing a marriage counselor.

Marsha
Not anymore.

George
Oh? Why not?

Marsha
It was pointless.

George
The point is to work on your marriage.

Marsha
Apparently, it was too much work.

George
Marsha, these things take t—

Marsha
The counselor was trying to hit on him.

George
Really?

Marsha
Yes, really.
(Pause)
They're sleeping together.

George
Ouch.

Marsha
I'm thinking about reporting her to the ethics board—a marriage counselor who tries to break up couples instead of helping them work out their problems. (*End Scene*)

Notes and scoring the scene

We can determine from the dialogue that George and Marsha are brother and sister and their mother is hospitalized with little hope of survival. Also, we know there is a lot of sibling rivalry going on. So, what should our first question be?

Recall that Chekhov tells us to begin with atmosphere. We literally feel tension from the very first line and the tension grows stronger as the scene progresses. If you decide to use the archetypal atmospheres, you could baptize the scene with the atmosphere of "fear" or "mad." It's a choice the director must make.

Yet, there is a trap here for actors and that is to play the atmosphere instead of playing actions and identifying a clear objective. It can't be a scene about George and Marsha just being mad at each other. The "trap" must be addressed in the artistic frames and what phrases we use. The way to combat the trap is to look for polarity in actions and qualities. By the way, do the characters, George and Marsha, remind you of another feuding couple from a famous play? I believe the names are meant to be reminiscent of George and Martha from *Who's Afraid of Virginia Woolf*. It is a similar rivalry.

While we should begin with atmosphere for scoring the excerpt, it would also be good (should you use this scene as an exercise) to have your students do "The Facts" exercise very early on.

You'll notice that I have not actually baptized the AoA with a phrase this time. Instead, I have suggested an overall PG for the AoA. I have sometimes found that doing this leads to a stronger collaboration between director/teacher and actors. The actors are "in" on the baptism. It is a good teaching tool to proceed this way. On the other hand, if you are doing an entire play, it is wise for the director to baptize the AoAs to save time. The director, as I have said earlier in the book, need not do this work for the entire script. Doing this work for the main and auxiliary climaxes will inform other scenes in the play.

As usual, artistic frames are enclosed in brackets and, as an exercise, read my scoring with all components aloud before speaking the actual line. Begin your exploration on your feet utilizing the QoM prior to speaking. (Create your own "director's secrets" as an exercise.)

Family Portrait — score

Lights come up on a hospital waiting area. **Marsha** *sits on one of the brightly upholstered chairs. She is a plump woman in her early forties, once quite beautiful, but beginning to rapidly fade. She is dressed quite fashionably. Her make-up and hair is done quite youthfully, almost as an attempt to hide her age. There is a tension to her mouth — as though she has trouble smiling. She is flipping through a magazine, but not really reading it. She looks uncomfortable and anxious, and keeps glancing off stage right and then looking at her watch. She looks at the clock on the wall comparing the time with her watch; there's no difference.*

Objective atmosphere = Mad

Marsha
[AoA = Wring. PG = I wring. Action = I bitch. Quality = Angrily.
 QoM = Molding.
(Under her breath)
Note: Again, I am not revealing the baptizing of the AoA with a
 phrase. Instead, I am naming it with an overall PG.
Where the hell is he?
Note: This is a very short artistic frame as George is yet to enter. It
 is logical, therefore, the personal PG and the PG for the AoA are
 the same.
*(She stands up and straightens her skirt. She puts the magazine
 down on a small table, and picks up a different one, returns to
 her chair and sits down again.* **George** *enters from upstage right
 without* **Marsha** *seeing him. He is in his late thirties and quite
 distinguished looking. He carries a leather briefcase and wears a
 three piece pin-striped suit.)*

George
(Crossing down to where Marsha sits)

APPENDIX III

[AoA = Close. PG = I open. Action = I apologize. Quality = Carefully.
QoM = Flowing.
Sorry I'm late.

Marsha
PG = I push. Action = I question. Quality = Condescendingly.
QoM = Molding.
Where have you been?

George
PG = I open. Action = I explain. Quality = Truthfully. QoM = Molding.
I came straight from the office.

Marsha
PG = I close. Action = I accuse. Quality = Unbelievingly. QoM = Radiating.
You said you'd be here by six.

George
PG = I close. Action = I defend. Quality = Irritatedly. QoM = Radiating.
Traffic was congested.

Marsha
PG = I penetrate. Action = I make my point. Quality = Winningly.
QoM = Molding.
It's six-thirty.

George
PG = I push. Action = I terminate. Quality = Firmly. QoM = Molding.
I can tell time. I said I was sorry.]
(Pause)
[AoA = Open. PG = I embrace. Action = I inquire. Quality = Politely.
QoM = Flowing.
How was your flight?

Marsha
PG = I pull. Action = I respond. Quality = Coolly. QoM = Flowing.
Expensive . . . and tiresome.

George
PG = I wring. Action = I separate (as in to separate her from him).
Quality = Joyfully. QoM = Flying.
Mom will be glad you came.

Marsha
PG = I throw. Action = I retaliate. Quality = Condescendingly. QoM = Flying.
I hope so.]

George
[AoA = Tear (Rip). PG = I lift. Action = I bait. Quality = Invitingly. QoM = Flowing.
I see you got here on your own.
Where's your suitcase?
Note: I justify this scoring because George knows that Marsha would never ask to be a guest at his house and he should revel in that fact.

Marsha
PG = I open. Action = I invite. Quality = Playfully. QoM = Flying.
I dropped it off at the hotel, then I took a taxi over.

George
PG = I open. Action = I invite. Quality = Baitingly. QoM = Radiating.
You know you could have stayed with us.

Marsha
PG = I pull. Action = I reel (him in). Quality = Teasingly. QoM = Molding.
You never offered.

George
PG = I open. Action = I invite. Quality = Baitingly. QoM = Radiating.
Well, I'm offering now.

Marsha
PG = I wring. Action = I twist (the knife). Quality = Hurtfully. QoM = Molding.
After I've already paid for the hotel room . . . .]
(Pause)

[AoA = Lift. PG = I open. Action = I invite. Quality = Genuinely (veiled sarcasm). QoM = Flying.
Besides, I don't think Sarah likes me.

George
PG = I open. Action = I reveal. Quality = Truthfully. QoM = Molding.
You've never been very nice to her.

Marsha

PG = I close. Action = I defend. Quality = Angrily. QoM = Molding.
That's not true.

George

PG = I penetrate. Action = I gouge. Quality = Headedly. QoM = Molding.
Marsha.

Marsha

PG = I lift. Action = I pretend. Quality = Truthfully (veiled sarcasm). QoM = Flowing.
I've always tried to be nice to her.

George

PG = I close. Action = I cut off. Quality = Honestly. QoM = Molding.
Your idea of trying baffles me.

Marsha

PG = I penetrate. Action = I inquire. Quality = Angrily. QoM = Molding.
What's that supposed to mean?

George

PG = I close. Action = I quit. Quality = Exasperatedly. QoM = Flying
Never mind.

Marsha

PG = I throw. Action = I bait. Quality = Calmly. QoM = Radiating.
She's never liked me.

George

PG = I lift. Action = I open (the door). Quality = Peacefully. QoM = Flowing.
Well, *she* thinks you don't like her.

Marsha

(Irritated)
PG = I close. Action = I finish (the subject). Quality = Determinedly. QoM = Molding.
Well, it doesn't matter. I'm staying at the Fairmont.]
(Pause)

George

[AoA = Penetrate. PG = I open. Action = I inquire. Quality = Knowingly. QoM = Flying.

How's Jim?

Marsha

PG = I close. Action = I shut down. Quality = Hurtfully. QoM = Radiating.

I don't know.

George

PG = I open. Action = Inquisitively. Quality = Salivatingly. QoM = Flying.

What do you mean?

Marsha

PG = I close. Action = I shut down (further). Quality = Angrily. QoM = Molding.

Exactly what I said.

George

PG = I penetrate. Action = I press. Quality = Inquisitively. QoM = Flying.

You don't know?

Marsha

PG = I open. Action = I create an opening. Quality = Hurtfully. QoM = Radiating.

No. I don't know how Jim is.

George

PG = I push. Action = I press (further). Quality = Accusingly. QoM = Molding.

I thought you guys were seeing a marriage counselor.

Marsha

PG = I open. Action = I create an opening (further). Quality = Hurtfully. QoM = Radiating.

Not anymore.

George

PG = I pull. Action = I pull her chain. Quality = Lovingly. QoM = Flowing.

Oh? Why not?

Marsha

PG = I open. Action = I confess. Quality = Truthfully. QoM = Radiating.
It was pointless.

George

PG = I wring. Action = I teach. Quality = Pointedly. QoM = Molding.
The point is to work on your marriage.

Marsha

PG = I open. Action = I reveal. Quality = Honestly. QoM = Radiating.
Apparently, it was too much work.

George

PG = I throw. Action = I throw (the ball back into her court).
Quality = All-knowingly. QoM = Molding.
Marsha, these things take t—

Marsha

PG = I close. Action = I quell. Quality = Firmly. QoM = Molding.
The counselor was trying to hit on him.

George

PG = I open. Action = I question. Quality = Baitingly. QoM = Flying.
Really?

Marsha

PG = I close. Action = I demand. Quality = Angrily. QoM = Molding.
Yes, really.]

(Pause)

[*AoA = Embrace. PG = I open. Action = I reveal. Quality = Woefully.*
QoM = Flowing.
They're sleeping together.

George

PG = I embrace. Action = I sympathize. Quality = Apologetically.
QoM = Flowing.
Ouch.

Marsha

PG = I embrace. Action = I lighten (the mood). Quality =
Humorously. QoM = Flying.
I'm thinking about reporting her to the ethics board—a marriage counselor who tries to break up couples instead of helping them work out their problems.] (*End Scene*)

In my above score, I hope you can determine from your own exploration that there is depth in the relationship of George and Marsha. The depth is discovered through polarity of actions, qualities of action, and qualities of movement. We should think there could be familial love between brother and sister, even though the given circumstances reveal a strained relationship at best.

How the World Began

Following is another scene for scoring purposes. It is from the play *How the World Began* (HTWB) by Catherine Trieschmann. Trieschmann is an award-winning playwright and one of my favorite contemporary writers.

HTWB takes place in a school room in a small town in Kansas. The town has just been devastated by a tornado. Susan, a teacher from Manhattan, begins work in the town partly because she is escaping from the city (she is pregnant and needs health insurance). Susan is a biology teacher and does not believe in God. She has to confront those beliefs with the 16-year-old Micah—a bright lad, yet disturbed.

Please read Catherine's entire play as it is a compelling one. It will be an interesting exercise to score the scene below and then read the play. When teaching a class in scene study, a stand-alone scene often will, and should, have a different score than when in context of the entire play. Again, compare your score with mine afterward.

Micah
I have it right here. You said, "the leap from non-life to life is the greatest gap in scientific theories of the Earth's early history."

Susan
Yes, I was talking about abiogenesis, how life on Earth could have risen from inanimate matter.

Micah
What you said about the gap? That's in the book too. I highlighted it.

Susan
Good to know someone's reading.

APPENDIX III

Micah
But then you said, "unless, of course, you believe in all that other gobbledy gook."

Susan
Gobbledy gook.

Micah
Yeah. That's not in the book.

Susan
No, I don't imagine it is. *(Pause)* That doesn't sound like something I'd say.

Micah
I wrote it down.

Susan
You did?

Micah
Yeah.

Susan
You must have misheard me. I probably said something that sounded like gobbledy gook.

Micah
Like what?
(Pause. Susan can't think of a single coherent phrase that sounds remotely like gobbledy gook. Can anyone?)

Susan
I don't know, Micah. It just doesn't sound like me.

Micah
It means gibberish. I looked it up.

Susan
I know what it means, but it's not something I'd say.

Micah
Except. You said it in third period.

Susan
I'll grant you: sometimes things just fall out of my mouth willy nilly, as you've observed, but the phrase gobbledy gook is not, you know, part of my vocabulary.

Micah
Do you think I'm lying?

Susan
No. God no. I just think we have a little misunderstanding.

Micah
You said, "unless, of course, you believe in all that other gobbledy gook."

Susan
I'm sorry, Micah. You must have misheard me. Is that all you wanted to talk about?

Micah
So you're saying there's no way you said "unless, of course, you believe in all that other gobbledy gook."

(Pause)

Susan
Yes. That's what I'm saying.

Micah
You know Helen Garrett? She's in third period, too. She has red hair.

Susan
Yes, I know Helen.

Micah
She said you said it too.

Susan
She did.

Micah
Yeah. And Cade Dinkel. He heard it. We could call them, if you want.

Susan
That won't be necessary. If you all thought I said gobbledy gook, then I guess it's conceivable I'm not remembering the moment exactly, but suffice it to say: I certainly didn't mean it.

Micah
Mean what?

Susan
I didn't mean to use the phrase.

Micah
But then, what did you mean?

Susan
I'm not sure I'm following. . .

Micah
You said, "The leap from non-life to life is the greatest gap in scientific theories of the Earth's early history. Unless, of course, you believe in all that other gobbledy gook." What is the other gobbledy gook.
(Pause)

Susan
I must have been referring to earlier scientific explanations. (*End Scene*)

How the World Began — Score

Objective atmosphere = Fear
[AoA = Push. PG = I push. Action = I prove (my point). Quality = Assuredly. QoM = Molding.

Micah
I have it right here. You said, "the leap from non-life to life is the greatest gap in scientific theories of the Earth's early history."
PG = I open. Action = I clarify. Quality = Matter-of-factly. QoM = Flowing.

Susan
Yes, I was talking about abiogenesis, how life on Earth could have risen from inanimate matter.
PG = I pull. Action = I reel in. Quality = Proudly. QoM = Flying.

Micah
What you said about the gap? That's in the book too. I highlighted it.
PG = I push. Action = I attempt (to end the conversation). Quality = Quickly. QoM = Molding.

Susan
Good to know someone's reading.
PG = I push. Action = I quote. Quality = I press (the issue). QoM = Molding.

Micah

But then you said, "unless, of course, you believe in all that other gobbledy gook."

PG = I close. Action = I deny. Quality = Unbelievingly. QoM = Molding.

Susan

Gobbledy gook.

PG = I push. Action = I make my point. Quality = Smartassedly. QoM = Flying.

Micah

Yeah. That's not in the book.

PG = I close. Action = I respond. Quality = Firmly. QoM = Molding.

Susan

No, I don't imagine it is.]

(Pause)

[AoA = Wring. PG = I push. Action = I defend. Quality = Assuredly. QoM = Molding.

Susan continued

That doesn't sound like something I'd say.

PG = I push. Action = I finalize. Quality = Strongly. QoM = Molding.

Micah

I wrote it down.

PG = I open. Action = I question. Quality = Condescendingly. QoM = Flowing.

Susan

You did?

PG = I close. Action = I defend. Quality = Firmly. QoM = Molding.

Micah

Yeah.]

[AoA = Open. PG = I open. Action = I offer (an explanation). Quality = Honestly. QoM = Flowing.

Susan

You must have misheard me. I probably said something that sounded like gobbledy gook.

PG = I open. Action = I open (the door). Quality = Baitingly. QoM = Flying.

APPENDIX III

Micah
Like what?
(Pause. Susan can't think of a single coherent phrase that sounds remotely like gobbledy gook. Can anyone?)
PG = I close. Action = I defend. Quality = Exasperatedly. QoM = Molding.

Susan
I don't know, Micah. It just doesn't sound like me.
PG = I push. Action = I defend. Quality = Proudly. QoM = Flying.

Micah
It means gibberish. I looked it up.
PG = I push. Action = I defend. Quality = Angrily. QoM = Molding.

Susan
I know what it means, but it's not something I'd say.
PG = I push. Action = I present (the facts). Quality = Confidently. QoM = Molding.

Micah
Except. You said it in third period.
PG = I open. Action = I concede then defend. Quality = Factually. QoM = Molding.

Susan
I'll grant you: sometimes things just fall out of my mouth willy nilly, as you've observed, but the phrase gobbledy gook is not, you know, part of my vocabulary.
PG = I close. Action = I challenge. Quality = Forcefully. QoM = Molding.

Micah
Do you think I'm lying?
PG = I embrace. Action = I offer (an explanation). Quality = Apologetically. QoM = Flying.

Susan
No. God no. I just think we have a little misunderstanding.
PG = I push. Action = I finalize. Quality = Forcefully. QoM = Molding.

Micah
You said, "unless, of course, you believe in all that other gobbledy gook."
PG = I close. Action = I finalize. Quality = Calmly. QoM = Molding.

Susan

I'm sorry, Micah. You must have misheard me. Is that all you wanted to talk about?

PG = I penetrate. Action = I bury (the knife). Quality = Twistingly. QoM = Molding.

Micah

So you're saying there's no way you said "unless, of course, you believe in all that other gobbledy gook."

(Pause)

PG = I Open. Action = I State (my final argument). Quality = Believingly. QoM = Radiating.

Susan

Yes. That's what I'm saying.]

PG = I push. Action = I tease. Quality = Invitingly. QoM = Flowing.

Micah

You know Helen Garrett? She's in third period, too. She has red hair.

PG = I close. Action = I answer. Quality = Carefully. QoM = Molding.

Susan

Yes, I know Helen.

PG = I penetrate. Action = I set (the hook). Quality = Winningly. QoM = Flying.

Micah

She said you said it too.

PG = I push. Action = I challenge. Quality = Piercingly. QoM = Molding.

Susan

She did.

PG = I push. Action = I present (further evidence). Quality = Giddily. QoM = Flying.

Micah

Yeah. And Cade Dinkel. He heard it. We could call them, if you want.

PG = I tear. Action = I acquiesce. Quality = Begrudgingly. QoM = Molding.

APPENDIX III

Susan

That won't be necessary. If you all thought I said gobbledy gook, then I guess it's conceivable I'm not remembering the moment exactly, but suffice it to say: I certainly didn't mean it.

PG = I push. Action = I capitalize. Quality = Knowingly. QoM = Flying.

Micah

Mean what?

PG = I open. Action = I admit. Quality = Quietly. QoM = Radiating.

Susan

I didn't mean to use the phrase.

PG = I pull. Action = I wind (up the argument). Quality = Hopefully. QoM = Radiating.

Micah

But then, what did you mean?

PG = I close. Action = I retreat. Quality = Fearfully. QoM = Molding.

Susan

I'm not sure I'm following . . .

PG = I penetrate. Action = I seal (the deal). Quality = Gleefully. QoM = Flying.

Micah

You said, "The leap from non-life to life is the greatest gap in scientific theories of the Earth's early history. Unless, of course, you believe in all that other gobbledy gook." What is the other gobbledy gook.

(Pause)

PG = I close. Action = I cover (my tracks). Quality = Unarguably. QoM = Molding.

Susan

I must have been referring to earlier scientific explanations.

(End Scene)

APPENDIX IV: ADDITIONAL EXERCISES AND HELPFUL DOCUMENTS

Partial list of qualities of action

Aggressively, Awkwardly, Bitterly, Blindly, Boastfully, Boldly, Bravely, Brightly, Calmly, Carefully, Cautiously, Clearly, Cheekily, Cheerfully, Chirpily, Completely, Courageously, Coyly, Crisply, Cruelly, Cynically, Defiantly, Desperately, Elegantly, Enthusiastically, Excitedly, Fearlessly, Fiercely, Firmly, Fondly, Forcefully, Frantically, Gently, Gladly, Gracefully, Greedily, Harshly, Hastily, Honestly, Humorously, Hungrily, Intensely, Invitingly, Joyously, Justly, Kindly, Lazily, Leadingly, Lusciously, Longingly, Loudly, Mischievously, Mysteriously, Obnoxiously, Openly, Passionately, Patiently, Piercingly, Pitifully, Pleadingly, Politely, Powerfully, Punctually, Quietly, Rapidly, Recklessly, Reluctantly, Roughly, Sarcastically, Seductively, Seriously, Sharply, Shrilly, Shyly, Silently, Slowly, Slyly, Smoothly, Softly, Stealthily, Sternly, Strongly, Suspiciously, Sweetly, Tenderly, Tensely, Tightly, Truthfully, Unexpectedly, Urgently, Vivaciously, Victoriously, Violently, Wearily, Wildly, Yearningly.

Further reading

For a comprehensive list of actions please see:

Caldarone, Marina, and Lloyd-Williams, Maggie, *Actions-The Actor's Thesaurus*, Drama Publishers, 2004.

APPENDIX IV

Definitions of the method of psychophysical action

Objective—What I want.
Action—What I do to get what I want (a verb).
Quality of Action—How I do what I do to get what I want (an adverb).
Obstacle—What is in the way of what I want.
Stakes—What I stand to lose or gain from what I want.

Exercise: Hunter and hunted

1. Players sit in chairs on opposite sides of a large and uncluttered playing space.
2. Players close their eyes at the beginning.
3. Two players are chosen silently by the moderator, one from either side. The moderator can walk from one side to the other and tap players on the shoulder.
4. A "weapon," a rolled newspaper, is tossed into the playing space by the moderator. (The moderator must warn the players not to rush into the space head first and to take ultimate care of themselves. When the players are chosen the moderator instructs the others to open their eyes.)
5. With their eyes closed the players scamper for the "weapon."
6. When one player has the "weapon" the moderator says "stop."
7. The moderator disorients the players by asking the others to make noise and placing the two players on opposite sides of the space after spinning them round and round.
8. Play begins. The "hunter" tries to find the "hunted." When the "hunter" finds the "hunted" the "kill" is made with the "weapon." (Should either actor inadvertently open their eyes begin again.)
9. The "hunted" can win the game by seating himself or herself in the vacated space of the "hunter" before being killed.

The game is played to help establish terminology: the playwright's given circumstances, obstacles, objectives, stakes, actions, qualities of action, emotions, relationship, using the senses, commitment. Guide actors to these terms in the spy-back.

Further exercise from Chapter 10

Score the following speeches:

Edmund
Thou, Nature, art my goddess; to thy law
My services are bound. Wherefore should I
Stand in the plague of custom, and permit
The curiosity of nations to deprive me,
For that I am some twelve or fourteen moonshines
Lag of a brother? Why bastard? wherefore base?
When my dimensions are as well compact,
My mind as generous, and my shape as true,
As honest madam's issue? Why brand they us
With base? with baseness? bastardy? base, base?
Who, in the lusty stealth of nature, take
More composition and fierce quality
Than doth, within a dull, stale, tired bed,
Go to th' creating a whole tribe of fops
Got 'tween asleep and wake? Well then,
Legitimate Edgar, I must have your land.
Our father's love is to the bastard Edmund
As to th' legitimate. Fine word—"legitimate"!
Well, my legitimate, if this letter speed,
And my invention thrive, Edmund the base
Shall top th' legitimate. I grow; I prosper.
Now, gods, stand up for bastards!

Macbeth
If it were done when 'tis done, then 'twere well
It were done quickly: if the assassination
Could trammel up the consequence, and catch

With his surcease success; that but this blow
Might be the be-all and the end-all here,
But here, upon this bank and shoal of time,
We'ld jump the life to come. But in these cases
We still have judgment here; that we but teach
Bloody instructions, which, being taught, return
To plague the inventor: this even-handed justice
Commends the ingredients of our poison'd chalice
To our own lips. He's here in double trust;
First, as I am his kinsman and his subject,
Strong both against the deed; then, as his host,
Who should against his murderer shut the door,
Not bear the knife myself. Besides, this Duncan
Hath borne his faculties so meek, hath been
So clear in his great office, that his virtues
Will plead like angels, trumpet-tongued, against
The deep damnation of his taking-off;
And pity, like a naked new-born babe,
Striding the blast, or heaven's cherubim, horsed
Upon the sightless couriers of the air,
Shall blow the horrid deed in every eye,
That tears shall drown the wind. I have no spur
To prick the sides of my intent, but only
Vaulting ambition, which o'erleaps itself
And falls on the other.

Hamlet

To be, or not to be—that is the question:
Whether 'tis nobler in the mind to suffer
The slings and arrows of outrageous fortune
Or to take arms against a sea of troubles,
And by opposing end them. To die—to sleep—
No more; and by a sleep to say we end
The heartache, and the thousand natural shocks
That flesh is heir to. 'Tis a consummation
Devoutly to be wish'd. To die—to sleep.
To sleep—perchance to dream: ay, there's the rub!
For in that sleep of death what dreams may come
When we have shuffled off this mortal coil,

Must give us pause. There's the respect
That makes calamity of so long life.
For who would bear the whips and scorns of time,
Th' oppressor's wrong, the proud man's contumely,
The pangs of despis'd love, the law's delay,
The insolence of office, and the spurns
That patient merit of th' unworthy takes,
When he himself might his quietus make
With a bare bodkin? Who would these fardels bear,
To grunt and sweat under a weary life,
But that the dread of something after death—
The undiscover'd country, from whose bourn
No traveller returns—puzzles the will,
And makes us rather bear those ills we have
Than fly to others that we know not of?
Thus conscience does make cowards of us all,
And thus the native hue of resolution
Is sicklied o'er with the pale cast of thought,
And enterprises of great pith and moment
With this regard their currents turn awry
And lose the name of action.—Soft you now!
The fair Ophelia!—Nymph, in thy orisons
Be all my sins rememb'red.

More speeches for characterization for Chapter 11

Puck
Thou speak'st aright;
I am that merry wanderer of the night.
I jest to Oberon and make him smile
When I a fat and bean-fed horse beguile,
Neighing in likeness of a filly foal.

Helena
Good Hermia, do not be so bitter with me.
I evermore did love you, Hermia,
Did ever keep your counsels, never wrong'd you;

APPENDIX IV

Save that, in love unto Demetrius,
I told him of your stealth unto this wood.
He follow'd you; for love I follow'd him;
But he hath chid me hence and threaten'd me
To strike me, spurn me, nay, to kill me too:

Lysander
I am, my lord, as well derived as he,
As well possess'd; my love is more than his;
My fortunes every way as fairly rank'd,
If not with vantage, as Demetrius';
And, which is more than all these boasts can be,
I am beloved of beauteous Hermia:
Why should not I then prosecute my right?

Bottom
Sweet Moon, I thank thee for thy sunny beams;
I thank thee, Moon, for shining now so bright;
For, by thy gracious, golden, glittering gleams,
I trust to take of truest Thisby sight.
But stay, O spite!
But mark, poor knight,
What dreadful dole is here!
Eyes, do you see?
How can it be?
O dainty duck! O dear!
Thy mantle good,
What, stain'd with blood!
Approach, ye Furies fell!
O Fates, come, come,
Cut thread and thrum;
Quail, crush, conclude, and quell!

Additional exercise for Imaginary Body: Magical Clay Imaginary Body Sculpture[1]

Transformation—that is what the Actor's nature, consciously or subconsciously, longs for.

MICHAEL CHEKHOV

I believe the major strength of this method of creating an imaginary body is its engagement of the willing center, the "do-er," the actor's own form. As the actor's hands reach into the never-ending mound of soft and pliable magical clay, his or her body moving and molding and twisting and reaching, it (the body) leads the creative imaginative process, allowing the thinking center to recede and to quiet.

The feeling center also becomes involved as sensations erupt from the discoveries offered to the ready actor regarding the fascinating and wondrous character's body that grows from the work of his/her fingertips. To begin the exercise, ask the participants to come to a quiet place, sitting on the floor.

Spend time in your imagination, thinking of the character. Allow for the opportunity to see the character in the business of the play, scene, or monologue. See the character in the context of the text, doing things, handling things.

You may, in your imagination, ask the character questions about these actions and pieces of business, and then listen carefully to the answers. No question is unimportant. Listen not only to the answers, but listen to the voice that speaks them.

Note how you might feel similarly to the character. Now note the differences.

After about 10 minutes of this imaginative concentration, bring yourself to a forward readiness position. Some will find this position as kneeling; some may sit back on their heels. The work can also begin sitting in a chair; the important part is to be forward, and active, and on or close to the floor.

---

[1] Contributed by Melissa Owens.

APPENDIX IV

Reaching out beside you, to the right or left, using your imagination, plunge your hand into a large mound of magical, pliable clay. Feel what it feels like on your skin; play with the clay, see the clay. When you feel the impulse to move some of the clay from the heap to the place directly in front of you, do so. Start to massage and mold the clay, knowing that the character's feet *need* this in order to become whole. You are moving the clay, and the clay is forming itself as well. Continue to work the clay while allowing for the surprise of what is quickly becoming a foot or feet. Note everything about these feet: the length, the width, the toes and toenails, the color, the age, any markings or scars. Begin with the smallest details, not the entire body. Store these observations in your center, and then reach back into the ever-replenishing pile of clay to bring new material for the legs. Proceed as before, both molding and responding to the clay's own lively building, finding joy in the process and discoveries.

As you reach the tops of the legs, stand up so you may continue building this amazing sculpture. Allow the tempo to increase, so that the magic clay is moving just ahead of you, offering you pieces of information about this character's body that you hadn't suspected before. Note the size, shape, color, markings, strengths, and weaknesses. Move up the torso, and down one arm, noting that the other arm materializes at the same time.

When you come to the hand, the tempo shifts again, slowing for you to be able to intimately study the character's hand—"experience Joy in the use of (y)our hand" (Michael Chekhov)—and find *their* hands using *your* hands.

Lastly, reach with both hands to take the last large mound of Magic clay, bringing it to rest in the position of the character's head. Moving the clay with both your hands, allow the face to peek out of the hair, eyes closed. Allow the harmonious blend of you molding and the clay creating to form a distinct head and face, with hair, ears, closed eyes, nose, mouth, and chin. Note everything about this face, and store it in your center.

Now walk around your sculpture, this body, seeing it in its entirety. Walk back to stand in front of the imaginary body and pause. Radiate energy from your Ideal Center toward the character's center, activating your sculpture, giving it life. You may choose to place your hands on your center and then reach out to place your hand on the character's center. When the character's center activates, see the character's eyes open, looking directly into yours. Feel what it feels like to have a connection between you and this character.

When you feel ready, step behind the imaginary body, to step in. Try reaching a hand in first and withdrawing it, to note how it feels differently than yours. Then try a foot. Eventually step completely inside, "clothe yourself, as it were, with this body . . . put it on like a garment." When inside, breathe. First, feel how even breathing is a new experience in this body. Close and open your eyes; receive sight through these new eyes. Move your awareness to your hands, seeing them, moving them for the first time. And so on until the character moves and explores the space.

To end the exercise, ask the participants to step backward out of their imaginary bodies, and take one more walk around them, with gratitude, noting specific information and logging feelings for spy-back and journaling.

APPENDIX V: A BRIEF HISTORY OF MICHAEL CHEKHOV

Mikhail Aleksandrovich Chekhov was born August 16, 1891 in St. Petersburg, Russia. He was the nephew of the great playwright Anton Chekhov. The work between Anton Chekhov, Stanislavski, and the Moscow Art Theatre is well documented and legendary. One would think that Anton would have had great influence on his nephew and that this influence would have helped inform Michael's young life in the theater. Rather, Michael was much more influenced by his father Alexander Pavlovich Chekhov than by his uncle. Alexander spent many hours with his son engaging—challenging—Michael's mind and, most important, his imagination. Chekhov the elder was a writer, philosopher, historian, caricaturist, and alcoholic. All of the attributes of his father would be inherited or cultivated by Michael Chekhov throughout his career. It is from these early encounters with his father that he would develop his theories in the Moscow Art Theatre and beyond. Chekhov's work is born in imagination and that is where the work in this book begins.

Chekhov experienced a tumultuous theatrical journey beginning with his being labeled a "sick-artist" in mother Russia. He was granted permission to immigrate to Germany with his wife and he never returned, probably out of fear, to his homeland. Fortunately, for us, after several famous stops in other countries, Chekhov was invited by Beatrice Straight to England and then to Connecticut and formed a company. Unfortunately for Chekhov, America entered the Second World War and the company had to be abandoned. Chekhov found his way to Hollywood and began a studio where he worked with many famous actors and others. Several of his students during this period went on to become oh so important in spreading his work in America and I am lucky to have studied with some of them. Chekhov's journey ended in September of 1955, when he succumbed to his third heart attack. Many years later, I began my journey with the Michael Chekhov Technique. In reality, I began the journey with Chekhov much earlier. I just didn't know it. After studying his work, I realized I was incorporating much of his philosophy in my own acting and directing. I began to have the power of his words in my own teaching and directing.

This brief history cannot do Chekhov justice. I would suggest the reader look at Franc Chamberlain's book (details below).

Further reading

Chamberlain, Franc, *Michael Chekhov*, Routledge, 2004.

APPENDIX VI: HOW THIS BOOK CAME TO BE

My artistic journey

My journey has taken me from playing in the wonders of the woods of North Carolina creating my own fantastic world to rediscovering how to do just that as an adult in the theater. Something terrible happens between childhood and adulthood that is a kind of death for artists. We are told to "grow up." Yes, I suppose we must. There is this thing of being responsible that is expected of us. Yet, when we create as artists we must find a path backward to that time when we created freely and without restraint. The Michael Chekhov Technique has been my path to return to that special place where fantasy is possible.

When I was in high school I began my journey in the theater. Thankfully, I had an outstanding mentor, teacher, and adopted father. Mr. Don Nance (Coach) founded a community theater in our small hamlet of Mount Airy, North Carolina. It began as an extension of our drama program at our high school and eventually grew into a theater of the entire community. I look back at those years now and realize how blessed I am to have had the experience in hanging and focusing lights, building and painting scenery, and being cast in plays and musicals. Coach taught me to do everything that needed doing. Those experiences were integral to my desire to direct and I encourage all young artists to delve into all aspects of the theater. Many young artists will eventually direct. It is so important to have experience in the scene shop, costume shop, and lighting lab. Directors must know "designer speak."

During this period, Coach produced summer seasons of three shows. I learned during those summers about collaboration. I learned that theater cannot be created by one person. Theatre can be likened to the team sport of football. Theatre and football cannot succeed without full team effort. I know this because I quit playing football to become a "drama freak." I was, and am, addicted to the community atmosphere that theater produces and I remain addicted to watching football. While I maintain that actors are theater's most important asset it is not just about the actors on the stage. Theater is family and it includes every name in the playbill. Now, many years later, I get to know everyone involved in a production I direct—including the running crew who come in late to the rehearsal process. I welcome them, on a first name basis, to the family of the show. Everyone is vital to the production.

In undergraduate school, at the University of North Carolina School of the Arts, lessons from Coach were reinforced from some outstanding teachers: Marty Rader, Lesley Hunt, Malcolm Morrison, and Bob Murray. These teachers gave me opportunities I don't think I deserved; yet they saw potential in me. I take these lessons to heart each time I walk into the acting studio or a rehearsal. An acting/directing teacher never knows when a student will blossom or "get it." I tell my students that they are on a journey and each of them, as am I, are on different points within the journey. The journey doesn't end until we expire. Recognizing that it is the journey that is the most important thing, not where you are on it, is paramount to a career in theater—and perhaps in any career.

About twelve years after my undergraduate experience my wife, Kathryn, convinced me to look into graduate school. She was tired of me being gone most summers while jousting in Renaissance faires with the Hanlon-Lees Action Theater. Kathryn knew I loved teaching and directing as that is what I had been doing for years—although not full-time. Accepted at West Virginia University (WVU) as an older MFA student, I dove headlong into the rigors of being a student again and teaching for my assistantship. The acting curriculum was based in the teachings of Uta Hagen. As my undergraduate training was extremely eclectic, I was pleased to get training in a specific technique. I thought this work would be a great way to boost my resume, balancing eclectic and specific methodologies. The work at WVU was excellent with another tremendous group of teachers: Jerry McGonigle, Joe Olivieri, Natalie Baker, and John Whitty (Doc). During my time there, I somehow became interested in Michael Chekhov.

APPENDIX VI

In 2001, I attended my first workshop in the Michael Chekhov Technique with the Michael Chekhov Association (MICHA). There I met and worked with Joanna Merlin, Jack Colvin, and Lenard Petit among others. Joanna and Jack worked with Chekhov in Hollywood in the 1950s. I was absolutely hooked. Later on, I had the privilege of working with Mala Powers in Los Angeles on several occasions. Mala was a very open and loving teacher. It is said that Chekhov hated criticism and taught in an extremely gentle manner. Mala taught this way and I learned a lot about teaching working with her. Since that time, I believe I teach like Mala and according to the principles of Chekhov.

My journey has taken me to my current position as president and producing artistic director of the Great Lakes Michael Chekhov Consortium, LLC (GLMCC). We exist to certify teachers in the Michael Chekhov Technique and to spread the word of Michael Chekhov to artists around the globe. GLMCC has been the most joyful part of my journey so far. I believe that GLMCC exemplifies what collaboration in fantasy is all about—what this book is about.

APPENDIX VII: ADDITIONAL NOTES ON *A MIDSUMMER NIGHT'S DREAM*

Plays are comprised of major events. I believe audiences attend plays to observe how writers, actors, directors, and designers struggle, or deal, with major events. This is true with tragedy and comedy.

Personally, in tragedy, I deplore seeing actors purge themselves of emotion on the stage. I prefer to see actors, as their characters, struggling with major events and to not completely be rid of the emotional experience. Once the actor begins to purge, I lose interest because my connection to the character is gone; my emotional contact with the character is gone. As an audience member I want to be taken along on the journey—to ride the roller coaster with the character and to purge myself of the ride after the play is ended by considering how the actor/character struggled with the journey. If the character emotionally purges the problem the journey is over. Why has the play *Hamlet* survived this long? Because audiences love to see how each actor playing Hamlet sorts through the struggle. We all know how the play ends. We all know how Hamlet solves his problem. In the genres of musical theater and comedy the problem is usually solved for the best but not until the end. It is the journey in which we're most interested. In comedy, I hate it when the director takes me on a journey of nothing but bigger, faster, funnier. Comedy should have as much nuance, or more, as tragedy. Tempo and rhythm is the essence of comedy. This equates to the changing of qualities of action frequently.

My directing philosophy is to keep the audience on the roller coaster, not let them fall off. That would be a real tragedy. The ride shouldn't stop until the house lights come up and the audience leaves the theater. Actually, it doesn't stop there. I want the audience to talk about the experience after the play.

To keep the audience on an exciting ride the director must discover the rhythmical wave, decide the superobjective, and then concentrate on the themes. Where do the major themes of the play illuminate themselves? Obviously, themes are revealed throughout the play, yet there is usually one chief occurrence for each major theme. The director should chart these occurrences in the rhythmical wave. I like to call these *atmospheric spikes*. They may or may not be in a major climax. Mid-rehearsal is the place to work on these atmospheric spikes. The actors are off-book and have a good understanding of their objectives, actions, and qualities. Now we can concentrate on making the choices specific. I consider the beginning and middle rehearsal periods longer than the final rehearsal period. I don't divide into thirds. Over the years, I have found that working this way makes the final rehearsal period, including tech, much easier. Actors are more prepared. They are finalizing—not still working on the nuts and bolts of the text.

The first major theme revealed in *Midsummer* is Feminism. And this particular one is in the first major climax. The director must identify for the actors exactly where the theme is at its apex because something big has to happen. It is usually wise to set a pause here. It gives the audience time to have an "ah-ha" moment. There can also be a subtle, or not so subtle, change in lighting. Whatever device is used the focus should be on the actor revealing the theme. Here is the dialogue surrounding the first theme:

Hermia
I would my father look'd but with my eyes.
Theseus
Rather your eyes must with his judgment look.
Hermia
I do entreat your grace to pardon me.
I know not by what power I am made bold,
But I beseech your grace that I may know
The worst that may befall me in this case,
If I refuse to wed Demetrius.

Theseus
Either to die the death or to abjure
Forever the society of men.

NOTE TO DIRECTOR

The following speech is the atmospheric spike and where the theme "Feminism" is revealed. Hermia is defying her father's wishes and is publically announcing it. It is an example of a theme occurring at the height of a major climax. There should be a pause at the end of the speech with all eyes on Hermia. Also, note how the speech is structured. It is short with no place to pause or breathe until the end. The actor should build this speech in intensity through to the last word.

Hermia
So will I grow, so live, so die, my lord,
Ere I will my virgin patent up
Unto his lordship, whose unwished yoke
My soul consents not to give sovereignty.
(Pause)

NOTE TO DIRECTOR

To keep the rhythmical wave moving in the proper direction, in this case downward, Theseus cannot respond in anger to Hermia. If he does then the theme is not as clear as it should be. This is another way to look at polarity. He should respond with reasoning. The threat is implied in his speech.

Block 4.

Theseus
Take time to pause; and, by the next new moon,
The sealing-day betwixt my love and me,

Upon that day either prepare to die
For disobedience to your father's will,
Or else to wed Demetrius, as he would;
Or on Diana's altar to protest
For aye austerity and single life.

Since this example is the pinnacle of the first climax we would have started here in early rehearsals. Regardless, we can add the rhythmical wave and theme in middle rehearsals. Early rehearsals are best to focus on actions, qualities, and objectives. Middle rehearsals are best to focus on the intricacies of themes, waves, and characterization. Directors make a mistake in cutting out the mid-rehearsal period altogether. I have witnessed and participated in countless productions that are blocked quickly, with no middle period, and run-throughs begin. There is so much more art to be mined.

Another major theme, "Love Is Blind," occurs early in the play and it is an example of a theme that does not reveal itself during a climax:

Block 9.

Helena

How happy some o'er other some can be!
Through Athens I am thought as fair as she.
But what of that? Demetrius thinks not so;
He will not know what all but he do know:
And as he errs, doting on Hermia's eyes,
So I, admiring of his qualities:

NOTE TO DIRECTOR

The theme "Love is Blind" is revealed in this speech. If Helena makes a huge discovery at the end of this section of the speech then the audience will discover it along with her. In the first part of the speech Helena is presenting a problem. After the discovery she seeks a solution and finds it. Her decision is illogical and therefore reinforces the theme. When in love we sometimes justify conclusions that simply make little sense.

Helena *continued*
Things base and vile, holding no quantity,
Love can transpose to form and dignity:
Love looks not with the eyes, but with the mind,
And therefore is wing'd Cupid painted blind:

NOTE TO DIRECTOR

After Helena makes her discovery (the climax of the entire speech) there should be a device to help point up the moment. In this production I had Helena move to center stage, where Cupid was painted in mosaic tiles, and physically point to the mask covering his eyes. I don't mind hitting the audience in the face to reveal a theme.

Helena *continued*
Nor hath Love's mind of any judgement taste;
Wings and no eyes figure unheedy haste.
And therefore is Love said to be a child,
Because in choice he is so oft beguil'd.
As waggish boys in game themselves forswear,
So the boy Love is perjured everywhere:
For ere Demetrius look'd on Hermia's eyne,
He hail'd down oaths that he was only mine;
And when this hail some heat from Hermia felt,
So he dissolved, and showers of oaths did melt.
I will go tell him of fair Hermia's flight:
Then to the wood will he to-morrow night
Pursue her; and for this intelligence
If I have thanks, it is a dear expense.
But herein mean I to enrich my pain,
To have his sight thither and back again.

NOTE TO DIRECTOR

There is quite a bit of speech left after the climax, which can be troublesome for the actor (and the audience who has to remain interested). To deal with this problem the actor has to find mini climaxes and build the speech around them. This is best done by breaking the speech into artistic frames with varied action and quality changes and, of course, polarity.

During the mid-rehearsal period I work on themes and rhythmical waves in the block format while allowing the actors to continue to discover. I also like to do what I call mini runs. We might work blocks 9–17 on a Tuesday night and before we leave I'll run those blocks. On Wednesday night, I would then work on blocks 18–26 and repeat the process. Thursday I would work blocks 27–30, run those, and then run 9–30. In this way we establish continuity without the pressure of doing full runs. I've discovered we really don't need full runs until the latter rehearsal period with the exception of the designer run-through. Once designers learn this block process, I often see them in the house during these mini runs. They are welcome.

About seven days before tech we'll begin work/runs of full acts. I like to run an act on a given night and go back and work through my notes. If there is time, we'll run the act again. I'll repeat this pattern for each act. If the director is diligent with the block process, three to four full runs are adequate prior to tech. Our tech for this production of *Midsummer* was completed in six hours, scheduled 10 of 12, and this was because of the tremendous collaborative effort from everyone in our family from the beginning.

Working with artistic frames and rhythmical waves requires the director to put in more preparation time, in a different manner, than he or she might be used to. In the end what this process will do is allow the director to say much less and give the actors freedom to accomplish much more. It is not how much the director says but how he or she says it. I often receive comments from actors that they have never experienced such freedom. This may give some directors pause. Actors don't necessarily know the craft of the director and the meticulousness of the process I have outlined in this book. This process does require the director to embrace the collaborative nature that makes great theater.

We have explored several of the themes and where they occur in the play. Directors should identify the main theme early and constantly reinforce it, at the proper points, throughout the rehearsal period. The major theme "Love Conquers All" is revealed throughout the play yet is completely unveiled at the end. The wedding is completed and we observe three happy couples. The mechanicals, through their love of each other and in performing, have found success and pure elation. In this production, as already pointed out, Egeus forgave Hermia for her disobedience—father and daughter are reunited. The actor playing Egeus also acknowledged Lysander as a viable son-in-law. Earlier Titania and Oberon made amends through their strong love. Through his/her persistence, love of Oberon, and humankind, Puck made all aright with the nobles, mechanicals, and the fairies.

In the final speech of the play, Puck appeals directly to the audience:

Puck
If we shadows have offended,
Think but this, and all is mended,
That you have but slumber'd here
While these visions did appear.
And this weak and idle theme,
No more yielding but a dream,
Gentles, do not reprehend:
if you pardon, we will mend:
And, as I am an honest Puck,
If we have unearned luck
Now to 'scape the serpent's tongue,
We will make amends ere long;
Else the Puck a liar call;
So, good night unto you all.
Give me your hands, if we be friends,
And Robin shall restore amends.

As director of this production I felt the audience was a character in the play. I consistently had actors interact with the audience and each performance proved that the audience appreciated the

APPENDIX VII

inclusion. I believe this last speech of Puck's to be a final plea for Love Conquers All. Puck is asking for forgiveness and inviting the audience to be friends. Everyone leaves the theater in the atmosphere of happy having observed the power of love conquering everything in its path. It was a powerful lesson for everyone involved.

INDEX

action, definition of 3
Actor's Ideal Center 47–9, 59, 64, 70, 71, 138
analysis and composition
 framework 1–4
 practice exploration 5–13, 16–17
archetypal gesture (AG) 67, 68
arc of action (AOA) 9, 12, 16, 88–9, 91–4, 103, 143–50, 154, 155, 173, 205, 209, 210
 clues to 13–15
 definition of 2–3
artistic frame 2, 6, 9, 12, 13, 17, 43, 50, 57, 59, 60, 64, 88, 97, 106–10, 126–9, 143–6, 148, 149, 153–4, 159, 160, 177, 209–10, 241, 242
atmosphere 9–13
 archetypes of 10, 79
 clues to 13, 79, 89
 definition of 2
 objective 2, 12, 15, 16, 79, 89, 91–3, 146–51, 185
 subjective 2, 10, 12, 15, 79, 92, 124, 132, 133, 159, 160, 167, 185–7
atmospheric spikes 185–6, 238, 239
auditions 20, 24, 33, 158, 199
 using Chekov Technique for directors and actors 186–7
auxiliary climaxes 3–5

baptism 177, 209
 of AOAs 94
 of frame 9
beats 2, 59, 139
Beckett, Samuel 157
beginning, middle, ending (B-M-E) 2, 59, 60, 75, 110
blocks 5–9, 12–16, 26, 51, 57, 87–9, 91, 93, 95, 100, 125–9, 143–4, 154, 165, 179, 193, 239–42
 definition of 3
 from PGs 82–4
 rehearsal 5–6
callbacks 20, 24, 26–33, 186, 197, 199
Callow, Simon 38
casting 16, 17, 37, 38, 44, 46, 51, 54, 67, 87, 88, 97, 100, 125, 135, 145, 148, 150, 178, 183, 235
 classwork, using archetypes 19–21
  character archetype determination and 24–31
  follow-up for directors and 33–5
  framework 19–21
  in-class/rehearsal exercise 22–4, 31–2
  pre-class/rehearsal exploration 21

INDEX

and concept statements 192–203
directors 186
characterization
  follow-up for actor 141–2
  framework 135–6
  in-class/rehearsal exercise 136–8, 140
  teacher/director instructions 140–1
  work analysis and 138–40
character relationships
  follow-up 120–1
  framework 99–100
  pre-class/rehearsal exploration 100
  in-class/rehearsal exercise 100–9, 112–15, 119–20
    atmosphere 113–14
    note to actors 109–10
    note to director/teacher 109
    relationships and sensations 118–19
    sensations 116–18
    speaking of action and quality aloud 110–11
    speaking of character name and action and quality 111–12
  relationship creation using polarity 102–3
Chekov, Anton 233
Chekov, Michael 4, 87, 164, 179
  To the Actor 1, 38, 142
  brief history of 233–4
  Lessons for the Professional Actor 9
  On the Technique of Acting 47
  The Three Sisters 34, 113, 118–19, 175, 200–3
Clarkson, H. G.
  Family Portrait 205–16
class and rehearsal
  exercises 55
  follow-up 65

framework 53–4
in-rehearsal and in-class exercise and 55–65
pre-class/rehearsal exploration and 54
climaxes 6, 9, 15, 17, 97, 194, 240–1
  auxiliary 3–5, 195, 209
  initial 2
  major 3–5, 154, 195, 209, 238, 239
  polar 2
Colvin, Jack 100, 236
composition 113; *see also* analysis and composition
  umbrella analogy and 16
concept statements and casting, from plays 192–203
costuming 124, 194–5, 199, 202
"Crossing the Threshold" exercise 181–2, 184

"Director's Book of Secrets" 155
eclectic technique 204
ensemble creation
  follow-up 51–2
  framework 37–8
  in-class/rehearsal first rehearsal 39–40
  in-rehearsal/class exercise 40–3
  director/teacher continued instructions 41–3
  "Ladies and Gentlemen" exercise and 44–6
  pre-rehearsal and class exploration and 38–9
  rehearsal/class exercise and 46–9
  spy-back and 43, 50–1
  working alone and 43–4

INDEX

fantasy 2, 40, 42, 46, 57, 59–60, 68, 70–2, 76, 80–2, 94–6, 113, 114, 125, 131, 136, 139, 140, 155, 234, 236
feeling center 34, 40, 46, 47, 56, 58–61, 64, 71, 99, 106, 109, 132, 137–9, 159, 183, 185, 230

gesture 9, 22–3, 34, 43, 44; see also psychological gesture (PG), as action
Great Lakes Michael Chekhov Consortium 69, 140, 158, 236
gut-level emotion 68

Higher Ego 4, 5, 10, 16, 17, 40, 47, 131, 139, 181–2, 184
hunter and hunted exercise 225–6

iambic pentameter 157, 158, 174
imaginary body 140, 141, 230–2
in-class/rehearsal 22–4, 31–2, 88–9, 144
   ball game and 55–65
   blocking and 82–4
   characterization and 136–8, 140–1
   character relationships and 100–16, 118–20
   first rehearsal 39–40
   psychological gesture for action and 69–70, 73–84
   qualities of movement and 46–9
   score 79–80
      speaking of 93–7
   soliloquies and 125–33
   spy-back and 182–3
   teacher/director continued instructions 41–3
   teacher/director's work 89–93
   tempo/rhythm and 158–74, 176–8
   working alone 77, 96–7
   written text addition 74

in-rehearsal/class exercise see in-class/rehearsal
inspired acting 87–8
   follow-up 97–8
   framework 87–8
   pre-class/rehearsal exploration 88
   in-class/rehearsal exercise 88–9
      speaking of score 93–6
   teacher/director's work 89–93
   working alone 96–7

Jones, Cherry 188, 189

"Ladies and Gentleman" exercise 44–6
Laws of Composition 1
Les Miserables 175

Mamet, David 157
Meisner, Sanford 187
Merlin, Joanna 236
Michael Chekhov Association (MICHA) 236
Midsummer Night's Dream 3–5, 21, 23, 24, 41, 44, 64, 87
   character archetype determination in 24–31
mini runs 241
Morrison, Malcolm 187
musical theater 40, 158, 174–5, 178–9, 237
Myss, Caroline
   Archetype Cards 20

Nance, Don 234

obstacles, definition of 113
operative words 148, 158, 162–3, 176, 178, 179

Palace exercise 40–4
Petit, Lenard 236
   The Michael Chekhov Handbook 19

INDEX

physical characterization 135, 136
polarity 1, 4, 5, 15, 26, 28, 50, 79, 93, 97, 99, 106, 108, 111, 126, 160, 173, 177, 179, 186, 198, 209, 239, 241
  definition of 2, 113
  relationship creation using 102–3
  tempo and 170
Powers, Mala 236
pre-rehearsal and class exploration 38–9, 54
psychological gesture (PG), as action 105, 106, 112, 209–16, 219–23
  clues to atmosphere and 79
  definitions 70–3
  follow-up 84
  framework 67–9
    pre-class exploration 69
    in-class exercise
      teaching of form 69–70
    in-class/rehearsal exercise 73–82
      blocking and 82–4
      score 79–80
      working alone 77
      written text addition 74
    inspired acting and 89–94, 96
    rules of forming 70
    tempos and 177

Qualities of Movement (QOM) exercise 46, 50, 120, 210
quality of action 10, 20, 22, 26, 33, 35, 53, 58–9, 61–4, 68, 75, 97, 102, 112, 128, 143, 154, 157, 159, 160, 162, 173, 177, 199, 216, 224, 237
  definition of 3, 113

radiation 22, 23, 42, 46–51, 60, 63, 68, 72, 73, 80, 82, 94–6, 121, 137, 139, 231
rehearsal 12, 15; *see also individual entries*
  blocks 5–6

rhythmical wave 3, 5, 15, 19, 93, 97, 130, 154, 160, 165, 166, 173, 179, 187, 238–42
  definition of 2
scenes and blocks
  follow-up 155
  framework 143–4
  in-class exercise 144
  scene score 144–55
score, definition of 113
sensations 47, 50, 99–100, 115, 120–1, 127, 132, 230
  and relationships 118–19
  and teaching of
    balancing 118
    falling 117–18
    rising 116–17
soliloquies
  framework 123–4
  in-class/rehearsal exercise 127–30
    expansion and contraction 125–7
    follow-up 131–3
    pre-class exploration 124–5
spy-back session 23, 34, 35, 43–5, 49, 50–1, 55, 60, 61, 63–5, 75, 80, 99, 103, 106, 109, 115, 125, 144, 145, 176, 226, 232
  atmospheric spikes and 185–6
  auditioning using Chekov Technique for directors and actors and 186–7
  framework 181
  in-class/rehearsal exercise 181–3
  status maintenance for directors and teachers through collaboration and 183–4
staccato-legato exercise 182
stage manager 6, 38, 39, 88, 100
stakes, definition of 113
Stanislavski, Constanin 2, 22, 39, 46, 56, 57, 59, 179, 188, 204, 233
Steinbeck, John

Grapes of Wrath 34, 192–9
style, significance of 174–5
superobjective 15, 16, 19, 43, 64, 154

teacher/director instructions 41–4, 48–51, 56–9, 61–4, 75, 87, 88, 103, 140–1
tempo/rhythm 1, 12, 49, 50, 63, 70, 72, 73, 75, 76, 82, 89, 117, 123, 130, 139, 141, 231, 237
   application to all genres framework 157–8
   definition of 2
   follow-up 178–9
   in-class exercise 158–63, 170–4, 176–8
      reading aloud with atmosphere imagination and working with tempos 164–70
   inner and outer 132–3
   operative words and 176
   pre-class exploration 176
   study of 163–4
thinking center 30, 39, 56, 60, 64, 71, 74, 75, 106, 109, 137, 139, 159, 177, 183, 197, 230
train analogy 62
transformation 1, 3, 5, 229
   definition of 2
trap speech 31–2
Trieschmann, Catherine
   How the World Began (HTWB) 216–23

umbrella analogy 16

veiling 46, 159, 160, 197

Williams, Tennessee 157, 175
willing center 56, 60, 71, 137, 139, 230
   and will power 74
workbook videos, links to 191